CW00957548

Algernon Charles Swinburne

MANCHESTER
1824

Manchester University Press

Algernon Charles Swinburne

Unofficial Laureate

Edited by
Catherine Maxwell and Stefano Evangelista

Manchester University Press
Manchester and New York

distributed in the United States exclusively
by Palgrave Macmillan

Copyright © Manchester University Press 2013

While copyright in the volume as a whole is vested in Manchester University Press, copyright in individual chapters belongs to their respective authors, and no chapter may be reproduced wholly or in part without the express permission in writing of both author and publisher.

Published by Manchester University Press
Oxford Road, Manchester M13 9NR, UK
and Room 400, 175 Fifth Avenue, New York, NY 10010, USA
www.manchesteruniversitypress.co.uk

Distributed in the United States exclusively by
Palgrave Macmillan, 175 Fifth Avenue, New York,
NY 10010, USA

Distributed in Canada exclusively by
UBC Press, University of British Columbia, 2029 West Mall,
Vancouver, BC, Canada V6T 1Z2

British Library Cataloguing-in-Publication Data
A catalogue record for this book is available from the British Library

Library of Congress Cataloging-in-Publication Data applied for

ISBN   978 07190 8625 0 hardback

First published 2013

The publisher has no responsibility for the persistence or accuracy of URLs, for any external or third-party internet websites referred to in this book, and does not guarantee that any content on such websites is, or will remain, accurate or appropriate.

Typeset
by Action Publishing Technology Ltd, Gloucester
Printed in Great Britain
by The MPG Books Group, Bodmin

For Dinah Birch

CONTENTS

III Influence

LIST OF FIGURES

ACKNOWLEDGEMENTS

We would like to acknowledge the British Library for permission to quote and reproduce passages from the manuscript of 'The Flogging-Block' (Ashley MS 2526), the Bodleian Library, Oxford, for the images from the *Athenæum* and the *Dark Blue*, and Senate House Library, University of London for the image from the *Magazine of Art*. We would also like to thank the Institute of English Studies, Senate House, London for hosting the Swinburne centenary conference from which this collection derives and the MHRA (the George H. Genzer Bequest), Queen Mary, University of London, Oxford University, and Portsmouth University for their financial support of this event. We thank Philip Bullock for his comments on the Introduction and Patricia Pulham for her contribution to the conference and assistance with the early stages of this collection.

NOTES ON CONTRIBUTORS

Laurel Brake is Professor Emerita of Literature and Print Culture at Birkbeck, University of London. She works on nineteenth-century media history and literature with special interests in Walter Pater and gender. She co-edited with Marysa Demoor the print and digital *Dictionary of Nineteenth-Century Journalism* (British Library Publishing Division, 2009), and directed the online Nineteenth-century Serials Edition (2008) (www.ncse.ac.uk). She was the co-founder and editor of the *Pater Newsletter*, and has published widely on Pater, including *Walter Pater* (Northcote House, 1994). Books on the press include *Print in Transition, Studies in Media and Book History* (Palgrave Macmillan, 2001), *Subjugated Knowledges* (Palgrave Macmillan, 1994), *The Lure of Illustration in the Nineteenth Century: Picture and Press*, co-edited with Marysa Demoor (Palgrave Macmillan, 2009), and *Encounters in the Victorian Press. Editors, Authors, Readers*, co-edited with Julie Codell (Palgrave Macmillan, 2005). She has restarted her biography of the Paters, *Ink Work*.

Stefano Evangelista is Fellow and Tutor in English at Trinity College and Lecturer in English at the University of Oxford. His research interests are in nineteenth-century English literature (especially aestheticism and decadence), comparative literature, the reception of the classics, and the relationship between literary and visual cultures. His monograph *British Aestheticism and Ancient Greece: Hellenism, Reception, Gods in Exile* was published by Palgrave Macmillan in 2009. He is the editor of *The Reception of Oscar Wilde in Europe* (Continuum, 2010) and, together with Catherine Maxwell, of a double issue of the *Yearbook of English Studies* (2010) devoted to the arts in Victorian literature.

Sara Lyons is a PhD student in the Department of English at Queen Mary, University of London. She holds a BA in English Literature from the University of Sydney and an MA in Victorian Literature and Culture from Royal Holloway, University of London. Her dissertation focuses on the relationship between Victorian aestheticism and secularism in the works of A. C. Swinburne and Walter Pater. She has recently published an essay on this subject in relation to the poetry of Mathilde Blind in the collection *Writing Women of the Fin de Siècle: Authors of Change*, eds Adrienne E. Gavin and Carolyn Oulton (Palgrave Macmillan, 2011).

Catherine Maxwell is Professor of Victorian Literature at Queen Mary, University of London, and author of *The Female Sublime from Milton to Swinburne: Bearing Blindness* (Manchester University Press, 2001), *Swinburne* in the British Council series Writers and Their Work (Northcote House, 2006), and *Second Sight: The Visionary Imagination in Late Victorian Literature* (Manchester University Press, 2008). She has edited a collection of Swinburne's poetry for the Everyman's Poetry Library Series (Orion, 1997), and with Patricia Pulham co-edited Vernon Lee's *Hauntings and Other Fantastic Tales* (Broadview Press, 2006), and a collection of essays *Vernon Lee: Decadence, Ethics, Aesthetics* (Palgrave Macmillan, 2006). She is guest-editor of the special issue 'Victorian Literature and Classical Myth', *Victorian Review* 34 (Fall 2008) in honour of Professor Margot Louis and guest-editor with Stefano Evangelista of the special double issue of *The Yearbook of English Studies* (2010) – *The Arts in Victorian Literature*. She has published essays on Browning, Christina and Dante Gabriel Rossetti, George Eliot, Ruskin, Swinburne, Thomas Hardy, Theodore Watts-Dunton, Arthur Symons, John Addington Symonds, and Vernon Lee.

Sarah Parker, a doctoral student at the University of Birmingham, recently completed her PhD thesis entitled 'The Lesbian Muse: Homoeroticism, Contemporary Muse Figures and Female Poetic Identity'. Her AHRC-funded project examined how re-imaginings of the concept of the muse, motivated by female homoerotic desire, play a central role in the construction of a poetic identity for women in the late nineteenth and early twentieth century, focusing on the poets H. D., Amy Lowell, Olive Custance, and Michael Field. Her article '"A Girl's Love": Lord Alfred Douglas as Homoerotic Muse in the Poetry of Olive Custance' was recently published in *Women: A Cultural Review* 22.2–3 (2011).

Yopie Prins is Professor of English and Comparative Literature at the University of Michigan. She is the author of *Victorian Sappho* (Princeton University Press, 1999) and *Ladies' Greek* (Princeton University Press, forthcoming), and she has published various articles on Victorian poetry, historical poetics, nineteenth-century Hellenism, and translation studies. She is co-editor with Virginia Jackson of *The Lyric Theory Reader: A Critical Anthology* (forthcoming from Johns Hopkins University Press). Currently she is completing *Voice Inverse*, a book on metre and music in Victorian poetry.

Charlotte Ribeyrol is Lecturer at the Sorbonne University in Paris where she teaches nineteenth-century English literature and art history. Her main field of research is Hellenism in Victorian literature and painting, more specifically in the works of A. C. Swinburne, Walter Pater, and J. A. Symonds. Her recent publications on Swinburne include 'L'Hermaphroditus' d'A. C. Swinburne, entre mythe et science', *Etudes Anglaises* (Paris, 2011); 'Swinburne et les peintres de son temps. Typologie des correspondances swinburniennes', in *Tombeau pour Swinburne* (Aden, Paris, 2010); 'A Channel Passage: Swinburne and France' for *A. C. Swinburne and the Singing Word* (Ashgate, 2010), and 'Filiations saphiques: de Swinburne à Woolf et H. D.', *Etudes Anglaises* (Paris, 2009). She is also involved in a research group on colour in Antiquity at the EHESS (Centre Louis Gernet) in Paris and is currently writing a book on colour and culture in the Victorian Age.

Dinah Roe is Senior Lecturer in Nineteenth-Century Literature at Oxford Brookes University. Her interests include the nineteenth-century novel, Victorian poetry, painting and illustration, and women's writing. She holds a BA from Vassar College and a PhD in English Literature from University College, London. She has taught English Literature at UCL, the University of Hertfordshire, and Brunel University. She is the author of *Christina Rossetti's Faithful Imagination* (Palgrave Macmillan, 2006), and has edited *Christina Rossetti: Selected Poems* (Penguin Classics, 2008) and *The Pre-Raphaelites: Selected Poems* (Penguin Classics, 2010). She has also written a biography of the Rossetti family and their circle (Haus, 2011).

Julia F. Saville is Associate Professor of English at the University of Illinois at Urbana-Champaign. She is the author of *A Queer Chivalry: The Homoerotic Asceticism of Gerard Manley Hopkins* (University of Virginia

Press, 2000) as well as various articles on nineteenth-century poetry, painting, and politics. She is currently working on a book manuscript provisionally entitled 'Cosmopolitan Republican Poets: Soul Poetics and the British Body Politic, 1840–1885'.

Marion Thain is Reader in English Literature and Culture at the University of Sheffield. Her expertise is primarily in nineteenth- and early twentieth-century poetry and poetics. Her publications include: *Michael Field (1880–1914): Poetry, Aestheticism, and the Fin de Siècle* (Cambridge University Press, 2007); *Michael Field, The Poet (1880–1914): Published and Manuscript Materials* (Broadview, 2009); *Fin-de-Siècle Literary Culture and Women Poets* (a special edition of *Journal of Victorian Literature and Culture*, 2006); and *Poetry of the 1890s* (Penguin, 1998). She is currently working on a monograph called *The Lyric and Modernity*.

Herbert F. Tucker is John C. Coleman Professor of English at the University of Virginia, where he also serves as associate editor for *New Literary History* and series co-editor in Victorian Literature and Culture for the University Press. He is the author of *Epic: Britain's Heroic Muse 1790–1910* (Oxford University Press, 2008), *Tennyson and the Doom of Romanticism* (Harvard University Press, 1988) and *Browning's Beginnings* (University of Minnesota Press, 1980), and has edited *A Companion to Victorian Literature and Culture* (1999), *Under Criticism* (Ohio University Press, 1998), *Critical Essays on Alfred Lord Tennyson* (G. K. Hall, 1993), and a teaching anthology (with Dorothy Mermin), *Victorian Literature 1830–1900* (Harcourt College Publishers, 2001). His interactive scansion tutorial 'For Better for Verse' is freely available at http://prosody.lib.virginia.edu.

A NOTE ON THE TEXTS

We use throughout the Harvard author-date system of referencing with full publication details given in the References at the end of this book. Where two or more works by the same author have been published in the same year, they have been identified by additional letters, e.g. 1862a, 1862b. In the case of certain key publications by Swinburne, we have provided a reference that indicates the original publication and/or standard edition and in some cases a modern edition as well. In the case of extended analyses of poems from *Poems and Ballads, First Series*, we state the initial page run in the standard edition of Swinburne's poems (1904) and the Penguin edition (2000) and give subsequent in-text line references to the Penguin edition which alone has line numbers.

1

INTRODUCTION

Catherine Maxwell and Stefano Evangelista

When, in 1895, various writers were asked who should be the next Poet Laureate after Tennyson, Oscar Wilde's reply was emphatic: 'Mr Swinburne is already the Poet Laureate of England. The fact that his appointment to this high commission has not been degraded by official confirmation renders his position all the more unassailable. He whom all poets love is the Laureate Poet always' (Wilde in Arnold et al. 1895, 403). Algernon Charles Swinburne (1837–1909), dramatist, novelist, critic, and late Victorian England's unofficial Poet Laureate, was admired by his contemporaries for his technical brilliance, his facility with classical and medieval forms, and his courage in expressing his sensual, erotic imagination. His first and best-known verse collection, *Poems and Ballads, First Series* (1866), notable for its consummate craftsmanship and provocative subject matter, created an unrivalled sensation. The radical republican views expressed in his later political collection *Songs before Sunrise* (1871) reinforced his reputation as a controversial figure. He was immensely important in his own day but, like several of his contemporaries, suffered neglect and misrepresentation during the first half of the twentieth century.

Now, however, Swinburne is acknowledged to be one of the most important Victorian poets, a founding figure for British aestheticism, and the dominant influence for many *fin-de-siècle* and modernist poets. Forging a vital link between French and English literary culture, he was responsible for promoting *avant-garde* poets such as Théophile Gautier and Charles Baudelaire who would have considerable impact on English decadent writers. Partly influenced by Gautier, he invented the impressionistic or 'aesthetic' prose style that, refined and made famous by Walter Pater, would leave its mark on a host of other considerable writers such as Oscar Wilde, John Addington Symonds, Vernon Lee, Arthur Symons, and

W. B. Yeats, as well as experimental modernists such as Virginia Woolf. Swinburne's critical essays on art helped shape the artistic tastes of the writers who succeeded him while his astute, perceptive, and wide-ranging literary criticism was responsible for introducing many new or previously neglected writings – such as Blake's poetry and Elizabethan and seventeenth-century drama – to a larger audience. A prolific dramatist, he is best known today for his classically inspired Greek plays, in particular the beautifully crafted *Atalanta in Calydon* (1865). His novels, the unfinished and fragmentary *Lesbia Brandon* (written 1864–6) and the brilliant and witty epistolary narrative *A Year's Letters* (completed in 1863, and first published in 1877), provide fascinating insights into the hidden sexual lives of the Victorian aristocracy. Swinburne's centenary in 2009 and the increasing interest in late Victorian literature and the nineteenth-century *fin de siècle* make this the perfect moment to re-evaluate his literary contribution.

This collection of essays by established and rising scholars aims to do just that. Stemming from the international centenary conference that took place in London in July 2009, this volume brings together some of the best new scholarship on Swinburne, resituating him in the light of current critical work on cosmopolitanism, politics, print culture, form, Victorian Hellenism, religious controversy, gender and sexuality, the arts, and aestheticism and its contested relation to literary modernism. It is our hope that these fresh perspectives will confirm Swinburne's central importance both to late Victorian culture and to contemporary academic interests in this period. We also hope the collection will generate new interest in Swinburne, invigorate scholarship on him, and stimulate further research.

Any scholarly reassessment has to take into account the poet's critical fortunes during the twentieth century. Swinburne was one of the most famous casualties of the modernist backlash against the Victorians. Damned by the faint praise of T. S. Eliot in an essay that even today still haunts Swinburne criticism (Eliot 1920a), the poet's reputation languished for nearly forty years. Swinburne's lead as an innovator made him too close for comfort for Eliot and others keen to demonstrate their own *avant-garde* credentials. However, as Catherine Maxwell shows in her chapter, although Eliot never revoked his relegation of Swinburne to the margins, this did not mean that he and other writers were not deeply indebted to him. Female writers in particular such as Renée Vivien, Radclyffe Hall, and Edith Sitwell proved receptive to Swinburne's legacy, as did the Imagist poet H. D. whose responsiveness to his influence has been extensively discussed by Cassandra Laity (Laity 1992, 1996) and Diana Collecott (Collecott 1999). Unlike their more grudging male peers, many women writers saw Swinburne as an enabling precursor. At a time when they were resisting the restrictions of contemporary masculine models, Swinburne's experiments with intricate patterns of sensory images, sounds, and rhythms, his acknowledgement of bodily pleasure and intuition, blurring of boundaries, celebration of fluid gender identities and polymorphous sexuality, and idolisation of the lesbian poet Sappho offered an alternative aesthetic practice that could help with the formation of a modern feminine poetics. As Charlotte Ribeyrol, another of our contributors, indicates in her chapter on Swinburne's Hellenism, it was his promotion of a markedly sensuous 'chromatic' classicism as opposed to the more austere, 'straight' version endorsed by men such as Ezra Pound and T. E. Hulme that women writers found appealing; and in her chapter Sarah Parker adds to the scholarly work of Laity and Collecott, by identifying another practitioner of Swinburnian-inspired Sapphic modernism in the Imagist poet Amy Lowell. Lowell, she argues, not only learns much from her precursor but also shares with him the experience of a critical backlash, much of it motivated by crude caricature, with a similar negative impact on the reception of her work.

While he commanded a select minority of admirers and supporters, Swinburne's own reception was muted until the 1960s when his fortunes began to revive owing to the good offices of scholars such as Cecil Y. Lang, editor of the monumental six-volume *Swinburne Letters* (Swinburne 1959-62) and Clyde K. Hyder, editor of important collections of Swinburne's prose (Swinburne 1966, 1972) and early reviews of his work (Hyder 1970). Since then he has benefited from the serious attention of a small but distinguished group of academics, mainly Americans, who have devoted monographs to him: Thomas E. Connolly (1964), Robert L. Peters (1965), Jerome McGann (1972), David Riede (1978), Kerry McSweeney (1981), Antony Harrison (1988), and the Canadian scholar Margot K. Louis (1990). The last twenty years have seen several useful selected editions of the poems by Catherine Maxwell (Swinburne 1997), and Jerome McGann and Charles Sligh (Swinburne 2004a), as well as Kenneth Haynes's indispensable edition of *Poems and Ballads, First Series* and *Atalanta in Calydon* (Swinburne 2000). In 1993 Rikky Rooksby and Nicholas Shrimpton published an important collection of ten essays by some noted scholars (Rooksby and Shrimpton 1993). One of Rooksby's own contributions to that collection provides a valuable detailed survey of Swinburne criticism in the twentieth century, although, published before the increased interest in modernist women's writing in the 1990s, it naturally could not take account of more recent scholarship that recognises Swinburne's importance to his female successors. (The same goes for the other many important critical works on gender and sexuality that have dominated Swinburne scholarship over the last twenty years.) In 1993 Rooksby's chief concern was the perceived encroachment of deconstructive criticism, his anxiety being that, following Eliot, such criticism might reclaim Swinburne merely as 'a poet of disembodied words'. Now, in the light of our current fascination with Swinburnian body matters, such anxieties look groundless, and Rooksby's desire for more diverse perspectives, 'other doors that need throwing open', has been fulfilled (Rooksby 1993, 19). Rooksby's new biography of the poet, which followed four years later (Rooksby 1997), was a landmark publication containing new material that enhances our understanding of the poet, especially in relation to his family and his formative years. That widening of knowledge has continued with the more recent appearance of Terry Meyers's excellent three-volume edition of Swinburne's *Uncollected Letters* (Swinburne 2004b), a worthy supplement to Lang's original project. These letters cast new light on Swinburne's relationships with other literary and notable figures and deepen our sense of his complex bond with his cousin Mary Disney Leith (née Gordon), now widely regarded as his 'lost love'.

Since 1990 there has been only one critical monograph – Catherine Maxwell's compact overview *Swinburne* (Maxwell 2006) in the British Council series Writers and Their Work. However, there has been a steady stream of chapters, essays, and articles published on Swinburne during this period, many of which have proved to be influential (e.g. Dellamora 1990; Zonana 1990; Morgan 1992, 1993a, 1996; Prins 1999; Kuduk 2001; Maxwell 2001 and 2003; Østermark-Johansen 2002a). As indicated above, many of these pieces have focused on sexuality and gender in Swinburne's writing, with Swinburne studies often ahead of the field in providing new insights with regard to nineteenth-century literary representations of non-normative ('queer') sexuality such as sadomasochism and same-sex love. In 1993, acknowledging the importance of Ian Gibson's 1978 account of 'Swinburne's experience of and predilection for the birch', Rooksby also welcomed Gibson's inadequately substantiated claim that the poet might in some ways conform to a more straightforward virility, clearly relieved that it 'made Swinburne's sexual abnormalities seem a little less abnormal' (Rooksby 1993, 14).[1] One sympathises with Rooksby's concerns about the reductiveness of commentators who 'made it seem that Swinburne's sexual life meant birching and nothing else' (15), although increased appreciation of the diversity of human sexuality means that efforts to mitigate Swinburne's 'abnormality' now look rather dated. That diversity is omnipresent in Swinburne's own writings where his understanding of desire is decidedly non-reductive, as can be seen in his epic *Tristram of Lyonesse* (1882). In a sensitive essay on its second canto, the late Margot K. Louis sees him 'undercutting the phallic model and substituting for it a model of sex based on the assumption of multitudinous centers of pleasure, in ways that highlight female sexuality and female desire' (Louis 2009a, 647).

Increasing awareness of the ways in which literary aestheticism is shaped and informed by queer or unconventional sexuality has in turn strengthened Swinburne's position as a foundational figure. There is a growing interest in the ways that sexuality itself might help shape, inform, or condition style, poetics, and other aspects of literary practice. Yopie Prins's chapter in this book, which reads Swinburne's flagellant verse as a prosodic primer of metrical discipline, is an excellent case in point. While Swinburne's style, themes, and subject matter have long been recognised as influential for his aesthetic and decadent successors, it is notable that many of those successors – Walter Pater, John Addington Symonds, Oscar Wilde, Arthur Symons, Vernon Lee, Michael Field, Mary Robinson, Charlotte Mew – are also sexual outsiders or dissidents. As 'founding father' and 'unofficial laureate' of this group, Swinburne can be seen to create literary models that appeal to, and are adopted and adapted by his likeminded followers – a process that, as already indicated, continues through into the twentieth century and bears fruit in the Sapphic modernism of his female inheritors. Moreover, as aestheticism – the major intellectual, artistic, and cultural movement from the 1860s to the turn of the century – continues to attract some of the best and liveliest criticism in Victorian studies, it becomes correspondingly more important to trace and evaluate Swinburne's pervasive influence.

Swinburne's centenary in 2009 saw a surge of critical activity in the form of two other notable collections. The first of these, a special Swinburne centenary issue of the academic journal *Victorian Poetry* (2009), is guest-edited by Terry Meyers and Rikky Rooksby and contains twelve essays, including pieces by Jerome McGann, Julia F. Saville, Margot

K. Louis, Catherine Maxwell, and Yisrael Levin. Levin is also the editor of the second book collection of eight essays (Levin 2010), which includes contributions by Charlotte Ribeyrol, Stephanie Kuduk, Nick Freeman, Catherine Maxwell, and Rikky Rooksby. The journal issue is heterogeneous and eclectic in its range. In contrast Levin's collection is more focused, concentrating on literary work from the late 1870s onwards, with the specific aim of introducing readers to 'Swinburne's often disregarded later achievements' while also considering 'the prevalent critical attitudes that have perpetuated this neglect' (Levin 2010a, 1).

Important though it is to promote Swinburne's later poetry, most readers nonetheless will, initially at least, be attracted to the earlier, better-known works about which, it should be added, there is still plenty to say. This current Swinburne collection aims to strike a careful balance between providing new readings of the more familiar works and encouraging readers to explore works that are comparatively less well-known. Thus, while readers will find discussion of some of Swinburne's most famous, not to say infamous, poems such as 'Anactoria' and 'The Leper' from *Poems and Ballads, First Series*, they will also find readings of late poems such as 'Off Shore', 'In the Water', and the 'Transvaal' sonnets, as well as consideration of his prose criticism including his diverting burlesque bogus reviews, and rare manuscript material from his flagellant collection 'The Flogging-Block'. *A Century of Roundels* (1883), a fine late collection that deploys Swinburne's innovative adaptation of the roundel and a delight in poetic form for its own sake, emerges in the work of three contributors as a volume richly deserving of a wider audience.

Our collection is organised into three individually distinct but interrelated sections which cover key aspects of Swinburne's work and situate its impact and significance within literary and cultural histories and the critical tradition. The first, 'Cultural Discourse', concentrates on understanding Swinburne's place in Victorian culture. During his lifetime Swinburne repeatedly took a crucial, if now often obscured, role in leading the public debate in spheres that range from classical studies to politics and print culture. The first two chapters in this book, for instance, examine Swinburne's involvement in the history of cosmopolitanism, a field of enquiry that is attracting growing attention among literary critics, especially within modernist studies (see Walkowitz 2006). Stefano Evangelista focuses on Swinburne's critical prose in order to examine his important role as cosmopolitan critic and cultural mediator between nineteenth-century England and France. Drawing on the early essays and reviews, Evangelista traces Swinburne's responses to Matthew Arnold, focusing in particular on the young Swinburne's challenge to the older critic who was held as the foremost English authority on French literature and cosmopolitan culture. Evangelista shows how Swinburne elaborated a unique form of critical writing, in which he staged a playful, hybrid dialogue between English and French voices, a form that he adopted in both his private and his public writings and that reached its most tantalising expression in two spoof reviews of fictitious French poets, unpublished during Swinburne's lifetime, which are here subjected to a detailed interpretation. Julia F. Saville, on the other hand, concentrates on Swinburne's poetry, in particular on his use of images of open-air swimming as a 'ubiquitous [trope] in nineteenth-century poetic meditations on democratic reform'. Juxtaposing early and late writings, Saville offers fresh insights into a problem that has vexed many readers of Swinburne: his turn from the progressive, cosmopolitan republicanism of *Songs before Sunrise* to the jingoism of some of his late verse. By means of sensitive yet clear-sighted reading of three sonnets that Swinburne composed during the Anglo-Boer War, Saville unveils the mobile and sometimes problematic allegiances of Swinburne's politics.

Intimately linked to cosmopolitanism is the question of Hellenism. In recent years, several critics have examined the importance of Hellenism as a productive area of collaboration and conflict between Victorian writers, artists, and intellectuals (see for instance Prins 1999, Goldhill 2002, Fiske 2008, Evangelista 2009, Louis 2009b, as well as the foundational Turner 1981). The Victorian culture wars over the meaning and value of ancient Greece assumed a particular importance for authors linked to aestheticism who looked to the classical past in order to develop transgressive readings of literary and material history, and new strategies of social and cultural dissent (Evangelista 2009, 11). Charlotte Ribeyrol shows that Swinburne took part in this important debate by seeking to draw the attention of his contemporaries to a marginal, darker Greece that was both entirely authentic and yet profoundly different from the ideal celebrated by Victorian institutional culture. She traces Swinburne's interest in the chthonic imagination of Greek antiquity from his early classical tragedy *Atalanta in Calydon*, through some of the best-known lyrics in *Poems and Ballads, First Series* to the later *Erechtheus* (1876), discovering the poet's pervasive fascination with colour as at once antidote and alternative to the sculptural, whitewashed classicism promoted by canonical nineteenth-century Hellenism.

In the last chapter in this section Laurel Brake argues for the importance of Swinburne's prose writings in our understanding of his overall achievement. Her specific interest, though, is in Swinburne's publication practices, a topic that has been neglected in the critical tradition. Brake reconstructs Swinburne's career as a journalist: she shows how journalism – a discursive practice quite distinct from the genre-determined field of criticism – provides an exciting new cultural context that broadens our sense of Swinburne's identity as author and public man of letters, revealing his ongoing relationship with the media and the material history of Victorian print culture. She presents a nuanced reassessment of Swinburne as professional man of letters through a detailed reconstruction of his participation in periodical and magazine publishing, a participation that involved both his poetry and his prose. She also considers his provocative negative pronouncements on the state of the press in Victorian Britain. All these chapters explicitly or implicitly refute the image of the disengaged and Parnassian Swinburne propagated by his modernist detractors: they reveal that, far from being a canon of 'disembodied words', Swinburne's writings present readers with multiple modes and layers of engagement with cultural and material history, politics, and the marketplace.

Centring our book as it must centre any discussion of Swinburne's writing is a section on form that encompasses a reconsideration of his thinking about metre, an exploration of a repeatedly used fixed form that he made his own, and a more general re-evaluation of the lyric impulse. Swinburne's pleasure in form and his mastery of it – his use of demanding metres and intricate poetic structures – have often caused his detractors to complain that he is the producer of style rather than substance, of 'empty' music without meaning. In fact Swinburne's poetry challenges the idea that poetry is essentially a message somewhat inconveniently packaged in a fancy wrapper and that reading poetry is merely a matter of extracting the meaning. Swinburne, more so perhaps than other poets, makes us read poetry as poetry. In his work verse form, metre, rhythm, rhyme, symbol, echo, allusion, and the rich texture of verbal patterning are an intrinsic part of the meaning, drift, or argument. In the first chapter in this section, Yopie Prins shows that a close analysis of metre and poetic form leads to a radical rethinking of how sexuality is encoded and expressed in Swinburne's poems. Through a detailed examination of Swinburne's unpublished flagellatory poem 'The Flogging-Block', Prins discovers a web of connections between the nineteenth-century culture of metrical discipline and the pedagogic discipline of minors portrayed through sexual fantasy. Prins persuasively urges us to read Swinburne's flagellant verses not as the signifiers of sexual perversions to be diagnosed but as 'closet prosody', and a 'subversion, or perversion of Victorian metrical culture'. In his chapter on *A Century of Roundels*, Herbert Tucker also asks modern readers of Swinburne to attend more carefully to the formal structures of his poetry. Tucker emphasises the need to 'refocus expectation so as to read our way not *past* form but *through* it, to grasp meaning as ingredient in verse structure rather than in spite or in lieu of it', adding that 'In poetry *the way* is the truth and the life'. Thus what in his analysis of the roundel form Tucker calls 'these poems' *reverberation*: a harboured difference maturing within the iteration of the same' is echoed in Marion Thain's reading of 'On an Old Roundel' where that reverberation is the resonant layering of the voices of François Villon, D. G. Rossetti, and Swinburne himself: 'Their poetic voices are bound, living and dead, through this form whose repetition makes both the dead return to life and what is living find community in death.' Thain uses the evocative notion of 'desire lines', a concept borrowed from urban geography, to argue that the lyric in Swinburne is not an expression of individuality but rather a desire for plurality and community, reflected in his extensive practice of retracing other poets' voices.

Our concluding section explores the topic of Influence in various ways. The first two chapters look at Swinburne in intellectual dialogue with two of the major poets of his age: Christina Rossetti and Robert Browning. The last two examine Swinburne's own influence on his modernist successors. Dinah Roe concentrates on Swinburne's transformative reworkings of the forms of an admired contemporary, Christina Rossetti. Swinburne strongly disagreed with Rossetti's espousal of a devout Anglo-Catholic faith. However, by a skilful juxtaposition of public and private writings by the two poets, Roe brings to light an intriguing relationship of simultaneous rejection and creative collaboration. She reconstructs the multiple ways in which these poets read each other and responded to each other's work, noting, for instance, Rossetti's debt to Swinburne in her adoption of the roundel form. The twin mechanics of poetic dialogue and cultural polemic is also the subject of Sara Lyons's chapter. Lyons argues that Swinburne's use of the dramatic monologue form associated with Browning, one of his key poetic precursors, was a way of interrogating the older poet's representations of religious doubt. Through a series of close readings, Lyons shows that Swinburne's own dramatic monologues

'Hymn to Proserpine' and 'The Leper' flaunt his own uncompromising atheistic position against both belief and respectable 'Victorian doubt', recasting atheism as 'a mode of Romantic transgression'.

Looking forward to the twentieth century, Sarah Parker and Catherine Maxwell explore the question of Swinburne's afterlife in the work of experimental poets linked to modernism. Parker adopts a gendered approach, comparing the use of Sappho as 'lesbian muse' in the work of Swinburne and the American Imagist poet Amy Lowell. She shows that Swinburne's controversial portrayal of lesbianism, sometimes attacked by late twentieth-century feminist critics, provided a positive model of poetic identification for Lowell, a poet who, like Swinburne, was also subjected to marginalisation and exclusion by the male modernists. Like Parker's, several chapters in the book go back to T. S. Eliot, whose ambivalence towards Swinburne left such a strong mark on twentieth-century criticism. Eliot is explicitly the subject of the last chapter, where Catherine Maxwell provides a detailed investigation of the mode and origins of Eliot's modernist hostility towards Swinburne. Focusing on the concept of Swinburnian 'vagueness' attacked by Eliot, Maxwell shows how Eliot's view of Swinburne's self-sufficient linguistic world, so often seen as an innovative assertion of modernist values, in fact derives from earlier critical formulations by the Georgian poets Edward Thomas and John Drinkwater, a dependence particularly surprising in the case of Drinkwater, whose poetry Eliot publicly despised. Read together, Parker's and Maxwell's chapters provide complementary accounts of the difficult and often invisible dynamics behind influence and marginalisation, unveiling narratives of problematic acceptance and problematic rejection, by a female and a male poet respectively. As in the first section, 'Cultural Discourse', with which the chapters here present several points of dialogue, the emphasis is on Swinburne's embeddedness and centrality in a culture from which he has been partly been written out. These studies of influence fittingly draw the present volume to a deliberately provisional and open-ended conclusion. In the early twenty-first century, as the modernist mentality has started to lose both its hold on educated readers and its primacy in academic institutions, Swinburne's work, with all its hidden complexities and immediate sensual appeal, its intellectual rigour and contradictions, stands more than ever open for new readings.

The range and variety of Swinburne's work do indeed speak to new generations, especially those working experimentally with new forms of expression. At the time of writing the contemporary filmmakers Andre

Semenza and Fernanda Lippi are in the final stages of completing *Sea without Shore*, a cinematic lyric narrative of love between women that unfolds in the remote forest landscapes of rural Sweden in the late nineteenth century.[2] An exploration of love and loss told through dance and movement, its haunting visual sequences are accompanied by a voiceover made of a collage of poetic fragments, the majority of them taken from Swinburne.[3] That these fragments are translated into and voiced in Swedish might at first seem incongruous, but the experience of hearing the strange yet often recognisably familiar words intoned aloud whilst seeing the original English in the subtitles seems like yet another version of that creative reverberation and layering that is so much a part of Swinburnian poetics. Swinburne's own practice of revoicing dead poets through translation, a process that often involves incorporation of their fragments into his own verse, means that Semenza and Lippi's film seems imaginatively true to his aesthetic as does their emphasis on the powerfully physicalised emotion of the dancers, its rhythms and compulsive repetitions. Swinburne believed passionately that the great poets he himself loved 'do not for us live only on the dusty shelves of libraries' (Swinburne 1904, 1.xxi) so it seems fitting that he continues to inspire new interpretations that mix 'memories' and 'metaphors' of his poetry (Swinburne 1904, 1.64; 2000, 53) to such extraordinary effect. T. S. Eliot was surely learning from examples such as Swinburne's 'On the Cliffs' from *Songs of the Springtides* (1880) when he mixed fragmentary poetic memories of his predecessors, Swinburne included, in *The Waste Land* (1922), although the modernist project seemed more funerary than celebratory. Swinburne mercifully has survived the modernist 'burial of the dead'. Though he himself acknowledged 'the two-edged spear of time' that eventually 'wastes all songs as roseleaves kissed and frayed', he declared Sappho's song a glorious exception: 'But thine the spear may waste not' (Swinburne 1904, 3.324, 325). How long Swinburne's own song will endure is unknowable, but it is consoling to recognise at the present time that there are many determined to cherish and 'waste not' his remarkable legacy.

NOTES

1 Gibson assumes with no real evidence that the female flagellators of the St John's Wood brothel who administered discipline to Swinburne in the late 1860s afterwards 'proceeded to assuage his desires in a more conventional

fashion' (Gibson 1978, 256–7, also cited in Rooksby 1993, 15). Both Gibson and Rooksby ignore the hints that Swinburne may have been impotent, perhaps as a result of an earlier riding accident; see Maxwell 2010a, 135, note 11.

2 *Sea without Shore* will begin its international festival life in 2013 and will be made available on DVD (produced by Maverick Motion Ltd and Zikzira Physical Theatre) in due course. For further details of festival / cinema screenings and the DVD, see www.zikzira.com.

3 Sources include 'Triads III', from *Poems and Ballads, Second Series* (1878), and the following poems from *Poems and Ballads, First Series*: 'Félise', 'April', 'Anactoria', 'A Ballad of Life', 'Madonna Mia', 'A Litany', 'The Triumph of Time', 'Phædra', 'Hesperia', 'A Leave-Taking', 'Laus Veneris', 'To Victor Hugo', and 'St. Dorothy'. The film takes its title from 'Hymn to Proserpine': 'Fate is a sea without shore' (Swinburne 1904, 1.69; 2000, 57, line 41).

Part I

CULTURAL DISCOURSE

1

SWINBURNE'S FRENCH VOICE:
COSMOPOLITANISM AND CULTURAL MEDIATION IN AESTHETIC CRITICISM

Stefano Evangelista

Swinburne's critical reception has, understandably, largely focused on the poetry, but criticism played a crucial if overlooked role in establishing his early reputation.[1] Swinburne is the author of an extensive prose output that ranges from reviews of English and French authors to literary criticism, art criticism, and polemical writings; among his most notable achievements are the public championing of authors who were at the time undervalued (such as William Blake and Charlotte Brontë), the study of Elizabethan drama, and the promotion in Britain of modern French literature, especially Victor Hugo, for whose work Swinburne nurtured a veritable idolatry.

Swinburne's debut as (anonymous) critic took place in the early 1860s in the *Spectator*, a liberal weekly then under the editorship of Richard Holt Hutton. It was here that Swinburne published his celebrated early review of Baudelaire (1862). Hutton was initially supportive of the young Swinburne but would in later years turn into an outspoken critic of what he saw as the 'indignity' of his poetry (Hutton 1896, 396). Even before these public hostilities, though, Swinburne had come to feel alienated by the moral bias of the *Spectator* and its editor, and had become eager to find a paper for which he could write more freely – 'at my own times and in my own way', as he wrote to Monckton Milnes in 1863 – on art and literature, especially on French writers (Swinburne 1959–62, 1.72). Such an opportunity arose in 1867, in the wake of the clamour over *Poems and Ballads, First Series* (1866), when Swinburne met John Morley, editor of the *Fortnightly Review*. The pages of the *Fortnightly* provided a progressive home for some of Swinburne's most important critical pieces of these early years, such as the essay on Matthew Arnold (1867) and 'Notes on Designs of the Old Masters at Florence' (1868). Aside from periodical contributions, Swinburne disseminated his criticism in pamphlets (*Notes on Poems and Reviews*, 1866), book form (*William Blake*, 1868), and collections (*Essays and Studies*, 1875). The criticism of these early years shows the strong influence of French literature, on which Swinburne would establish himself as a paramount authority in years to come: French writers are not only a favourite topic but also a stylistic model on which Swinburne draws in order to create a highly distinctive critical idiom. Following the examples of Baudelaire and, especially, Gautier, Swinburne pioneered an experimental type of critical writing rich in vivid pictorial imagery, lyrical texture, and synaesthetic effect, which translated into poetical prose the complex emotional response triggered in the sympathetic critic by the encounter with a literary work or art object. Swinburne's friend and biographer Edmund Gosse speaks of it as the first attempt in English 'to produce a concrete and almost plastic conception of the work of an author, not minutely analysed or coldly condensed, but presented as if by an inspired neophyte, proclaiming a religion in an ecstasy' (Gosse 1917, 169). Swinburne's groundbreaking criticism thus folded together two otherwise distinct and apparently mutually exclusive categories: specialisation and emotion or, to put it differently, the cold eye of the critic and the receptive enthusiasm of the poet. This critical style brought to England by Swinburne was embraced, on both sides of the Channel, by the advocates of the doctrine of art for art's sake.

This new critical idiom, better known through Walter Pater's formulation as 'aesthetic criticism' (Pater 1980, xix), was a style that twentieth-century modernism would come to dislike. T. S. Eliot, for instance, was disturbed by the hybrid of critical prose and poetic technique which he described in a language redolent of psychoanalytic theories of sublimation: in 'The Perfect Critic', Eliot tried to determine whether Swinburne 'found an adequate outlet for the creative impulse in his poetry' or whether such impulse was 'forced back and out' through the, to him, clearly inappropriate medium of critical prose (Eliot 1920a, 5). Eliot's verdict was positive in the end: Swinburne did manage to separate between the two and his critical writings were therefore not 'the satisfaction of a suppressed creative wish'; even so, Swinburne's criticism remained impressionistic and sentimental – which is a damning judgement from a critic for whom bad criticism was 'nothing but an expression of emotion' (Eliot 1920a, 7, 14). This confused analysis might well be the result of Eliot's discomfort about Swinburne's frank treatment of sexual perversion, a topic that Eliot struggles to keep out of his assessment but that emerges as a displaced diagnosis of repression. Swinburne, of whom Eliot holds a higher opinion than he does of other late Victorians such as Pater or Arthur Symons, is nonetheless for him an 'imperfect critic'. While possessing a very good command of his material and sound judgement, he was let down by his stylistic faults, in particular his ornate language and syntax, which Eliot, in his essay 'Swinburne as Critic', again reads psychologically as 'the index to an impatience and perhaps laziness of a disorderly mind' (Eliot 1920a, 15).

Eliot's bias is symptomatic of the modernists' generational suspicion towards their late-Victorian precursors. In the first half of the twentieth century Swinburne's critical works were first demolished and then progressively forgotten, so much so that Robert L. Peters, at the outset of his 1965 study of Swinburne as critic, stated that his aim was 'to rescue [Swinburne's criticism] from near oblivion' (Peters 1965, 9). Since then, though, critics have elaborated positive ways to frame Swinburne's achievement in criticism, focusing openly on eroticism and sexual complexity, highlighting the clarity of judgement that even Eliot had to concede, and reassessing Swinburne's hybrid technique as an important experiment in formal innovation: Swinburne is now recognised as an influential early proponent of the aesthetic prose style that would, from the 1870s onwards, be perfected by Pater and that would become one of the most effective platforms for the expression of an English decadent sensibility (see Maxwell 2006). In this chapter I argue that Swinburne's early critical writings promote a theory of aesthetic cosmopolitanism that emerges from a sustained polemical dialogue with Matthew Arnold. In a recent article Julia F. Saville has placed Swinburne in a tradition of cosmopolitan republicanism active in Britain between the 1850s and 1870s. Saville's interest is in the way in which Swinburne's cosmopolitan poetics fuses macro-politics and body politics (Saville 2009a, 692–3). I believe that Swinburne theorises criticism as a space of cosmopolitan interchange and fluidity, where the poet-critic participates in networks of cross-national alliances that enable him to experience multiple subject positions, imaginatively embracing antithesis and contradiction. In this way not only are the critical essays intimately related to the experiments in cultural translation that Swinburne undertook, more famously, in his poetry, but they also make an important intervention in the evolving understanding of cultural mediation in Victorian criticism. My focus is on the critical work of the 1860s. It is in these early essays that the young Swinburne established his well-deserved reputation as an authority on French literature and it is here that we find his most compelling reflections on the dynamics of translation and cultural exchange. From the 1880s an inward-turning seems to take place: just as Swinburne's poetry gives up the impulse towards transgression that had made it popular in the 1860s, his criticism becomes decidedly more insular.[2] While his near-idolatry of Hugo remained constant, his public writings gradually lost interest in the newest trends in French literature, concentrating instead more and more on the English Elizabethans (as foundational of a mythology of Englishness), just as his prose style abandoned poetic flair in favour of rhetorical and oratorical display.[3]

Paramount in any account of Swinburne's career as critic is his 1862 essay on Baudelaire, a short but influential work that effectively launched the reception of the French poet in Britain. Swinburne gives a complete sketch of Baudelaire's achievement, including his important work as critic and translator of American and English writers, but the main focus of the piece is on some of the poems in *Les Fleurs du mal*, published in 1857 and immediately subjected to public attacks and censorship, which, as various critics have pointed out, would have a strong impact on the development of Swinburne's own poetry.[4] Swinburne includes several extracts from Baudelaire's poetry, praising it with that element of extravagance that would become a hallmark of his critical style, placing particular emphasis on the French poet's talent for capturing elements of sorrow and strangeness, and for bringing together apparently antithetical registers of emotion. For Swinburne the verses in *Les Fleurs du mal* enlarge the boundaries of modern poetry by giving expression not to 'the luxuries of pleasure in their simple first form, but the sharp and cruel enjoyments of pain, the acrid relish of suffering felt or inflicted, the sides on which nature looks unnatural' (Swinburne 1862a, 999; 1972, 30). As an example of this modern complexity Swinburne reproduces two stanzas from 'Une Charogne' ('A Carcass'), where, he argues, Baudelaire is able to make 'noble' material out of the repulsive themes of putrescence and decomposition thanks to his great technical command of the poetic medium. The essay therefore introduces not simply a new poet but a new way of writing. At the same time it functions as an English manifesto for the doctrine of art for art's sake, which believes that the artist's primary responsibility is towards medium rather than subject matter, and as an early theorisation of decadent poetics, captured by Swinburne in his paradox about the unnatural side of nature. Most importantly, the essay on Baudelaire heralds a new literary culture in which poetry is divorced from didacticism and morality, and in which it is the artist's prerogative to set his or her work *against* the standards of middle-class readers. These characteristics, which we now associate with *fin-de-siècle* writing and experimental modernism, are already discovered by Swinburne in Baudelaire's poetry of the 1850s.[5] His essay identifies France as a source of literary modernity that is worthy of serious study and imitation, which was particularly provocative at a time in which popular perceptions of modern French writing, especially of French novels, were dominated by generalised impressions of libertinism and cheap sensationalism. It was a matter of popular wisdom that women and young people should be screened from this potentially pernicious influence. Gosse, for instance, relates how Swinburne incurred the wrath of Sir Walter Trevelyan for presenting his wife with a copy of a French novel (Gosse 1917, 71–2); and we know that Pater got into trouble for recommending Gautier to an Eton schoolboy (Evans 1970, 16).

In the 1860s, though, Swinburne was not the only British critic intent on redressing this popular prejudice about the negative influence of reading in French. Through the first half of that decade Matthew Arnold promoted his own version of British Francophilia in a series of influential articles published in various magazines and later collected in *Essays in Criticism* (1865). Arnold was already an established poet at that time, as well as having been Professor of Poetry at Oxford. His interventions therefore carried a great deal more authority than those of the considerably younger, virtually unknown, and decidedly more maverick Swinburne, whose essays in the *Spectator* were moreover published unsigned. But it is possible to reconstruct a dialogue between the older and the younger critic – a debate over what exactly is to be got from France and why – that is a crucial episode in the early history of aestheticism, establishing its roots, cultural mission, and future directions as they would appear in the better-known critical writings of Pater and Oscar Wilde.

The dominant note of Arnold's criticism in this period is his impatience with his perceived narrowness of nineteenth-century English culture. In order to overcome this narrowness Arnold urged critics and writers to look abroad, specifically to France. Arnold's cosmopolitanism is evident everywhere in his critical writings – in the 'Preface' to *Essays in Criticism*, for instance, he describes himself as 'a plain citizen of the republic of letters' (Arnold 1962, 288) – but it is best encapsulated in his famous definition of culture in the 'Preface' to *Literature and Dogma* (1873) as 'the acquainting ourselves with the best that has been known and said in the world' (Arnold 1968, 151): in Arnold's ideal, culture is not a function of national character (as in the standard formulations 'British culture' or 'French culture') but a shared property of trans-national communities. It is easy to see how this ideal should have fallen out of favour with twentieth-century critics, less keen to adopt hierarchical or value-driven definitions of what counts as culture; and it is also easy to feel how readers of Arnold then and now could at times have felt alienated by his voice, with its propensity for high-mindedness and its often patronising tones. This is why, in the 'Introduction' to *The Sacred Wood*, T. S. Eliot not implausibly speaks of Arnold's criticism as 'destructive work', bent first and foremost on attacking the uncritical rather than building new structures of thought (Eliot 1920a, xi); even though later in that volume Eliot undoes his own metaphor by calling that same criticism 'a bridge across the Channel', recognising its historical importance in creating a dialogue with France (Eliot 1920a, 1).

Arnold's cosmopolitan ideal and the characteristics of his style are evident in his essay on Heinrich Heine (1863). The choice of a German author seems surprising at first, until we realise that Heine is in fact partly an authorial projection, an alter ego of Arnold himself, just as Heine's early nineteenth-century Germany is a displaced version of Arnold's mid-Victorian Britain. Arnold admires Heine's ability to effect a harmonious synthesis of the different national traditions of Germany and France and prophesies, with a touch of immodesty, a time in the near future when British critics will take stock of the beneficial effects of his own work of cultural mediation.

> It is because he thus operates a junction between the French spirit, and German ideas and German culture, that [Heine] founds something new, opens a fresh period, and deserves the attention of criticism far more than the German poets his contemporaries, who merely continue an old period till it expires. It may be predicted that in the literature of other countries, too, the French spirit is destined to make its influence felt, – as an element, in alliance with the native spirit, of novelty and movement, – as it has made its influence felt in German literature; fifty years hence a critic will be demonstrating to our grandchildren how this phenomenon has come to pass. (Arnold 1962, 120)

Arnold argues that the contact with France was a motor for modernity in Heine's Germany, whose native culture was caught in the long aftermath of a lingering, spent Romanticism. It is this same French 'spirit' – Arnold uses this word all through the essay in relation to France and his usage has a marked French intonation: it is the French 'esprit' rather than the German 'Geist' – that he wants to import into Victorian England, a country likewise grappling with the legacy of its own Romanticism, a movement Arnold associates with the failed aristocratic poetics of Byron and Shelley. In order to define his notion of the 'French spirit', Arnold argues that foreigners looking to France will find that its people have shown 'more accessibility to ideas than any other people', more readiness to overthrow 'prescription and routine', and, most importantly perhaps, 'most readiness to move and to alter at the bidding (real or supposed) of reason' (Arnold 1962, 112). This promise of freedom, rather than the influence of any specific writer or thinker, is the antidote that Arnold prescribes to his compatriots as a corrective to what, borrowing Heine's use of the word 'Beschränktheit', he calls the 'narrowness' of the English Victorian frame of mind and its impatience with ideas. One can see in this argument, which juxtaposes sets of national characteristics associated with France on one side and with England/Germany on the other, the germ of the famous dialectic structure deployed in *Culture and Anarchy* (1869), with France acting as the new Hellas for Hebraic Germany and England.

Arnold's most lasting borrowing from Heine is the concept of Philistinism – a notion that would come to assume paramount symbolic significance in the English culture wars of the late nineteenth century. Heine had used the Biblically inspired concept of Philistinism to describe the conservative and anti-intellectual German tradition against which he pitted his French-accented authorial voice. In Arnold's definition, Philistinism is an 'inveterate inaccessibility to ideas' (Arnold 1962, 120) or, in other words, the ideological resistance to modernity and the modern spirit which is the reverse of the cosmopolitan ideal he was seeking to promote. Arnold argued that the absence of the term Philistinism from the English language could be explained only by the fact that its ubiquity had made the English effectively blind to it. But once imported and diagnosed by Arnold, Philistinism invaded the late Victorian press where it was used both by its enemies, like Arnold and the aesthetes, and by those who identified with it positively, and thereby tried to reverse its negative connotations. While Arnold's attack on Philistinism (so widespread as to be one of the unifying elements of his work as a critic) championed a vision of modernity founded on cosmopolitan culture, self-styled Philistine critics would, from the 1860s until the end of the century, gather their opposition to the cosmopolitan stance around an ideal of Englishness that they invoked as a conservative antidote to the cultural dislocation and the anti-patriotic forces of cosmopolitanism and what they saw as its excessive liberalism, affectations, and elitism. In Arnoldian terms, the tension between philistinism and cosmopolitanism is a further displacement of the dialectics of Hebraism and Hellenism: the Philistine camp believed in the Hebraic value of singleness, the adherence to one predetermined and constant tradition in national as well as moral terms, while cosmopolitan critics like Arnold and Swinburne advocated multiplicity and the Hellenic 'spontaneity of consciousness' (Arnold 1965, 165): their position was across nations and boundaries, their allegiances mobile.

The young Swinburne, passionate about modern France and classical Greece, was understandably drawn to Arnold from an early age. He used to memorise Arnold's verses when he was still a boy and later attended Arnold's Oxford lectures although, Gosse tells us, he was disappointed by their moderation (Gosse 1917, 52). To the emergent poet and critic Arnold offered an important model of how to manage successfully two distinct modes of authority. There is no doubt that, after the publication of his own essay on Baudelaire, Swinburne would have followed closely the development of Arnold's theories of cosmopolitanism and his views on French culture as they appeared in the articles published in the periodical press in the early 1860s, which would eventually make up *Essays in Criticism*.

In 1867 Swinburne took the decision to enter into a public conversation with Arnold in his review 'Matthew Arnold's New Poems', published in the *Fortnightly Review* in October and later reprinted in *Essays and Studies*. Swinburne's essay comes at a crucial time in Arnold's career as critic, between the publication of *Essays in Criticism* and *Culture and Anarchy*, and, in spite of its title, actually devotes considerable attention to the criticism. Swinburne acknowledges Arnold's role as the critic who launched the Victorian reaction against Philistinism and takes sides with his rejection of intellectual and moral narrowness. Swinburne claims that one of Arnold's greatest merits as a critic is his injunction to the English to learn from French culture and his strife 'to purge them of the pestilence of provincial thought and tradition, of blind theory and brute opinion, of all that hereditary policy of prejudice which substitutes self-esteem for self-culture, self-worship for self-knowledge' (Swinburne 1867a, 436; 1875a, 167; 1972, 83). Swinburne endorses Arnold's diagnosis that chauvinism and provincialism prevent English culture (and by extension, any national culture) from embracing modernity, and in so doing he effectively subscribes to Arnold's cosmopolitan ideal. But the rhetoric of praise and alliance is modified in the course of the essay as Swinburne tries to assert the independence of his own critical voice modelled, partly, on Arnold's, but also radically distinct from his. He regrets that Arnold, because of his ingrained loyalty to institutions, cannot be a real rebel: Arnold 'has smitten the Janus of Philistine worship on one face; under the other, if he has not himself burnt a pinch or two of adulterate incense, he has encouraged or allowed others to burn' (Swinburne 1867a, 435; 1875a, 165; 1972, 82). Arnold's importance as a critic is strategic, but his judgements are faulty, especially when it comes to French literature: he is, Swinburne cuttingly claims, 'not a sure guide over French ground' because he lacks 'the sudden and sensitive intuition of an innate instinct: he thinks right, but he feels wrong' (Swinburne 1867a, 437; 1875a, 168; 1972, 84). Swinburne, who was a passionate admirer of Hugo's verse, strongly objects to Arnold's claim that the highest achievement of French literature is in prose rather than poetry. He questions both Arnold's ability to hear French and his general competence in modern French literature, accusing him of being too ready to follow the judgement of George Sand. Most importantly, he plausibly challenges Arnold's overpraise of a minor poet like Maurice de Guérin, to whom Arnold had devoted one of his studies in *Essays in Criticism*, while ignoring the really vital developments in modern French literature that he, Swinburne, had spotted in his review of Baudelaire. At the end of what started as a positive review, the reader is left with the image of a deaf and confused Arnold, an amateur ageing Francophile ready to be dethroned from his position as leader of the cosmopolitan movement and of the anti-Philistine war by the present critic, author of *Atalanta in Calydon* (1865) and *Poems and Ballads* (1866) and now, as he was not in 1862, a signed critic.

Swinburne's staging of his succession to Arnold reaches its climax when he turns Arnold's own terms against himself, accusing him of provincialism. In Swinburne's essay Arnold becomes a champion of insular taste, not only deaf to French verse but blind to his own narrowness. Swinburne's target is Arnold's celebration of the French Academy, an institution that Arnold had praised in *Essays in Criticism* for its role in setting and maintaining a 'high, correct standard in intellectual matters' (Arnold 1962, 243) and curbing the eccentricities that, he worryingly observed, proliferated in England. Swinburne, by deliberate contrast, belittles the Academy's role in overseeing the best French literature and criticism and exposes its failure to admit really talented modern writers among its members – a point that he would reiterate to Arnold in private.[6] For him literary academies, in France or anywhere else, block the very influx of modernity that Arnold was allegedly trying to welcome and that, for Swinburne, must come from below, the margins, and unexpected places rather than be regulated from the top down. For Swinburne, Arnold's misjudgement is the giveaway blunder of a provincial critic who is determined to argue that things are always better on the other side of the fence: this Francophilia is more a form of social snobbery than a sign of progressive cosmopolitanism. Swinburne exposes the paradox whereby Arnold praises the nimbleness of the French spirit on the one hand but idolises stuffy institutions on the other, promoting a vision in which writers and intellectuals of an entire nation are subjected, like schoolchildren, to the supervision of a body of supreme teachers who police their work, in Arnold's words, 'checking and rebuking those who fall below [the] standards' (Arnold 1962, 241) – projecting, in fact, on a gigantic scale the pedagogical ideals of public school education with which Arnold was well acquainted, so that the whole national culture comes to resemble a phantasmagoric version of Thomas Arnold's Rugby.

Swinburne knew very well that Philistinism was as rampant in France as it was in England. He had started the essay on Baudelaire with an extended tirade on how modern French writers are subjected in their country to the same expectations of moral conformity prevalent in England. In the essay on Arnold he cautions readers against the great critic who might pass as a cosmopolitan in England but would be a Philistine in France. Swinburne puts himself forward as the English critic who, to paraphrase his words on Arnold, 'feels right' about France, guided by instinct rather than study in his promotion in England of the real innovators from across the Channel: Hugo, Gautier, and Baudelaire. The power of this instinctive knowledge was recognised by some of the most authoritative French voices of the second half of the century, from Baudelaire to Mallarmé (see Swinburne 1959–62, 1.87 and 3.114).[7]

So what was Swinburne's own ideal of cosmopolitan criticism? And how did he practise cultural mediation in his critical writings? We have already seen how Swinburne achieves a dynamic dialogue with his French

sources: his relationship with French writers transcends the usual
hierarchy between so-called primary and secondary texts (evident for
instance in Arnold's essay on Maurice de Guérin, in which Arnold is
straightforwardly a critic of the French poet) and moves instead to the
level of intertextuality, so that his critical writings of the 1860s explain the
French doctrine of art for art's sake but at the same time already assimi-
late it into their own language and style. His review of *Les Fleurs du mal*
overtly divulges Baudelaire's radical poetics but it does so by silently
imitating and endorsing the experimental fusion of the idioms of poetry
and criticism pioneered by Gautier in his critical writings. As his percep-
tive critic Georges Lafourcade remarks, in this early period Swinburne is a
'disciple original' of both Gautier and Baudelaire (Lafourcade 1928,
2.378). In his own essay on Baudelaire, Gautier had stressed the impor-
tance of the formative encounter with the work of Edgar Allan Poe, in
which Baudelaire had seen a powerful corrective of French provincialism
and which, Gautier claims, exerted on him an intimate, almost physical,
influence (Gautier n.d., 12.85–91). Mirroring the narrative described in
Gautier's essay, the French writings of Baudelaire become for Swinburne
what the Anglophone Poe had been for Baudelaire. In other words,
Swinburne describes a circular pattern of influence that goes from
English to French and then back to English (and so forth), showing that
cultural mediation does not move in a straight line but moves dialectically:
through entanglement rather than imitation. True innovators such as
Baudelaire and, Swinburne immodestly implies, himself, are necessarily
cosmopolitan because of their position of alienation from and antithesis
to their national readership (famously expressed by Baudelaire in his
address to the 'Hypocrite lecteur' of *Les Fleurs du mal*). This is counterbal-
anced by a desire to forge virtual communities in print across borders and
languages built on shared countercultural values. This ideal is very
different from the notion invoked by Arnold in *Essays in Criticism*, of a
modern republic of letters based on civilised values and Hellenism.

  Swinburne's capacity to 'feel' in French also led to a curious phenome-
non in these early years: the invention of a number of fictitious French
voices that he inserted into his critical writings. In the essay on Arnold, for
example, Swinburne quotes an extract from an unspecified French critic
who cuttingly remarks on Arnold's 'suspect' habit of praising French
'poëtes manqués' (Swinburne 1867a, 438; 1875a, 170; 1972, 85).
Swinburne uses the authority of the anonymous French critic to support
his criticism of Arnold, without giving the precise details of his source.

Pressed by Arnold in a letter, Swinburne had to admit that the critic was in fact his own invention, giving a revealing explanation for his ploy: 'I so often want French words for my meaning & find them easier & fuller of expression that I indulge the preference, as I write prose (I know) quicker & (I think) better in French than in English'; adding that 'writing as from a French standpoint I had been able to put things more clearly' (9 October 1867; Swinburne 2004b, 1.111). Swinburne, secure in his excellent command of the French language, claims that writing in French gives him a critical distance from the English material that enhances his clarity of judgement. Finding the right French words is not necessarily 'easier' as Swinburne implies here; it is more like a form of self-discipline, a mental exercise by means of which the cosmopolitan critic purges his idiom of the provincial or one-sided perspective. In her analysis of Swinburne's Francophilia, Charlotte Ribeyrol has argued that Swinburne, like his idol Hugo, occupied an 'interspace' between the two countries that enabled him to 'adopt a critical perspective' on England (Ribeyrol 2010, 108). Switching to French, Swinburne enters a different mentality and a land of greater expressive freedom. Seen from this perspective, the Arnold essay therefore contains an experiment in bilingualism in which Swinburne stages a conversation between his English voice – the one that publicly bears his signature as critic – and his disguised French voice, which here appears bracketed and displaced into anonymity. Indeed, in the otherwise lightly revised version of the essay published in *Essays and Studies*, Swinburne would add a substantial new quotation from his fictitious French source, in which the critic attacks the English poetry of religious doubt, prevalent in the mid century, and the attempt by modern English writers to reconcile what ought to remain irreconcilable quantities: reason and religion, philosophy and poetry (Swinburne 1875a, 128–32; 1972, 57–9). The French voice is richer in poetic and rhetorical intensity, and frank in its espousal of a symbolist take on religion ('toute véritable religion, sombre ou radieuse, tragique ou riante, est une chose essentiellement poétique'; Swinburne 1875a, 131; 1972, 58);[8] and the more sober and admittedly much more prevalent English voice is sufficiently detached from it to be able to chastise its 'flippancy' and its attack on English political institutions. It is difficult to gauge shades of irony and, as in all dialogic writing, it is ultimately left to the readers to extract their own meaning from the piece, balancing the differences in opinion and tone expressed by the two critical alter egos.

The quicker and more expressive French prose that Swinburne

described to Arnold is abundantly preserved in his private correspon-
dence, where Swinburne clearly finds French particularly congenial when
approaching risqué topics. Here French is the language of fantasy and of
a sort of playful daring, full of references to the writings of de Sade,
which Swinburne shares with a clique of likeminded men that includes
Richard Burton and the bibliophile Richard Monckton Milnes. In his
numerous asides in French, and in letters entirely written in that language,
although addressed to English recipients, Swinburne plays with the possi-
bility of adopting an alternative identity or creating a different, freer self
by switching language, emphasising the element of *mise-en-scène* that is of
primary importance in his early writings, in poetry as well as prose.
French is a language of freedom for Swinburne but the evident pleasure it
gives him is also, importantly, connected, as in his words to Arnold cited
above, with discipline and mastery – the same mastery over language that
Swinburne loves to exert in his choices of complicated or unusual
prosodic structures.

The most extreme experiment with the French voice is contained in
two critical essays composed for the *Spectator* in the early 1860s, soon after
the review of Baudelaire, which were to introduce English readers to two
bogus French writers, Ernest Clouët and Félicien Cossu, supposedly
modern French authors of daring works that had made a sensation in
their country. The essays were not published in the end although one of
them, the one on Clouët, was even set up in proofs before Hutton
pronounced it unprintable, not because he had spotted the hoax but
because he objected to the immorality of the French material. Their
manuscripts, however, were preserved and Gosse brought them out as
pamphlets after Swinburne's death; they were later collected by the critic
Cecil Lang (Swinburne 1964). The hoax reviews follow the usual pattern,
also adopted by Swinburne in his essay on Baudelaire, of providing a brief
contextualisation for the author's work and then interspersing generous
amounts of quotations with relatively succinct critical commentary. Just
as he would do in the essay on Arnold, Swinburne here uses the French
language to create different personas or aliases for himself that he sets
against each other in dialogic form: a modern French author of obscene
verse and a broadly censorious, anonymous English critic. Neither of the
two voices adopted by Swinburne can be straightforwardly called his own,
although the French one clearly comes much closer to his artistic beliefs.
The dialogues between the bogus libertine French writer and the fictive
priggish English reviewer are meant to be amusing but their light-heart-

edness in fact masks a complex negotiation of authority that throws light on Swinburne's practice of cultural mediation.

Of the two pieces, the one on Cossu is the more sophisticated, as the poetic French extracts are longer and more polished. These are clearly modelled after Baudelaire (*Les Fleurs du mal*) and Hugo (*Les Châtiments*) and bear such openly decadent titles as 'Une Nuit de Sodôme' and 'Messaline', which reflect their symbolist technique and their treatment of sexual perversion, moral corruption, and paganism. The English reviewer admires the technical accomplishment of the French poet but professes himself disturbed by the subject matter towards which he would anyway be compelled by the prevailing moral conventions of Victorian criticism to adopt a censorious tone. In order to negotiate this difficult position, Swinburne's fictitious critic reproduces carefully selected extracts, stopping short where the material allegedly becomes unacceptable. Playing against each other the voices of the transgressive French poet and the cautious English reviewer, Swinburne was hoping to keep just on the safe side of the borderline of Victorian respectability. But the various protestations that 'not one of the poems in question is fit to be read aloud in the hearing of Englishwomen' (Swinburne 1964, 88), the constant allusions to the unspeakable, and the abrupt interruptions of the quotations where the material becomes unprintable, create a distinctive type of eroticism: like Aubrey Beardsley in *Under the Hill* (1896), Swinburne uses his fragments from the fictive Cossu to stimulate the readers' erotic imagination, encouraging them to fill the textual gaps with their own perverse fantasies, and in fact urging them to go on where textual censorship overtly asks them to stop.

Gosse reads the reviews of Cossu and Clouët as outlets for the frustration that Swinburne the *enfant terrible* felt with English Victorian narrowness: they were, in his view, meant to shock readers by making fun of 'the Podsnappery of the age which supposed all French literature to be of a fantastic and horrible immorality' (Gosse in Swinburne 1916, 6). But the hoax reviews are also satires on the pervasive power of Victorian censorship: the moral censorship exercised by the liberal press, to which, ironically, they fell victim; and the self-censorship adopted by authors and critics who tried to negotiate the demands of public morality (if they had been published, the essays would of course have managed to subvert public censorship by means of fake self-censorship). Swinburne dramatises the internal mechanism of self-censorship through the dialogue between the French and English voices, representative of the conflicting psychological impulses towards expressive freedom and public restraint, transgression and convention, which operate within the individual consciousness but are here displaced in space, across national borders. The hoaxes therefore reflect the mechanism at work in the genesis of the lyrics in *Poems and Ballads*, many of which were being composed at this very point: they not only set the parameters for those poems' challenge to the critical establishment but, most strikingly, anticipate with uncanny accuracy the terms of the public controversy that erupted after 1866. There is moreover a clear correspondence in technique between the spoof reviews and poems such as 'Anactoria', where Swinburne weaves together Sappho's poetic voice (albeit in English translation) and a lyric 'I', creating a lyrical dialogism that destabilises assumptions of a unified authorial voice and makes moral censorship problematic. The spoof essays show us just how deliberate and self-conscious Swinburne's poetics of transgression was at this point. When Swinburne's fake English reviewer accuses Cossu of priapic obsession, monotony, and 'base effeminacy of feeling' (Swinburne 1964, 95) he foreshadows the accusations that Buchanan and others would make against Swinburne himself in the infamous 'Fleshly School of Poetry' controversy of 1870. Because of this extreme self-consciousness, Swinburne's French aliases additionally function as vehicles for self-parody directed not only at the poet's own penchant for symbolist excess but also at his practice of imitating French sources: as the voice of the English reviewer puts it, Cossu's poetry 'constantly recalls the verse of greater men, whose noble ideas, passed through the unclean filter of his fancy, reappear under some loathsome and devilish parody' (Swinburne 1964, 94). Swinburne here captures an important dilemma of English symbolist and decadent literature, whose poetics of deliberate imitation and exaggeration rides the dangerous line between earnestness and pastiche, as is best exemplified by Wilde's *Salomé* (1893), another French work by an Anglophone author that became caught in a long history of public censorship.[9]

The ultimate object of Swinburne's parody, though, is the institution of Victorian criticism with its investment in the values of accuracy and truthfulness. Inventing Cossu, Clouët, and their disapproving English critic(s), Swinburne meant to make fun of the intellectual and moral earnestness with which critics like Arnold approached their profession. The hoax reviews break the contract that regulates the relationship between the Victorian sage and his public, leading readers into a virtual labyrinth supported by bogus bibliographical references, footnotes, and travesties of all the paraphernalia of precise attribution. Readers keen to find out more about Cossu and Clouët would moreover have been able to chase further references to their non-existent works in other essays previously published by Swinburne in the *Spectator*, where the names of Cossu and Clouët had already been mentioned in the context of otherwise earnest reviews of Hugo, and in Swinburne's own poem 'The Four Boards of the Coffin', also published in the *Spectator* in 1862, ostensibly as a translation of *Recueil de Chants Bretons*, edited by Félicien Cossu, Paris, 1858.[10] These inquisitive readers would only eventually find out that they had moved all along inside a self-referential edifice, a fantastic library within the author's mind.

Even once Swinburne's hoax has been unmasked, though, the problem of authorship remains. For what status should readers attribute to Cossu's poems? As we have seen, it is not easy to determine if they should be read as parodies. Are they French poems written by Swinburne under a pseudonym? The question is complicated by the existence of the voice of the English reviewer, another authorial persona of Swinburne's, who edits and controls the texts. It is undeniable that the poems possess an identity of their own as literary texts. 'Messaline', for instance, the most developed of Cossu's fragments with over seventy lines of French Alexandrines, exists in a separate manuscript entitled 'Messaline au cirque', which suggests that Swinburne might have planned for it an independent life from the Cossu hoax (see Lang in Swinburne 1964, 221). It would certainly be possible to give a straight reading of a poem like 'Messaline', which has as its subject the wife of the Roman Emperor Claudius famed for her cruelty and sexual voracity, testimonies of which have been passed down to us by Seneca and Juvenal. Messalina is an ideal symbolist icon – a *femme fatale* who embodies the excesses of Roman decadence and offers a perfect antithesis to the nineteenth-century ideal of female virtue and Christian values more generally – and as such she would later become the subject of a well-known painting by the leading French symbolist artist Gustave Moreau. Cossu's 'Messaline' contains the themes, imagery, and register that would become the hallmarks of *Poems and Ballads*, and it would be possible to see it as a French-language companion piece to 'Faustine', a poem about another Roman *femme damnée* with a special fondness for the gladiatorial circus that Swinburne composed in the same year as the Cossu hoax. By doing this, though, we would be missing the point. For by relinquishing the authority of the poem to the fictional Cossu, Swinburne intended precisely to question the primacy in Victorian criticism of what, in the twentieth century, structuralist critics would call the author-function. As the attacks on *Poems and Ballads* would shortly demonstrate, Victorian critics were heavily invested in reading literary texts as leading straight into the author's psychology or ethical values, and evaluating literature on that basis, simplifying the interpretative art of criticism as a thermometer of morality. Once again, Swinburne seems to be one step ahead of his future critics in his literary puzzles, by challenging them to unravel the paradox of real poems by a fake author. Deconstructing his own authorial voice into a dialogic structure (critic and poet, English and French, anonymous and 'signed', etc.), Swinburne explodes the integrity of authorship, creating a play of multiplicity and contradiction that goes beyond the possibilities of the dramatic monologue as practised for instance by Browning and Tennyson, where it is comparatively easy for modern readers to reject the identification between the authorial voice and the lyric 'I'.[11]

Writing to Arnold about the hoax review, Swinburne compared himself to Carlyle who in *Sartor Resartus* (1833–34) had invented a bogus German authority, Professor Teufelsdröckh, whose idiosyncratic philosophy of clothes he set out to translate and interpret for English readers (Swinburne 2004b, 1.111). Like Carlyle's fictive review essay, Swinburne's pieces employ playfulness and satire to reflect on the difficulty of translation and cultural mediation. Reading the essays on Cossu and Clouët together with the essay on Arnold reveals that they are more than a ludic intermezzo in Swinburne's career as critic: they belong to his extensive preoccupation in the 1860s with the practices of cosmopolitanism and cultural translation, and with the relationship between public print culture and the unsayable – a set of concerns that Swinburne works out at the same time in his better-known early poetry. In the 1820s Carlyle established himself as a crucial figure for the reception of German culture in Britain in the form of essays and translations. In the mid-century, Arnold's work as sage-promoter of French literature took over from Carlyle's in its cosmopolitan ambition. Swinburne's self-identification with Carlyle is apt because it reveals a line of influence in Victorian cosmopolitan criticism that goes from Carlyle to Arnold to the young Swinburne, who is determined to take it in new directions with his knowledge of modern French writing and with the unsettling energy of the *enfant terrible*. In the genealogy of Victorian critical lineages, though, Swinburne's essays also occupy an important middle point between Carlyle and the Oscar Wilde of *The Decay of Lying* (1889), in the progressive self-deconstruction of the figure of the sage by the means of irony, dialogism, and playfulness.

NOTES

1 The most notable exception to this scholarly neglect is Peters 1965. The most comprehensive recent selections of Swinburne's critical prose are Swinburne 1966, 1972, and 2004a.

2 In Chapter 2 below, Julia F. Saville traces the same shift in relation to Swinburne's poetry, which, she argues, abandons cosmopolitan republicanism in favour of a dour form of patriotism.

3 Cecil Y. Lang describes this evolution in uncompromising political terms: 'The most cosmopolitan of English poets was transformed into the most parochial and chauvinistic of British jingoes' (Swinburne 1959–62, 1.xxviii).

4 The most thorough study of Baudelaire's influence on Swinburne is in Clements 1985; for a revisionist account see Garland 2009.

5 It is therefore even more remarkable, if not altogether surprising, that Eliot does not even mention the Baudelaire essay in his study of Swinburne's criticism. Thaïs Morgan argues that Eliot's failure to acknowledge this essay is a form of anxiety of influence, as Eliot was himself invested in being the first to have 'discovered' Baudelaire as a source of poetic modernity (Morgan 1993b).

6 Writing to Arnold on 9 October 1867, Swinburne complains of the French Academy's 'ultra-Philistine' decision not to elect Gautier, provocatively adding that its English equivalent 'would elect Mr. John (or say Jacob) Bright & Mr. Coventry Patmore rather than you, were you a candidate' (Swinburne 2004b, 1.111).

7 Swinburne's honorary place among French men of letters was confirmed by the invitation to contribute to the Tombeau de Théophile Gautier (1873). Charlotte Ribeyrol shows that, after absorbing French influences in his work, Swinburne in turn became a model for French poets of Mallarmé's generation. It is also notable that Swinburne has been the subject of serious study in France, from the early Lafourcade 1928, published at the nadir of his reputation in England, to the recent Tombeau pour Swinburne (Bonnecase and Scarpa 2010).

8 Translation: 'All veritable religion, sombre or radiant, tragic or cheerful, is an essentially poetical thing.'

9 In the history of the reception of Salomé, several critics have argued that the play should be read as a parody of Decadence, most influentially Mario Praz in La Carne, la morte e il diavolo nella letteratura romantica (1930), translated as The Romantic Agony in 1933 (Praz 1970, 312).

10 This poem was republished in Poems and Ballads, First Series as 'After Death', with no reference to Cossu's 'original'. Other mentions of Cossu and Clouët are found in Swinburne's Spectator essays on Les Misérables of 21 and 26 June 1862 (see Swinburne 1964, 218).

11 On Swinburne's idiosyncratic use of the dramatic monologue form, see Shrimpton 1993.

2

SWINBURNE'S SWIMMERS: FROM INSULAR PEACE TO THE ANGLO-BOER WAR

Julia F. Saville

In his editor's introduction to the six-volume *Swinburne Letters*, Cecil Y. Lang describes the insularity that came to dominate Algernon Charles Swinburne's thinking particularly after the mid-1870s: 'The most cosmopolitan of English poets was transformed into the most parochial and chauvinistic of British jingoes. The republican-turned-"English Republican" became English first and last, and remained republican only by a semantic sophistry that would be as much at home in *1984* as in *Through the Looking-Glass*' (1959–62, 1.xxviii). In this chapter, I consider Lang's terms 'cosmopolitan' and 'republican' in the light of recent critical theories of 'rooted cosmopolitanism' while revisiting the poet's change in perspective during the late years of his career. In doing so, I pursue further the explorations of Swinburne's evolving cosmopolitan republicanism I have begun elsewhere (Saville 2009a and 2011). Did he indeed become an insular jingoist, or did he continue to explore the challenging intellectual problems that preoccupied him as a young man?

The Swinburne of the 1860s and early 1870s was a practitioner of hybrid republicanism.[1] In part a classical republican emphasising independent civic virtue, he was also an anti-monarchist red republican who assimilated the cosmopolitan London ethos cultivated by post-1848 European exiles such as Giuseppe Mazzini, Louis Kossuth, and Louis Blanc. Like other republican poets – Elizabeth Barrett Browning, Arthur Hugh Clough, and Walt Whitman, to name a few – Swinburne envisaged republicanism as leading to a trans-Atlantic, trans-European, and potentially world-scale federation. Like them too, he was suspicious of imperialism and the progressivist commercial enterprise driving many imperialist projects. Cosmopolitan republicans were dedicated to balancing individual well-being with that of the body politic, and reconciling the interests of emergent nations (such as Italy,

Hungary, and Poland) with the broader international community. They thus faced challenges that have a special resonance when compared with today's consciously paradoxical concept of 'rooted cosmopolitanism'.

A negotiative social practice, rooted cosmopolitanism was developed in response to the shortcomings of cosmopolitanism conventionally conceived – for instance, the tendency to think in idealised universal terms, or the potential disregard for local alliances and gravitation toward detachment and privileged immunity.[2] As they addressed these limitations, critical theorists such as Kwame Anthony Appiah found new interest in social practices that balance the need both to honour commitments to local ties, and to foster broad alliances with other nation-states.[3] Appiah consciously rejects humanism's universals, celebrates diverse views, and believes that 'sometimes it is the differences we bring to the table that make it rewarding to interact at all' (Appiah 2005, 271). Recognising values as social, rather than individual, Appiah emphasises the importance of imaginative engagement and conversation as vital supplements to abstract theory (Appiah 2006, 27, 85). For this reason, he treats conversations about literature as a powerful corollary to moral and political philosophy (Appiah 2005, 22, 214, 245; Appiah 2006, 28–9, 92–3). The power of literature and in particular poetry to clarify ethical choices through narrative, to enrich the literal with the figurative, or to confront the visceral experience of cultural prohibitions is well suited to advancing the rooted cosmopolitan's efforts to negotiate between local interests and more distanced, cosmopolitan affiliations (Appiah 2006, 56, 78).

Like rooted cosmopolitans today, cosmopolitan republicans in the mid-nineteenth century counted poets and novelists among their warmest allies and, in Britain, Swinburne was among the most colourful and imaginative. During the 1860s and 1870s, his poetry was filled with tropes of illumination, literal as well as figurative. As Stephanie Kuduk Weiner has shown, tropes of light – be they of dawn, sunshine, beacons or watch-fires – are characteristic of republican verse because they convey well the intellectual dimensions of this political enterprise, for instance, the plain-speaking rationalist's clear vision, or poetic insights that unveil the deceptions of priestcraft and kingcraft (Weiner 2005, 24–5, 32–3). But Swinburne also used another trope, perhaps less widely recognised as republican but nonetheless ubiquitous in nineteenth-century poetic meditations on democratic reform: images of open-air swimming or bathing in large bodies of water. The bathing body, divested of the sartorial markers of identity such as socio-economic or national indicators and immersed in water, was well suited to representing the common man engaging with life's vicissitudes and to exploring physical and aesthetic dimensions of republican reform. While tropes of enlightenment portrayed liberation of the mind, swimming tropes could explore bodily freedom and the imaginative or spiritual well-being from which it was, for many republicans, inseparable.

Inflected by the seventeenth- and eighteenth-century health regimens of bathing at spas, in rivers, and at seaside resorts, swimming tropes could bring with them classical republican associations of athletic self-training and civic virtue.[4] The figure lent itself to portraying the heroic potential of the individual, but equally well it could represent simple pleasures that many republicans sought as basic civil rights; for instance, in poets such as Clough and Whitman, it could be used to express the liberating, eroticised sociability of male companions *en plein air*. Furthermore, the singer as swimmer could mediate poetry's own aesthetic contribution to a self-critique of the Enlightenment reason from which democratic movements like republicanism itself arose.[5]

Diverse tropes of swimming and inundation can be found balancing the deliberative narrative moments in Barrett Browning's *Casa Guidi Windows* (e.g. 1.398–403), Clough's *Bothie of Toper-Na-Fuosich* (e.g. 1.1–8 and 3.58–83) and *Dipsychus and the Spirit* (6.206–25), and, most famously, Whitman's *Leaves of Grass* (e.g. 'Song of Myself' 22.448–60). In dialogue with these poets and others, the republican Swinburne immersed his swimmers in ocean rhythms, conveying his faith in the capacity of poetic song to vitalise the imagination through rhythms and rhymes, and to move the sympathies of the body politic through images of literal feeling.[6] Often individualised and athletic, his swimming bodies convey alternating self-command and self-overcoming embrace of Fate, an alternation mirrored in his crafted classical prosody.

Many critics have interpreted Swinburne's swimmers as reflecting his fascination with boundary-crossing and erasures of difference: for Jerome McGann such figures dramatise the experience of 'seeing into two worlds at once' (McGann 1972, 172). To Catherine Maxwell, swimmers represent the submission of the male poet to 'the sublime elemental rhythms' of a more powerful feminised sea (Maxwell 2001, 215), while for Herbert F. Tucker they enact the self, merging with 'the beauty of the world's body' (Tucker 2008, 531). Yet the political implications of the trope for a cosmopolitan republican ethos call for further study, particularly with relation to the poet's post-1879 work. For, during the last three decades of his career,

Swinburne's poems increasingly faltered in negotiating the tension between cosmopolitan and republican sensibilities: between, on the one hand, principles of broad-mindedness and inclusiveness and, on the other, strong-minded individualism, heartfelt patriotism, and immersiveness in the particular. In part these difficulties can be attributed to his withdrawal from a metropolitan intellectual community to his more secluded life at Putney, but they can also be interpreted as reflecting the changing political mood in Europe.

Cosmopolitan intellectuals who had relished the prospect of democracy throughout Europe became increasingly disappointed after the passage of the Second Reform Bill of 1867. Not only did many republicans experience a reactive disillusionment at the failure of reform to produce vigorous democracy, but challenges from other European powers (including the 1879 alliance of Prussia with Austria against Russia) and demands for autonomy by Britain's colonies (such as Ireland, the Transvaal, Egypt along with the Sudan, and India) also displaced the earlier collaborative spirit with debates about defending the cohesiveness of the Empire and national, especially commercial interests abroad (Shannon 1974, 142–71). By the 1880s, as Jonathan Parry succinctly explains, 'the fourfold increase in the franchise ... raised many questions about how to guide and discipline the democracy and to prevent sectional and disintegrative pressures on domestic and foreign policy' (Parry 2006, 398). In this shifting climate, the republican principles that were pertinent in mid-century Europe began to lose coherence: for instance, commitment to fraternity or unity in the Commonwealth could not be sustained alongside commitment to liberty and equality when the latter were demanded by disaffected colonised communities like the peoples of Ireland or India, or by settler colonies like the Boers in the Transvaal.

As he struggled to adapt his poetics to these new debates during the 1880s and 1890s, Swinburne produced volumes of poems lacking aesthetic and ethical subtlety. Polemic barely modified by aesthetic control and the absence of open-minded engagement with alternative perspectives often, as Lang declares, mar this poetry. Yet, even as he published ineptly partisan verse, Swinburne also produced poems that reflect intriguing transformations both in his border-crossing fascination with the strange and his investment in principles of freedom, equality, and communal well-being. Among these, swimming songs reminiscent of the radical republican ballads and sea songs of the early period, such as 'Les Noyades' and 'A Song in Time of Order. 1852' from *Poems and Ballads, First*

Series (1866), and 'To Walt Whitman in America' from *Songs before Sunrise* (1871), are worthy of close attention.

Songs of the Springtides (1880), the first volume Swinburne published after his move to Putney, reasserts his treatment of the sea as origin and end-point of life, an 'elemental voice' with 'elemental rhythms' (Maxwell 2001, 214–5).[7] Following the inaugural 'poetic tale' of the poet as inherently 'of the sea' ('Thalassius'), swimming scenes proliferate in Swinburne's corpus: some, like the two in *Tristram of Lyonesse* (1882), are memorable episodes in epic narratives.[8] Others, like 'Loch Torridon' from *Astrophel and Other Poems* (1894) or 'The Lake of Gaube' from *A Channel Passage and Other Poems* (1904), are descriptive, attentive to local detail, and reminiscent of holidays spent at secluded venues at home and abroad such as Lancing-on-Sea in West Sussex, the Highlands of Scotland, or the Cauterets valley in the Pyrenees. Most prolific and of special interest here are the swimming songs – rhythmically distinctive lyrics in regular stanza forms long favoured by republican poets (Weiner 2005, 8, 17, 20–34) – such as 'Off Shore' (*Studies in Song*, 1880), 'In the Water' (*A Midsummer Holiday and Other Poems*, 1884), and 'A Swimmer's Dream' (*Astrophel and Other Poems*, 1894). Republican principles and cosmopolitan receptiveness to the strange persist in these poems, but the reformist calls for revolutionary restructuring of state and ecclesiastical power which characterised volumes like *Songs before Sunrise* now give way to intellectual preoccupations and aesthetic experiments using impersonal singer-swimmers within unspecified littoral topographies.

Weiner has recently described such songs as 'sound-driven', that is, concerned with insights gained by attending to 'the sensuous qualities of language itself' and thus foregrounding 'the poet's and reader's experience of following patterns of sound toward unexpected meanings' (Weiner 2010, 12).[9] In this respect, these lyrics continue the radical experiments in harmonic poetry that date back to Swinburne's border-crossing engagements with the theories of Richard Wagner and Charles Baudelaire in the early 1860s (McGann 2009). One such poem is 'Off Shore', which Yisrael Levin perceptively reads as a myth of creation and a development of 'Hertha', one of the *Songs before Sunrise*, whose metrical effects it replicates (Levin 2010b, 58).[10] Levin argues that 'Off Shore' replaces republican with natural imagery, going beyond the human to a broader mythopoeic vision, but I wish to scrutinise republican rhetoric and principles in this song more closely, especially the trope of the singer-swimmer. For, like 'Hertha', 'Off Shore' advocates universal spiritual freedom, performing the sensual process by which poetic song conjures unorthodox conceptions from a field of free imaginative play. It thereby rejects the tyranny of prescriptive dogma in favour of a cultivated spiritual vitality and displaces hierarchised oppositions (light/darkness, land/sea, man/nature, and literal/figurative) with imagined border-crossings, liminal spaces, and engagements with the strange. Yet close reading reveals shifts in the framing of this song that, when translated into a political context, exert pressure on a negotiative cosmopolitan republican ethics.

In *Songs before Sunrise*, tropes of dark, stormy seas are commonly used to suggest the turmoil of revolution and overwhelming adversity in which the swimmer as common man is immersed. Sunrise promises the dawning of peace and enlightened liberty: for instance, in 'To Walt Whitman in America', Swinburne sings to the republican advocate from freedom-fighting Europe: 'Here, with hope hardly to wear, / Naked nations and bare / Swim, sink, strike out for the dawn' (Swinburne 1904, 2.123). By contrast, 'Off Shore' (Swinburne 1904, 5.46–54) opens with a calm pre-dawn sea, performed in lulling anapaests, and feminised as rapturously submissive to summer's 'royal enchantment':

> When the might of the summer
> Is most on the sea;
> When the days overcome her
> With joy but to be,
> With rapture of royal enchantment, and sorcery that sets her not free
> . . .
>
> Then only, far under
> In the depths of her hold,
> Some gleam of its wonder
> Man's eye may behold,
> Its wild-weed forests of crimson and russet and olive and gold.
>
> (Swinburne 1904, 5.46)

Peace conveyed by the sea's calm gives the amphibious singer-swimmer and his listeners access to a strange underwater seascape inaccessible in the storms of revolution. Depth and darkness beautify the submarine vegetation which, impervious to seasons, 'knows not of sunshine and snow'. As if habituated to radical republican thought patterns, the swimmer associates the darkness with imprisonment and yearning for light ('Soft blossomless frondage / And foliage that gleams / As to prisoners in bondage / The light of their dreams'), but the unanticipated sensuality and vitality of the 'flowerage', 'frondage', and 'foliage' thriving in this gloom prompt revision: 'Not as prisoners entombed / Waxen haggard and wizen, ... / the flowers of them shine / Through the splendour of darkness that clothes them of water that glimmers like wine' (Swinburne 1904, 5.47). This is fecund darkness that prompts leisurely wonder, one of Swinburne's 'divine contraries of life' ('Genesis', Swinburne 1904, 2.118) whose counterpart is the suddenly emerging, energising sunrise.

A force associated with imaginative liberty, sunlight 'gives forth his word, / And the word that he saith, / Ere well it be heard, / Strikes darkness to death; / For the thought of his heart is the sunrise, and dawn as the sound of his breath' (Swinburne 1904, 5.49). Displacing 'the Word' of Christian dogma, light initiates a network of reciprocal elemental processes represented rhetorically through strings of interactive similes. The waves, for instance, responding to the sunrise through the breeze are represented as voices which 'take part / In the sense of the spirit / That breathes from his heart, / And are kindled with music'. Taking up this semantic and auditory harmonic motif, verbal transformations (for instance, 'the wind ... enkindles the wings of the ships' (Swinburne 1904, 5.50)) produce the image of sails, in turn prompting an association with flocking seabirds ('White glories of wings / As of seafaring birds') that transmute first into sheep ('That flock from the springs / Of the sunrise in herds / With the wind for a herdsman') then back to birds ('scatter as wild swans'), even as the sails' tackle suggests clouds ('So glimmer their shrouds and their sheetings as clouds on the stream of the wind' (Swinburne 1904, 5.51)).

Echoing with sound patterns, these air and flight metamorphoses resonate with poetic associations of breath, inspiration, and sublime flight, finally returning to the wind-wings that initiated them: 'the flight of them past / Is no more than the flight / Of the snow-soft swarm of serene wings poised and afloat in the light' (Swinburne 1904, 5.51). Then, in a final synaesthetic coup, the singer-swimmer uses his border-crossing amphibious perspective to yoke together the strange fecundity of the gloomy underwater and the familiar sun-drenched marine scene to

produce the unanticipated climactic image of sea-butterflies, hovering
between literal and figurative:

> Like flowers upon flowers
> In a festival way
> When hours after hours
> Shed grace on the day,
> White blossomlike butterflies hover and gleam through the snows of
> the spray.
>
> Like snow-coloured petals
> Of blossoms that flee
> From storm that unsettles
> The flower as the tree
> They flutter, a legion of flowers on the wing, through the field of the sea.
>
> Through the furrowless field
> Where the foam-blossoms blow
> And the secrets are sealed
> Of their harvest below
> They float in the path of the sunbeams, as flakes or as blossoms of snow.
>
> (Swinburne 1904, 5.51–2)

The sea butterflies seem both familiar, yet tantalisingly mysterious. In
the sunshine of enlightened reason their associations with snow suggest
the ephemerality of a fleeting insight, 'blossomlike' resonating with
Walter Pater's epiphanic 'gem-like flame'. As gatherings of 'flowers upon
flowers' or 'a legion of flowers on the wing' their fluttering also evokes
anthologies (Greek *anthos*: flower + *logia*: collection), or pages of poetry.
This is the image's association in the 'Envoi' of *A Century of Roundels*
(1883): 'Fly, white butterflies, out to sea, / Frail pale winds for the sea to
try' (Swinburne 1904, 5.193). Yet the butterflies do not yield their
meanings readily for they do not belong only to the world of cultivated
enlightenment on shore, but also to the submarine 'furrowless field'.
Indeed when they reappear in *Tristram of Lyonesse*'s second canto ('Fleet
butterflies ... / White as the sparkle of snow-flowers in the sun';
Swinburne 1904, 4.52) they represent meanings of which the sleeping
lovers seem oblivious.[11] Reminiscent of the hovering butterflies in Dante
Gabriel Rossetti's painting *Soul's Beauty*, and of Robert Browning's
'strange butterfly! Creature as dear as new' in 'Amphibian' (*Fifine at the
Fair*, 1872), Swinburne's image suggests the soul as imaginative vitality

that to the atheist republican has no materiality but what the senses and poetic language conjure for it.[12] In this he implicitly follows the precedent of the ancient Greeks for whom the term *psyche* represents both soul and butterfly.[13]

As the effect of the singer-swimmer's immersion in the rhythmic borderland off shore, the sea-butterflies allegorise transformative lyrical meanings, appearing and disappearing for the reader's vicarious sensual and imaginative revitalisation. They perform the process that encourages us to extend our imaginations beyond the comfortable paths of conventional thought to attempt new meanings and thereby offer a recreative peacetime counterpart to a revolutionary activist spirit. The song's transformative dynamism thus follows the precedent of 'Hertha'. However, there is a crucial difference. The vitality of 'Hertha', as McGann shows, depends on identifiable allusions to spiritual texts as diverse as the Hindu *Upanishads* and the Scandinavian *Eddas*, which merge or displace each other in the course of the poem (McGann 2008, 287–90). Swinburne's point is less to negotiate the cultural conflicts that may arise within such diversity than to invoke the spiritual richness to be found in difference as a means of critiquing the uncompromising narrowness of Christian dogma and its spiritually impoverishing effects in mid-nineteenth-century Europe. In 'Off Shore', however, alterity is allegorised by the submarine garden whose strange beauty, while sensually experienced, is universalised, foreclosing attention to particular differences necessary for stringent comparative and self-reflective critique. Furthermore, the impersonality of the swimmer-singer limits the psychologised self-reflection possible in the more developed contexture of *Tristram of Lyonesse*.[14] Thus, what Swinburne the cosmopolitan republican intellectual gains in the imaginative vitality of this recreative, sound-driven poem, he stands to lose in critical stringency valuable for activist, reformist contexts.

Similar negotiations occur in sound-driven songs like 'In the Water'. One of a suite of nine lyrics dedicated to Theodore Watts and entitled *A Midsummer Holiday* (Swinburne 1904, 6.5–25), 'In the Water' appeared in summer 1884. As a group, the suite has an intimate tone, each lyric containing a closing address to a companion ('Friend') reminiscent of Wordsworth's asides to Dorothy in 'Tintern Abbey'. In several of the poems, the landscape is marked as specifically English through allusions to literature ('Because thy passage once made warm this clime, / Our father Chaucer, here we praise thy name'; Swinburne 1904, 6.9), landmarks ('Where the waste Land's End leans westward'; Swinburne

1904, 6.23), and landscape: ('Moor and copse and fallow', or 'the scarred cliffs downward sundering drive and drown'; Swinburne 1904, 6.16–17). Most of the lyrics suggest a sober interval of stock-taking. They meditate on goals and limits ('The Seaboard'), boundaries and borders ('The Cliffside Path', 'On the Verge') where elemental forces of wind, water, and sun meet land, and where man confronting his fleeting inconsequence seeks comfort ('A Haven', 'A Sea Mark'). Some, by contrast – 'The Mill Garden', 'In the Water', and 'The Sunbows' – suggest spiritual refreshment through physical recreation.

'In the Water' (Swinburne 1904, 6.18–20) is striking for its ebullient galloping rhythm. It opens with a musical summons from the sea: 'The sea is awake, and the sound of the song of the joy of her waking is rolled / From afar to the star that recedes, from anear to the wastes of the wild wide shore. / Her call is a trumpet compelling us homeward' (Swinburne 1904, 6.18). Like 'Off Shore', the song is structured by sound patterns such as echoes ('awake', 'waking'), internal rhymes ('afar to the star'), and alliterations ('sea', 'sound', 'song', 'wastes', 'wild', 'wide'). Catching the ear of the listener, these harmonies invite desire for a reciprocal awakening prompted by the singer-swimmer: 'From the sea shall we crave not her grace to rekindle the life that it kindled before, / Her breath to requicken?' (Swinburne 1904, 6.18) Thus the listener (addressed variously as 'us', 'the twain of us', 'we', and 'Friend'), and by extension a community of listeners, is encouraged to cross from the quotidian world of land with its oppressive pressures and anxieties to the sensual immersiveness of the sea-song's 'measureless music of things'.

Suspending the textures of temporal difference, the allusions to the past of 'Knights' and 'pilgrims' ('A Haven', Swinburne 1904, 6.7), or the nebulous 'goal' or 'aims' of the future ('The Seaboard', Swinburne 1904, 6.5), the song privileges the present moment: 'Life holds not an hour that is better to live in: the past is a tale that is told, / The future a sun-flecked shadow, alive and asleep, with a blessing in store' ('In the Water', Swinburne 1904, 6.18). Initially this might seem mere hedonism, a transformation of the body into a politically disengaged aesthetic object. Yet a republican ethics persists here, for the song uses swimming to trope the spiritual invigoration that accompanies sensory pleasure. It thus lyrically performs recreation as a holiday's common good: 'As we give us again to the waters, the rapture of limbs that the waters enfold / Is less than the rapture of spirit whereby . . . / Our souls and the bodies they wield at their will are absorbed in the life they adore' (Swinburne 1904, 6.19).

To be 'in the water' is therefore to celebrate freedom as an equal and universal right, a justifiable need to which all should respond, regardless of socio-political station: 'For albeit he were less than the least of them, haply the heart of a man may be bold / To rejoice in the word of the sea as a mother's' (Swinburne 1904, 6.19). The singer-swimmer acknowledges that 'There are cliffs to be climbed upon land, there are ways to be trodden and ridden', thereby recognising the challenges and obligations of quotidian life elaborated in the other lyrics of the suite. Nonetheless, he insists in the four-times repeated chorus-line that his community of listeners should 'Strike out from the shore as the heart in us bids and beseeches, athirst for the foam' (Swinburne 1904, 6.20).

Despite this egalitarianism, the classical republican associations of athletic self-training and civic virtue are more pertinent to this song than the potentially radical imaginative vitality suggested in 'Off Shore'. Moreover, the bracing call to respond to visceral instincts is implicitly appropriated to the Englishness of the coastal context. Cultural alterity of gender, religion, or race is singularly absent from this song. The presence, for instance, of a companion swimmer has little of the eroticised male sociability that we might find in even the manliest exhortations of Whitman's singer-swimmers, while the embrace of the sea, to enlist Catherine Maxwell's terms, has little suggestion of castrative feminised difference. On the contrary, it is maternally reassuring and restorative with emphasis on the boyish delight and rejuvenation of a swim pervaded by 'laughter', 'glee', and 'joy'.

'In the Water' belongs to the genre of inspiriting republican songs in which ocean swimming tropes coupled with sound patterns urge physical refreshment as a universal good; yet, when this form and the swimming trope are displaced from a recreational to a politically vexed context, the ethical liabilities of universalised principles and depersonalised swimmers become apparent. This is the problem Swinburne wrestles with in the face of dissenting republicanisms emergent during the 1880s. To Swinburne, whose model of republicanism was largely shaped by Mazzini's Risorgimento theories, Irish Nationalists and Boer settler communities who invoked republican rights rhetoric were impostors and outlaws. Mazzini, as the champion of Italian unification, privileged unity as an ideal and associated Irish Nationalists with the Roman Catholic Irish supporters of Pope Pius IX who had fought against Italian republicans in the first Risorgimento. Ireland, in his view, was rightly a part of the British Commonwealth, and this was the opinion that Swinburne continued to respect long after Mazzini's death (Swinburne 1959–62, 5.188–90). Encouraged by the ageing Karl Blind, the poet insisted on unity as a founding principle of republicanism jeopardised in the British Commonwealth by those who sought their independence (Swinburne 1959–62, 5.190–3). Such insistence conflicted with the border-crossing receptiveness to difference that he valued also in the republican poetics of both Barrett Browning and Whitman.

These are the contradictions into which Swinburne drifted as he sought to balance a republican's defence of universal liberty, equality, and unity with a cosmopolitan's respect for diversity in a rapidly changing *fin-de-siècle* modernity. They emerge with painful clarity, for instance, in his treatment of ocean and swimming tropes in a cluster of would-be inspiriting republican sonnets published in *The Times* in the first years of the Anglo-Boer War. Ironically, these poems are written almost simultaneously with one of his most cosmopolitan and republican swimming lyrics, 'The Lake of Gaube', which appeared in *The Bookman* of October 1899 and later in *A Channel Passage and Other Poems*, troubling any too decisive condemnation of Swinburne's political ethics.

ENGAGING RADICAL STRANGENESS: THE TRANSVAAL SONNETS AND
'THE LAKE OF GAUBE'

The Anglo-Boer War (1899–1902) was a notoriously complex tangle of conflicting interests in which Britain pursued economic and geopolitical benefits opposed by determined republican farmers, who fought less for democratic principles than for the mineral wealth and land they themselves had wrested from native peoples (Nasson 2010, 30 and 64). Swinburne's letters make clear his susceptibility to British propaganda which promoted war as a noble defence of disenfranchised 'Uitlanders' (foreigners) and Africans from the oppressive, autocratic Boer regime. The poet's antipathy to 'that unspeakable old villain Paul Kruger and his lying thieving murdering Boers' (Swinburne 1959–62, 6.142) fuelled his belief that the Boers would, if victorious, 'establish a reign of terror and slavery and torture for all dark races from Cape Town to the Zambesi' (Swinburne 1959–62, 6.154). His sonnets express similar sentiments. I am, however, less interested in the location of his sympathies, for debates about Britain's foreign policy, especially in the Transvaal, were notoriously overdetermined, and impatience with the Boer perspective was by no means unusual.[15] My concern lies with what Swinburne's ocean and swimming tropes in these sonnets show about the thinking behind his antipathies, and thus the continuities and shifts in his political ethics.

Swinburne's first sonnet, 'The Transvaal', appeared in *The Times* of 11 October 1899, the day the allied Boer republics, goaded for years by British brinksmanship, opened hostilities against Britain with a formal declaration of war (Nasson 2010, 56).[16] A classical republican call to arms, the sonnet personifies abstractions in the interests of moral clarity:

> Patience, long sick to death, is dead. Too long
>   Have sloth and doubt and treason bidden us be
>   What Cromwell's England was not, when the sea
> To him bore witness given of Blake how strong
> She stood, a commonweal that brooked no wrong
>   From foes less vile than men like wolves set free
>   Whose war is waged where none may fight or flee –
> With women and with weanlings. Speech and song
> Lack utterance now for loathing. Scarce we hear
>   Foul tongues that blacken God's dishonoured name
>   With prayers turned curses and with praise found shame
> Defy the truth whose witness now draws near
>   To scourge these dogs, agape with jaws afoam,
>   Down out of life. Strike, England, and strike home.

> (Swinburne 1904, 6.385)

Notably here, Swinburne launches his reflective critique of 'England' not through a border-crossing invocation of another ethically exemplary culture (such as Victor Hugo's France or Whitman's America), but of England's own republican origins. The moral strength of Cromwell's 'commonweal', exemplified by the prowess of the navy under General at Sea Robert Blake (1598–1657), is used to denounce diplomacy as moral equivocation. This view of Britain as the founder of democracy, and therefore a world leader in political ethics, is reminiscent of Barrett Browning's rhetorical efforts to shame England into military intervention on an emergent Italy's behalf in *Casa Guidi Windows* (2.373–424). However, where Barrett Browning writes from the position of one immersed in the fine ethical nuances of Italian politics, Swinburne shows no such textured understanding of Boer, Uitlander, or African interests and concerns.

Furthermore, his sound patterns, performed in 'Off Shore' to evoke counter-intuitive meanings, are now marshalled to polarise positions, as in the alliterative description of the Boers as '**w**olves ... / **W**hose **w**ar is **w**aged ... **W**ith **w**omen and **w**ith **w**eanlings'. Likewise, the concluding exhortation, 'Strike, England, and strike home', ironically reminiscent of 'In the Water''s ebullient call to listeners to respond to visceral impulse ('Strike out from the shore as the heart in us bids and beseeches, athirst for the foam'), now devalues the fellow-feeling cultivated through 'Speech and song' in favour of decisive activism. Indeed, it is on this exhortation that Swinburne's contemporary George Gissing focuses in his patient, respectful, but forceful critique of the poet of 1889 (Gissing 1974), a critique privately applauded by Thomas Hardy as 'the right word at the right time' (Millgate 2004, 370).

Keeping his focus resolutely 'literary and ethical', Gissing acknowledges the classical republican genre of warrior poetry to which the sonnet belongs: an incitement to honourable warfare for the common good exemplified by the Spartan Tyrtaeus, believed to have exhorted his fellow Spartans to military action against the Messenians toward the end of the seventh century BC. Yet this encouragement of 'brute strife', Gissing argues, is beneath the dignity of poetry, which should support modernity's 'ascendency of reason' (Gissing 1974, 2). The easily aroused 'old blood-thirst', he warns, has itself no respect for poetry, for 'the singer incautiously advancing, is hustled in a howling mob'. In other words, it is precisely poetry's contribution to a democratising Enlightenment modernity – the appeal to the senses to encourage unanticipated meanings and unwonted sympathies – that Swinburne's poetics endangers with such polemical verse.

A few days after Gissing's critique was published, Swinburne's second sonnet, 'Reverse', appeared in response to an article in *The Times* entitled 'The Reverse at Ladysmith' (Anonymous 1899a).[17] In brief, British forces defending Ladysmith in Natal sent a column to reconnoitre Boer positions. They came under fire and, because of an ammunition shortage, suffered great losses, eventually capitulating to the enemy. The octave of 'Reverse' first invokes the English Commonwealth's reputation for military courage, then Swinburne uses the volta and sestet in a biting rush to judgement that indicts the troops' surrender as despicable fawning to an ignoble enemy. Thus the sonnet opens in the declarative voice with an idealised image of courage in adversity: a lone swimmer battling heavy seas.

> The wave that breaks against a forward stroke
>   Beats not the swimmer back, but thrills him through
>   With joyous trust to win his way anew
>   Through stronger seas than first upon him broke
>   And triumphed.

(Swinburne 1904, 6.386)

This swimmer embodies the same contrarian courage portrayed in the first swimming scene of *Tristram of Lyonesse*, but the texture of the experience evident in *Tristram* is minimised here. The representation of national fortitude that follows in phrases such as 'England's iron-tempered oak' or 'lion-like from sleep her strength awoke' is likewise abstract, subsuming diverse individualised experience into a universalised valour. Moreover, in the sestet, the consequences of failing to conform to such nationalised sentiment are dire:

> As bold in fight as bold in breach of trust
>   We find our foes, and wonder not to find,
>   Nor grudge them praise whom honour may not bind:
> But loathing more intense than speaks disgust
>   Heaves England's heart, when scorn is bound to greet
> Hunters and hounds whose tongues would lick their feet.
>   (Swinburne 1904, 6.403)

Here enemy courage, while acknowledged, is under-rated as the rash, arbitrary boldness of those unmotivated by any longstanding traditions of honour. Consequently, officers and troops ('Hunters and hounds') who surrender to such an enemy are guilty of fawning that warrants unanimous national disgust. Such rhetoric has the effect of grossly exaggerating both the differences between British and Boer troops, and the unanimity of the patriotic perspective. Thus Swinburne's republican ideals, no longer internationalist let alone potentially worldscale, are also detached from any meaningful English republican project.

The rashness and crudity of this poem are especially evident when read alongside the telegraphed verbatim account of events by the commanding officer, General Sir George White, which appeared in *The Times* the following day (Anonymous 1899b): the troops, a diverse, indeed 'British' rather than 'English' column, lost their ammunition in a stampede of supply mules prompted by falling boulders.[18] They nonetheless fought until overwhelmed and forced to surrender. Far from public scorn, they deserved respect. The Boers, moreover, behaved with an ethical integrity that Swinburne's poems nowhere acknowledge. In White's words, they treated the British wounded 'with great humanity', offering British doctors prompt opportunity to tend and retrieve the fallen. Within this context, Swinburne's swimming trope becomes empty moralising, capturing neither the chaos faced by the British forces in a poorly administered war nor the dogged persistence of the Boers determined to defend their farmlands.

The last sonnet I will consider, 'The Turning of the Tide', is a celebra-
tion of the British victory at Paardeberg on 27 February 1900 – the date of
the sonnet's composition. As in 'The Transvaal', the octave invokes the
English past to evaluate the present, but now to applaud moral heroism.
In familiar republican fashion, the opening quatrain marshals stormy seas
with epic phrasing ('As when') to trope overwhelming adversity:

> Storm, strong with all the bitter heart of hate,
> Smote England, now nineteen dark years ago,
> As when the tide's full wrath in seaward flow
> Smites and bears back the swimmer.

> (Swinburne 1904, 6.387)

No longer a trope for the sensory immersiveness of the common man or
the heroic individual, the swimmer is a simile for the English
Commonwealth's body politic. The 'dark years' past allude to the disas-
trously brief First Anglo-Boer War and the British military humiliation at
the Battle of Majuba Hill on the same date, nineteen years earlier (27
February 1881). Swinburne, conforming to the widespread British view
that Paardeberg avenged Majuba, uses republican images in the sestet to
announce the restoration of liberty and enlightenment with Boer defeat.
Yet sound patterns such as '**free**dom **free**', 'laid low', or 'light on land and
sea' fail to engage the fraught ethics of Paardeberg that have troubled
historians of the war ever since. Questions such as the fate of Boer
women and children trapped with General Piet Cronje's forces, or the
harshness of British commanding officers not only to the Boers but to
their own troops are not raised.

Unable to use the Boer perspective to modify his patriotism,
Swinburne apparently failed to recognise the similarities between the
Transvaal Boers fighting for their own republic and the Italian patriots of
the mid-century Risorgimento, nor could he see that the British treatment
of the Boers bore many resemblances to Austrian intolerance to Italian
patriots. And where Barrett Browning recognised the commercial
interests motivating British non-intervention in Italy's plight, Swinburne
along with many others failed to recognise the economic motivations of
the European enterprise in Africa.[19]

Ironically, for all the insular dogmatism he displayed in defending what
he believed were ideals under attack by renegade factions, Swinburne was
nonetheless capable of sustaining a negotiative ethics when meditating on
radical philosophical and ontological difference (such as fate or death).

This capability is borne out by one of his last swimming poems, 'The Lake of Gaube' (Swinburne 1904, 6.284–7), published only days before the outbreak of the South African war. A masterful synthesis of the strengths of both descriptive and sound-driven poems, this lyric has prompted exemplary recent readings, so mine need only be brief (see Maxwell 2001, 216–17 and Weiner 2010, 18–20). Set abroad in a non-English (but nonetheless very European) landscape, the poem meditates on poetry's relation to the strange, represented here by the amphibian salamanders inhabiting the lakeside terrain and the dark waters of the lake itself. As in 'Off Shore', Swinburne uses Apollo's world of poetic song and aesthetic delight to transform irrational fear of strangeness, which too easily becomes 'hate and horror' (ironically exemplified by his own aversion to the Boers), into curiosity that approaches the unknown as imaginative possibility.

The local myth – that anyone who swims in the lake courts death – masks a more intractable fear than the salamander myth: a fear of one's fate as the radically unknowable. Such fear not only is impervious to reason but inhibits the imagination. Swinburne challenges it with the swimmer's dive into the lake waters: an athletic and self-overcoming embrace of Fate from which other poets customarily shrink (Maxwell 2001, 217). The plunge is cast as personal and immediately visualised even as it is also narrated as applicable to common humanity. Yet the swimming trope by no means domesticates the interpretative aporia of death or fate, but transforms it into the grounds for poetry's creative and equal freedom. In this context, the trope thus implicitly endorses the earlier cosmopolitan republican ideals of border-crossing and imaginative openness to difference even of the most threatening variety. At the same time, it gives more contexture to abstractions such as 'fear', 'freedom', and 'strangeness' than do poems like 'Off Shore' or 'In the Water', both figuratively at the level of simile, and sensually at the level of poetic form. Swinburne thus tracks the process whereby poetic art may explore the limits of knowledge, heightening the senses not simply for art's own sake, but, as Weiner argues, to illustrate 'his conviction that the limitations of human knowledge in sense experience are matched by the expansive powers of the mind' (Weiner 2010, 20).

That Swinburne fails to exercise those expansive powers in the swimming tropes of the Transvaal sonnets might remind us today not simply of the flaws apparent in this poet's contribution to a *fin-de-siècle* political ethics but also of the challenges involved in negotiative ethical

practice itself. Today's rooted cosmopolitans rightly place great faith in
the power of literary conversation to educate us in balancing universal
aspirations with many-sided deliberation and an immersive respect for
diversity. Reading Swinburne the cosmopolitan singer of the strange
alongside Swinburne the under-informed, intolerant patriot is sobering
evidence that even among the most imaginative and creative thinkers
viscerally felt prejudices may prove resolutely resistant to rational conver-
sation.

NOTES

1 Recent studies of British republicanism to which this chapter is especially
   indebted include Weiner 2005 and Prochaska 2000.
2 See for instance Anderson 1998, Appiah 1998, Hollinger 1995, and Cohen 1992.
   For discussions in a specifically Victorian literary context, see Anderson 2001
   and Keirstead 2011.
3 For an incisive overview of the criticisms levelled at cosmopolitanism, see
   Calhoun 2002.
4 For more on this topic, see Saville 2009b.
5 In Swinburne's poetry we may thus find the kind of 'complex dialectical rela-
   tionships between political and aesthetic modernity' to which Anderson invites
   us to pay more attention (Anderson 2005, 201).
6 For a fine discussion of the associations Swinburne's poetry evokes between
   his own rhythms and those of the ocean, see Prins 1999, 165–73; for
   Swinburne's ability to move his readers literally with the sensuality of his style
   and thus seduce them into sympathetic response, see Maxwell 2003 and Blair
   2006a.
7 John A. Walsh uses digital media to demonstrate the intensity of Swinburne's
   post-1879 preoccupation with nodes of marine rhetoric (Walsh 2010).
8 For an explication of the radical republican value of the 'poetic tale' in
   Swinburne and Blake, see Weiner 2005, 160–1.
9 My own readings of the swimming trope owe much to Weiner's exemplary
   interpretations of Swinburne's synaesthetic language patterns.
10 See also Swinburne 1959–62, 4.138n; Weiner offers an illuminating interpreta-
   tion of 'Hertha' in relation to Swinburne's early religious critiques (such as
   'Hymn of Man' and 'Christmas Antiphones') and his responses to precedents,
   such as Blake (Weiner 2005, 166–70).
11 Margot Louis makes this point in her moving reading of the butterflies in
   Tristram (Louis 2009a, 654–7). For exciting new readings of the butterflies in
   'Envoi' see Weiner 2010, 22–4, and Herbert F. Tucker in Chapter 6 below.
12 Herbert F. Tucker describes Swinburne and D. G. Rossetti as implicit followers
   of Blake's 'incarnationist psychotheology' (Tucker 1996, 158).

13 My thanks to Stefano Evangelista and Catherine Maxwell for drawing this connection and the Pater echo to my attention.

14 As I show in another context, *Tristram of Lyonesse* is dense with allusions to other cultures and literatures: Irish, French, Italian, and Hellenic (Saville 2011, 494).

15 Widely divergent and ethically flawed perspectives on the war ranged from the idealised view of the Boers held by Welsh Liberals and Irish Nationalists, who saw them as 'a small democratic people resisting English domination' (Shannon 1974, 335–6), to derogatory attitudes like John Buchan's claim that appalling conditions in British-administered Boer concentration camps were attributable to 'mentally and bodily underbred' Boer victims of 'a class of people who have somehow missed civilisation' (cited in Nasson 2010, 268). Added to these was the Radical theory 'heavily spiced with anti-semitism' that the war was a conspiracy of Johannesburg capitalists (Shannon 1974, 328).

16 The Transvaal was supported by the neighbouring Boer republic of the Orange Free State. Nasson offers a compelling account of Milner's hawkishness in the years immediately prior to the war (Nasson 2010, 51–6).

17 'The Reverse at Ladysmith' was published in *The Times* of 1 November 1899, while Swinburne's sonnet appeared on 7 November.

18 The advance column included the 10th Mountain Battery, companies from the Gloucesters, and the Royal Irish Fusiliers, *The Times* (2 November 1899), 5. The loyalties of the Irish in this war were notoriously vexed: many, like Field Marshall Lord Frederick Roberts, were loyalists while others, Irish Nationalists, volunteered in support of the Boers (Nasson 2010, 307).

19 *Casa Guidi Windows* 2.577–655; Nasson recounts the blame cast on rapacious capitalism by dissidents such as British Fabians, Ramsay MacDonald and Bertrand Russell, and the Radical Liberal J. A. Hobson (Nasson 2010, 39).

3

SWINBURNE: A NINETEENTH-CENTURY HELLENE?

Charlotte Ribeyrol

Swinburne was a learned Hellenist, trained at the best institutions offering a classical education in nineteenth-century Britain, from Eton to Oxford. Although wary at first of the 'idols of Oxford Hellenism' (Swinburne cited in Lafourcade 1928, 170), the poet soon came to be very proud of his mastery of the ancient Greek language, boasting in one of his letters to Sidney Colvin in 1872 that some of his Greek poems had been mistaken for Hellenistic originals (Swinburne 1959–62, 2.203). Indeed, lines from his early play *Atalanta in Calydon* (1865) could almost be fancied to be 'a direct translation from the Greek' according to a critic impressed by Swinburne's pseudo-Greek archaisms (Hyder 1970, 10).

The question raised by this chapter is not the genuineness of Swinburne's Hellenism but its relation to the more official and orthodox Victorian 'hellenomania' (Bernal 1987). I wish to explore Swinburne's liminal and transgressive excursions into marginal Hellenic territories, often obscured by the exclusively Olympian vision of Greece extolled by most Victorians in their quest for secure ideological foundations. In the nineteenth century ancient Greece was a Western utopia to which European countries (mainly France, Britain, and Germany) laid claim. If the Homeric texts belonged to all nations, works of art such as the Parthenon frieze associated with the Golden Age of Greece (i.e. the Classical Athens of Pericles) were safely appropriated by, transplanted to, and secured in the main European museums: the Louvre, the British Museum and the Glyptothek in Munich. In keeping with the harmonious proportions of these marbles celebrated by Winckelmann in his *History of Ancient Art* (1764), Greek Antiquity progressively appeared through-out the nineteenth century as a powerful signifier of rationality, purity, and order.

Matthew Arnold's *Culture and Anarchy* (1869), which exhorted his contemporaries to 'Hellenise' their way of life (Arnold 1869, 63), helped to spread this belief in the Greek ideal supposedly made up of 'sweetness and light', to quote the title of the first chapter. In his *Lectures on Art* (1870), John Ruskin also heralded the Greek school as 'the school of light' (Ruskin 1903–12, 20.105). In his review of Swinburne's *Poems and Ballads, First Series* (1866), William Michael Rossetti summed up the Victorian Hellenic craze in the following way: 'everything Greek has become to us as a compound of beauty and of thought, a vestige and an evidence of human soul infused as into Parian marble, marble-like in its purity of appeal to us' (Hyder 1970, 65). This ideological faith in the Greek canon – meaning on the one hand the sacred masterpieces of Greek culture which all artists should emulate and on the other, following the Greek etymology of the word *kanon*, a religious and military order or law never to be infringed – lasted far beyond the Victorian age, at least until the Second World War, when the prestige attached to classical studies started to wane. Many writers in the second half of the nineteenth and early twentieth centuries were thus fascinated by the perfection of the Doric body, in particular that of the antique Spartans, a race of warriors associated with the victory at Thermopylae, who were known to have paid great attention to physical training, 'cut[ting] and carv[ing]' their own form in preparation for war as if it were 'a work of art' to take up Walter Pater's description of the Lacedaemonians in *Plato and Platonism* (1893) (Pater 1910, 6.257). But the hellenophilia of aesthetically inclined authors such as Swinburne, Pater, Symonds, and later Wilde did not draw exclusively on these virile solar figures of crystal-clear purity such as the 'sun-child whiter than the sunlit snows' of 'Thalassius' (Swinburne 1904, 3.296). Like Wilde's Antinous-like Dorian Gray, Hellenic beauty appeared to these authors both as colourful rather than marmoreal and as dappled, mingling light and shade. My aim here is to show how Swinburne's shady and dappled Greek poems on the one hand jar more often than not with this mainstream ideal Hellenism, and on the other echo or anticipate the provocative Hellenism displayed in the works of his fellow aesthetes.

In his 1931 book *Swinburne, A Nineteenth Century Hellene*, William R. Rutland strove to defend the purity of Swinburne's Greek inspiration, which he probably thought might be a good way of drawing attention back to his poetry which most modernist writers had rejected as neoromantic and decadent. Rutland's strategy was to re-evaluate Swinburne's Greekness in a period when ancient Greece was still a powerful ideological symbol of authority. But this implied of course a selection of

Swinburne's 'proper' Greek works such as – mainly – *Atalanta in Calydon* and *Erechtheus* (1876). Rutland dismisses Swinburne's more subversive poems on Hellenic subjects:

> If *Anactoria* were enough to make the angels weep, *Dolores* might well raise a smirk from the Father of lies. It happily does not concern us here, for the vices of Nero and the underground shrine of his Excellency de Sade make no pretence to kinship with anything Hellenic. (Rutland 1931, 292)

This comment, which significantly attributed 'Anactoria' and 'Dolores' to some decadent Roman or French, rather than Greek, influence, may seem surprising given the obvious Sapphic echoes in 'Anactoria' and the Greek origins of Dolores, daughter of Priapus, the ithyphallic fertility god (Swinburne 1904, 1.156; 2000, 124). Rutland's biased reading of Swinburne's works reveals clearly that Swinburne's Hellenism was the locus of conflicting moral interpretations, and is less enlightening as to Swinburne's actual Greek sources than to the ideological expectations of his modern readers. Rutland therefore chose to focus on Swinburne's apparently less provocative Greek poems, in which the poet toyed with the Greek reference in order to gain cultural and moral immunity in the eyes of his critics. Indeed, as Linda Dowling has explained, 'The prestige of Greece among educated middle-class Victorians ... was so massive that invocation of Hellenism could cast a veil of respectability over a hitherto unmentionable vice or crime' (Dowling 1994, 28). But Swinburne deliberately stretches this 'veil of respectability' to his more questionable verse, including 'Anactoria', later discarded by Rutland. With regard to 'Anactoria' Swinburne ironically reminds his readers that pupils from the best public schools are asked to learn Sappho's fragments by heart: 'We in England are taught, are compelled under penalties to learn, to construe, and to repeat, as schoolboys, the imperishable and incomparable verses of that supreme poet; and I at least am grateful for the training' (Swinburne 1866, 9; 2000, 406).

However, some critics were not blinded by the formal perfection of his Greek poems. This was the case of John Morley reviewing *Poems and Ballads, First Series* in August 1866. Morley accused Swinburne of 'glorify[ing] all the bestial delights that the subtleness of Greek depravity was able to contrive' (Hyder 1970, 23). This denunciation of Swinburne's 'Greek depravity' sounds almost oxymoronic in the context of Victorian 'hellenomania'. But it shows that Swinburne's Hellenism is dual, Janus-like. His Hellenic inspiration exceeds the limits of Olympus to offer readers shocking glimpses of Chthonian and Dionysian depths (closely linked within the Eleusinian Mysteries), revealing repressed features of ancient Greek culture, in particular colour as opposed to marmoreal whiteness, darkness as opposed to Apollonian light, suffering as opposed to health and innocent joy. Related to this provocative shift of aesthetic paradigm, Swinburne's fascination with dissident marginal and liminal figures such as Persephone, Tiresias, Hermaphroditus, or Atalanta, similarly questions the centrality of Greek authority.

What is striking in Swinburne's poems is the instability of the Greek reference which constantly shifts from the archaic to the later, Hellenistic periods or from the mystery gods (Demeter, Persephone, and Dionysus) to the deities of Olympus. This is the case for example in the 'Last Oracle' in which the Olympian god Apollo, competing with the '*Galilean*' (Swinburne 1904, 3.5) is only partly defined by the light which he sheds on the world: 'Thou the word, the light, the life, the breath, the glory' (Swinburne 1904, 3.8). A sort of dramatic chiaroscuro veils Apollo's power: 'Dark thou satest, veiled with light, behind the morning' (Swinburne 1904, 3.9). 'Dark', 'veiled', 'behind': all these words belong to the lexical field of the hidden rather than of spiritual revelation, and evoke a mysticism more reminiscent of the Mysteries of Eleusis (to which Swinburne also dedicated a poem in *Poems and Ballads, First Series*) than of the official solar worship of Olympian religion. Moreover, the God Apollo is repeatedly said to be both 'Destroyer and Healer' – a curing divinity and the ruthless slayer of Python, whose face is an oxymoronic 'shining shadow' (Swinburne 1904, 3.9). Indeed, in Swinburne's poems the Greek gods often appear as ambiguous *pharmakoi*, to use the antanaclastic Greek word meaning both the poison and the remedy, just as Althea reflects on her name in *Atalanta in Calydon*:

> I am severed from myself, my name is gone,
> My name that was a healing, it is changed,
> My name is a consuming.
>
> (Swinburne 1904, 4.317–18; 2000, 309)

The Greek word *pharmakon* also means 'colour', as it was frequent in Antiquity to prescribe certain pigments to cure illnesses. The status of colour in Greek culture was hotly debated in the Victorian age as it did not quite fit the marmoreal requirements of the Apollonian cults. Since the late eighteenth century many travellers had noticed traces of colour on the sculptured reliefs of Greek temples. In 1851, the Franco-German archaeologist J. I. Hittorff provided serious scientific evidence as to the general practice of polychromy on Greek sculpture in *L'Architecture poly-*

chrome chez les Grecs. However, in spite of these archaeological discoveries, the Elgin Marbles were 'scrubbed' and cleaned with acid in 1858 to remove all traces of colour (Jenkins 2001, 5) on the grounds that polychromy was alien to the neoclassical ideal as defined by J. J. Winckelmann, still the supreme authority on Greek art and aesthetics, who believed that white sculptural bodies reflected light best. Colour was thus perceived by many Victorians as a primitive stain on the perfect marmoreal surface of the Greek ideal. This Victorian refusal of Greek colour sheds light on the provocative aspects of some of Swinburne's apparently measured Hellenic texts which were also attacked for their dubious colouring. The mistrust of colour is illustrated once again by Morley's 1866 review, which brings together Dionysian wine-induced ecstasy and chromatic excess:

> It was too rashly said, when *Atalanta in Calydon* appeared, that Mr. Swinburne had drunk deep at the springs of Greek poetry, and had profoundly conceived and assimilated the divine spirit of Greek art ... But the new volume shows with still greater plainness how far removed Mr. Swinburne's tone of mind is from that of the Greek poets. Their most remarkable distinction is their scrupulous moderation and sobriety in colour. Mr. Swinburne riots in the profusion of colour of the most garish and heated kind. He is like a composer who should fill his orchestra with trumpets, or a painter who should exclude every colour but a blaring red, and a green as of sour fruit. There are not twenty stanzas in the whole book which have the faintest tincture of soberness ... Unsparing use of the most violent colours and the most intoxicated ideas and images is Mr. Swinburne's prime characteristic. (Hyder 1970, 26)

Indeed, Swinburne often evokes vivid hues rather than whiteness which he seems to link less to purity than to morbidity. For instance, in the Chthonian poem 'At Eleusis', Demeter compares her bringing nature back to life in spring with a Greek artist colouring a statue:

> I make the lesser green begin, when spring
> Touches not earth but with one fearful foot;
> And as a careful gilder with grave art
> Soberly colours and completes the face,
> Mouth, chin and all, of some sweet work in stone,
> I carve the shapes of grass and tender corn
> And colour the ripe edges and long spikes
> With the red increase and the grace of gold.
> (Swinburne 1904, 1.209–10; 2000, 167)

But even in his later and apparently more formally Hellenic play *Erechtheus*, the poet inverts the usual chromatic polarities: whiteness is no longer the supreme aesthetic ideal, and colour becomes synonymous with life and creation. Swinburne seems particularly wary of whitening practices. When Chthonia (symbolically *not* an Olympian figure) is about to be sacrificed, nature undergoes morbid changes from colour to a dangerous whiteness: 'its olive-leaf whiten[s] and wither[s]' (Swinburne 1904, 4.364). The verbs 'wither' and 'whiten' are graphically very similar, so that death and whiteness appear as closely intertwined. J. A. Symonds, who was a regular correspondent of Swinburne's and an admirer of his works, also seemed to have shared the poet's fears of the 'whitewashing' of 'the imagination of the Greeks' (Symonds 1902, 1.56).

Similarly in his *Notes on Poems and Reviews*, Swinburne denounced another dangerous form of whitening, whereby Greek poetic texts underwent the same fate, as it were, as the Elgin Marbles: some Victorian exegetes of the Homeric texts believed in the total absence of colour in Greek literature, on the grounds that the Hellenes were 'colour-blind'. William Gladstone, for instance, used this pejorative adjective in an article on the Greek 'colour-sense', published in 1877. The real question was not whether the Greeks of Antiquity perceived colour or not, but what terminology they used to describe the phenomenon of colour, as Symonds explained:

> The sense of colour cannot be judged by colour-nomenclature. People in a primitive state of society, may be acutely sensitive to colours, as indeed they have all their senses in fine working order, and yet may have no names to denote the shades of hues. That is due mainly to the fact that colours are not connected with utility ... Suppose the currency were established, not on varying weight of precious metals, but on varying tints of red, blue, yellow; then we should soon find a nomenclature springing up to denote the finest gradations of those colours ... The shifts we submit to in order to communicate sensations of colour ought to teach us that in the Homeric or other early ages colours were fully appreciated by the senses, but had not found their analogue in language. (Symonds 1890, 307)

Pater agreed with Symonds's conclusions, which he applied to his own reading of Plato, an author whose works were then being rediscovered thanks to new translations and reclaimed by many thinkers. Rather than underline the purely abstract dimension of Plato's thought, Pater chose to stress the colourfulness of the philosopher's genius:

Plato's richly coloured genius will find a compromise between the One which alone really is, yet is so empty a thought for finite minds; and the Many, which most properly is not, yet presses so closely on eye and ear and heart and fancy and will, at every moment ... Prefer as he may in theory that blank white light of the One – its sterile, 'formless, colourless, impalpable,' eternal identity with itself – the world, and this chiefly is why the world has not forgotten him, will be for him, as he is by no means colour-blind, by no means a colourless place. He will suffer it to come to him, as his pages convey it in turn to us, with the liveliest variety of hue. (Pater 1910, 6.46–7)

Swinburne also rejected the monochrome or chromatically limited vision of ancient Greek literature and art. In *Notes on Poems and Reviews*, he considered the Latin translations of Sappho 'colourless and bloodless' (Swinburne 1866, 9; 2000, 406). In his Sapphic poems, the fragments he significantly adapts are those in which controversial and untranslatable colours are mentioned. For instance the most frequently quoted passage from Sappho's 'Ode to Aphrodite' (Fragment 1) in Swinburne's poems corresponds to the first line of her fragment: 'a mind of many colours' ('Anactoria', Swinburne 1904, 1.59; 2000, 49), '*O thou of divers-coloured mind*' and '*Thou of the divers-coloured seat*' ('On the Cliffs', Swinburne 1904, 3.321) – as if Swinburne could not possibly choose a single translation for the very first word of the Greek poem: *poikoltron* – the Greek adjective *poikilos* meaning polychrome, of many colours, diverse. Pater uses the noun *poikilia* extensively in his *Greek Studies* (1895) in reference to the Ionian rather than Dorian pole of Greek art: 'traceable all through Greek art – an Asiatic curiousness, or *poikilia*' (Pater 1910, 7.216). This 'many-faced, multifarious' (Swinburne 1866, 6; 2000, 404) aesthetic similarly characterises Swinburne's *Poems and Ballads* and Pater's subversive conclusion to his essays on the Renaissance. As Linda Dowling has argued, this term suggesting variety was also part of a 'Victorian homosexual code' understandable to readers in the know (Dowling 1989, 1). Pater thus uses the Greek term *poikilos* or *poikilia* in relation to Eastern sensuality and sexual permissiveness, and Symonds, in 'A Problem in Greek Ethics' (1883), mentions Plato's use of the term in the *Symposium* (182b), with reference to Greek homosexual love as a multifaceted form of desire (Symonds 1975, 185, 188).

However this interest in *poikilia* did not prevent Pater from praising on several occasions the whiteness of 'sexless' (Pater 1980, 176) Greek statues as if in need of 'sanitizing' (Pulham 2008, 59) and erasing the taint of homoerotic desire in order better to fit in with the Doric aesthetic and moral demands of his age. Symonds similarly strove to contrast the 'immaculate white-winged desire' described in his homoerotic 'Eudiades' (Symonds 2005, 25) with the '"libidinous joys" [which] present themselves under seductive colour' mentioned in his *Memoirs* (Symonds 1984, 240). In contrast, the perfect body of Venus in Swinburne's 'Laus Veneris' is described as 'naked' rather than 'nude' (Swinburne 1904, 1.22; 2000, 19) and bears the stain of sin from the outset:

> Asleep or waking is it? for her neck,
> Kissed over close, wears yet a purple speck
>   Wherein the pained blood falters and goes out;
> Soft, and stung softly – fairer for a fleck.
>
> (Swinburne 1904, 1.11; 2000, 9)

Swinburne deliberately chooses fleshliness and colour over marble-like purity. In 'Anactoria' he also stages the act of wounding and therefore staining of the perfect Greek body: 'the flowerlike white stained round with blue' (Swinburne 1904, 1.58; 2000, 48). The poet, who had a perfect grasp of the French language, might have been here thinking of the double meaning of the word blue in French as both a colour and a bruise. A few lines later this colour is mentioned again: 'dyed round like night with blue' (Swinburne 1904, 1.58; 2000, 48). Blue was the colour of death in Antiquity (Pastoureau 2002, 23 and 27), a 'dead blue' to which Swinburne refers in his poem 'Faustine' (Swinburne 1904, 1.111; 2000, 90), in which Faustine is described as both a votary of Bacchus and a Lesbian disciple of Sappho. This colour was indeed also frequently associated with same-sex desire, in particular with Uranian love (as homosexuality was sometimes called in the Victorian age), as Ouranos was the sky-god (Matthews 1999, 185) and, in keeping with Pausanias's speech in Plato's *Symposium* (180e–181c), the Uranian Aphrodite the tutelary divinity of a higher spiritual form of love than that offered by Aphrodite Pandemos. This Uranian connection certainly led Symonds to name one of his homoerotic collections of poems *In the Key of Blue* (1893): here nearly every poem or 'word picture' opens with a highly Whistlerian first line offering synaesthetic variations on the colour blue, such as 'A symphony of black and blue' or 'A symphony of blues and white', etc. (Maxwell 2010b, 239). Purplish blue was moreover the colour of the highly homoerotic figure of Hyacinthus often conjured up in Pater's, Symonds's, and Wilde's essays, poems, and letters. As Patricia Pulham has underlined in her analysis of Olive Custance's 'tinted' poetry, the colours of Hyacinthus would later be equally appropriated by female poets, from Custance, who included two homoerotic poems entitled 'Hyacinthus' and 'Blue Flowers' in her collection *The Inn of Dreams* (1911), to H. D., who also believed violet and purple to be eminently Sapphic colours: '"Little but all roses" true there is a tint of rich colour ... violets, purple woof of cloth, scarlet garments, dyed fastening of a sandal, the lurid, crushed and perished hyacinth, stains on cloth and flesh and parchment ... I think of the words of Sappho as these colours' (cited in Pulham 2007, 174).

Swinburne refers to this colourful hyacinth – 'For thy sweet priests to lean and pray upon / Jasper and hyacinth and chrysopras' (Swinburne 1904, 1.241; 2000, 193) – in association with the sensuous cults of Venus, the pagan goddess 'painted with face red' in 'St Dorothy' (Swinburne 1904, 1.241; 2000, 193). This cosmetic reference mingles archaeological evidence (that of vivid paint applied to the eyes, cheeks, lips, and hair of antique statues as exemplified by John Gibson's 1862 reconstitution of a *Tinted Venus*) with the iconography of the prostitute with alluring painted lips, as in Dante Gabriel Rossetti's *Bocca Baciata* (1859), modelled on his mistress Fanny Cornforth. Swinburne's poems thus seem to pave the way for the gendering of colour terminology by deliberately associating colour and provocative sensuality. Besides, his use of the verb 'dye' in 'Anactoria', homophonically evoking death as well as artificial colouring, clearly suggests a reflection on the metapoietic role of colour. It is as if Swinburne, Pygmalion-like, consciously staged the creative process of colouring, bringing back life, flesh, and desire to inert Hellenic marble figures, as in his poem 'The Two Dreams':

> ... refit
> The fair limbs ruined, flush the dead blood through
> With colour, make all broken beauties new.
> (Swinburne 1904, 1.256; 2000, 206)

Moreover, numerous occurrences of the compound adjective 'coloured' in *Poems and Ballads, First Series* convey the creative impulse rather than any colour notation in particular: 'summer-coloured', 'clean-coloured', 'leper-coloured', 'subtle-coloured', 'sea-coloured'. These colours are made to appear as 'strange dyes' reminiscent of those mentioned by Pater in his highly sensuous and sensual conclusion to his essays on the Renaissance:

While all melts under our feet, we may well grasp at any exquisite passion, or any contribution to knowledge that seems by a lifted horizon to set the spirit free for a moment, or any stirring of the senses, strange dyes, strange colours, and curious odours, or work of the artist's hands, or the face of one's friend. (Pater 1980, 189)

Pater's and Swinburne's 'troubled colouring' (Pater 1980, 154) and deliberate chromatic excesses introduce a sensuality, verging at times on sexual violence, which could hardly coincide with the calmer and more sanitised vision of Greek culture extolled by their contemporaries. In 'Anactoria', Swinburne's intertwining of desire and pain clearly antici-pates Friedrich Nietzsche's aesthetics of suffering developed in *The Birth of Tragedy* (1872), which explores the Dionysian pole of Greek culture, as opposed to the Apollonian – an opposition which Linda Dowling describes as 'cognate' with the 'Dorian/Ionian antithesis' (Dowling 1989, 4).

This Dionysian inspiration is particularly felt in many of Lawrence Alma-Tadema's paintings, including *The Roses of Heliogabalus* (1888), which draws on the legend of the decadent and Hellenophile Roman Emperor Heliogabalus who supposedly smothered his guests to death with a shower of violets and roses similar to the 'roses of vice' described by Swinburne in 'Dolores' (Swinburne 1904, 1.156; 2000, 124). In the background of the painting a dancing maenad, wearing a pied leopard-skin, illustrates this Dionysian force. In addition to the music played by the maenad, the evident focus on the synaesthetic flowers (associating smell, colour, and touch) in the painting also heightens the sensual ecstasy. This sensuality is also present in Simeon Solomon's 1866 depiction of *Heliogabalus, High Priest of the Sun and Emperor of Rome, 118–122 AD*. Ironically both works probably draw on Swinburne's late Hellenophile affinities (exposed in 'Dolores' and in 'St Dorothy'), subverting and displacing the Doric solar worship of Apollo in favour of more decadent figures.

This subversive sexual drive is also hinted at in Swinburne's correspon-dence. In a letter to William Michael Rossetti of 2 December 1869, he mentions a poem which he claims 'bawdier in Greek' (Swinburne 1959–62, 2.62). In another addressed to Richard Monckton Milnes in 1863, he invokes flagellating Greek divinities, 'scourge-bearing Aphrodite or Minerva bearing the rod' (Swinburne 1959–62, 1.76), to quote his own translation from the Greek. Swinburne creates his own pantheon of Greek punitive gods congenial to his sadomasochistic tendencies. The ecstatic suffering described in Swinburne's more Dionysian poems is thus further emphasised, as it were, by a series of sadistic Olympian divinities, including Venus in 'Laus Veneris' or Apollo the 'Destroyer' in 'The Last Oracle'. The depiction of the Olympians as cruel gods was indeed becoming more and more frequent in the second half of the nineteenth century as the primal rituals associated with Chthonian divinities were arousing the interest of an increasing number of scholars and artists. This shift of cultural paradigm has been well analysed by Margot K. Louis in *Persephone Rises*, in which she pays particular attention to this 'anti-Olympian topos' (Louis 2009b, 14) and reads Pater's essays on the myth of Demeter and Persephone and Swinburne's Proserpine poems as responses to, and illustrations of, this progressive change of focus.

Swinburne's interest in liminality and marginality in these Chthonian poems has more rarely been commented upon. It is as if the poet were trying to decentralise the Greek reference in favour of an 'interspace' ('A Ballad of Death', Swinburne 1904, 1.7; 2000, 8) in which ambivalent figures take their place – in particular the adolescent 'maiden' Persephone ('At Eleusis', Swinburne 1904, 1.210; 2000, 167), torn between earth and the underworld, between inside and outside in her garden 'beyond porch and portal' ('The Garden of Proserpine', Swinburne 1904, 1.170; 2000, 136), between the rites of Eleusis and Christian worship ('Hymn to Proserpine'). In *Atalanta in Calydon*, the poet's use of negative prefixes in words such as 'disfleshed' or 'disallied' (Swinburne 1904, 4.258; 2000, 258) thus reveals more than just a mimetic impulse to follow the Greek canonical texts, from Homer to the Attic playwrights. The Hellenic façade reflected in the perfectly ordered sections of the play (parodos, stasimon, exodus) is flawed by a series of dissonances, to use the same negative prefix, referring to a deathly presence – that of 'Dis', the Chthonian god of the underworld in classical mythology. Just as Nietzsche tried 'to enlist fellow revelers and to tempt them into secret alleys, onto mysterious dancing grounds' (Nietzsche cited in Louis 2009b, 20), Swinburne's deviant Hellenic fantasies stray from the moral path dictated by his compatriots in search of a Greek model of formal rectitude and sexual straightness – a paradigm embraced later by the modernists, such as Ezra Pound, who wished to be as 'straight as the Greeks' (cited in Collecott 1999, 113). But romantic wandering was already a crucial heuristic process in ancient Greek culture, reinforced on the one hand by the quasi-homography of the Greek word *alèteia* (meaning 'wandering, erring') and *alètheia* (meaning 'truth') (Montiglio 2005, 93) and on the other by the profusion of myths involving such straying, among them the myths of Tiresias and Ulysses. Swinburne explicitly mentions Ulysses' wandering fate in his poem 'By the North Sea': 'the wise wave-wandering steadfast-hearted / Guest of many a lord of many a land' (Swinburne 1904, 5.95). Moreover, the scene from the *Odyssey* which Swinburne significantly evokes here refers to Ulysses' near-experience of death in the realm of Hades where his mother Anticleia was held. Swinburne's Hellenic utopia is not a secure, defined, or confined space: his Hellenic heroes explore its extreme margins horizontally and vertically, as it were, with the recurring *topos* of the descent into hell which is perfectly illustrated in his liminal Persephone poems. These poems in turn inspired Dante Gabriel Rossetti's multiple pictorial versions of 'Proserpina' in the 1870s, in which the overall gloom is only partially relieved by a discreet bright opening offering a glimpse of the upper world. Rossetti wrote his own Persephone poems to accompany these paintings, inscribing them on to the canvas, as if to blur the frontiers not only between light and darkness, and life and death, but also between text and image.

Tiresias, in Swinburne's eponymous poem, is also one of these errant mythological figures who transgress Hellenic frontiers in quest of more barbaric margins. Tiresias carries the staff of Hermes, the god of cross-roads, and 'prophes[ies] with feet upon a grave' (Swinburne 1904, 2.178). The blind prophet only accesses poetic truth in a liminal fashion: 'I stand a shadow across the door of doom, / Athwart the lintel of death's house, and wait' (Swinburne 1904, 2.178). Swinburne 'Hellenises' the Miltonic myth of the revelation of the blind bard but here truth does not come from a central authority or divinity (the blind Homer), but rather from a delving into strange, untrodden depths. In her analysis of the female sublime, Catherine Maxwell has convincingly linked blindness, poetic vision, and castration (Maxwell 2001). The liminality Tiresias experiences may thus be understood in gendered as well as in spatial terms. According to one of the versions of the myth, Tiresias changed sex each time he encountered snakes mating – snakes being yet another attribute of the wandering Hermes and a powerful symbol of hermaphroditism (Brisson 1997, 111), as Swinburne himself suggests in 'Fragoletta', which describes an androgynous youth, both 'sightless' and 'sexless' (Swinburne 1904, 1.82; 2000, 67): 'Thou hast a serpent in thine hair, / In all the curls that close and cling' (Swinburne 1904, 1.84; 2000, 69). Swinburne may also be hinting at the ambivalent gender of Tiresias: 'I have seen this, who saw long since, being man, / As now I know not if indeed I be' (Swinburne 1904, 2.179). Swinburne could here be implying that Tiresias is no longer a man but an androgynous figure, which would be consistent with

Swinburne's own provocative bisexual claims ('Great poets are bisexual; male and female at once', Swinburne 1881, 130) and his fascination for figures of doubtful sex combining the physical perfections of both sexes, like 'Hermaphroditus':

> There is nothing lovelier, as there is nothing more famous, in later Hellenic art, than the statue of Hermaphroditus ... At Paris, at Florence, at Naples, the delicate divinity of this work has always drawn towards it the eyes of artists and poets ... Odour and colour and music are not more tender or more pure. How favourite and frequent a vision among the Greeks was this of the union of sexes in one body of perfect beauty, none need be told. (Swinburne 1866, 17–18; 2000, 411–12)

Perception and in particular perception of colour are here closely intertwined in this celebration of generic ambiguity: 'Odour and colour and music are not more tender or more pure.' But this fleshly rather than sculptural idealism ('the idea thus incarnate') was of course quite remote from the ideas of most Victorians concerning the muscular bodies of Doric athletes and warriors.

Swinburne was clearly drawn to these myths of effeminacy or gender instability, like other aesthetically inclined painters such as Solomon, whose androgynous figures (such as *Heliogabalus* or *Bacchus*) in blurred watercolours rather than in assertive oils the poet described as 'supersexual' (Swinburne 1871a, 574). The story of Atalanta also attracted the attention of Swinburne as it appeared equally subversive in terms of the codification of gender roles. According to Ovid, Atalanta was, like Salmacis in the myth of Hermaphroditus, one of the armed devotees of Artemis, the goddess of hunting but also of adolescence. This detail is essential given that, from the opening lines of *Atalanta in Calydon*, Swinburne calls Artemis 'mistress of the months' (Swinburne 1904, 4.247; 2000, 249) – that is the moon, a symbol of androgyny. Artemis, according to the Greeks, was 'Kourotrophos' (Vernant 1996, 19), meaning that she 'carried' the young, that she had the charge of adolescents on the verge of becoming adults. Young boys and girls were submitted to initiatory rituals which consisted in the blurring of gender boundaries and which enabled them to confront the barbaric and bestial Other in the wilderness. But it happened that this ritual led some adolescents like Atalanta to rebel. In his play, inspired by a fragment from Euripides entitled *Meleager*, Swinburne deliberately shifts attention to Atalanta, who is described throughout as 'strange' because of her refusal to conform to gender roles: 'She the strange woman … even she / Saw with strange eyes and with strange lips rejoiced' (Swinburne 1904, 4.307; 2000, 300). This adjective encoding homoeroticism (Pulham 2007, 162) is significantly used in both 'Hermaphroditus' and 'Fragoletta'. By refusing the *telos* of marriage and social conformity, Atalanta embodies a dangerous otherness, verging on the barbaric. There is even confusion about which 'beast' is being hunted down: Artemis's wild boar or her androgynous devotee. Here are the words of Plexippus, who wishes to kill the 'unwomanlike' Atalanta (Swinburne 1904, 4.265; 2000, 264) for her transgression of gender norms:

> Let her come crowned and stretch her throat for a knife,
> Bleat out her spirit and die, …
>
> But thou, O Zeus, hear me that I may slay
> This beast before thee and no man halve with me
> Nor woman.
>
> (Swinburne 1904, 4.281; 2000, 278)

By the end of the play Meleager himself is feminised, as he comes into contact with Atalanta (like Hermaphroditus when he 'melts into' Salmacis) – the burning of the brand by his mother acting as symbolic castration according to Maxwell (Maxwell 2001, 183): 'And minished all that god-like muscle and might / And lesser than a man's' (Swinburne 1904, 4.331; 2000, 320).

By focusing on myths of androgynous adolescent heroes and on liminal Chthonian divinities, Swinburne was in search of the Greek other rather than of the Greek forefather. He chose to subvert the classical tradition and *kanon*, and to go beyond the well-defined utopian space of the Victorian Hellas imagined and projected as 'the revered ancestor of the west, the origin of western civilisation' (Wallace 1997, 6). Under the veil of his mastery of Greek language and culture, Swinburne explored the frontiers of the other, the unknown margins which archaeologists, anthropologists, and the Cambridge Ritualists at the end of the nineteenth century would attempt to exhume and reveal.

Swinburne was certainly not as well-read as Pater or Symonds in the new sciences of archaeology and anthropology and yet his Hellenic writings inspired professional classicists such as Gilbert Murray and Jane Ellen Harrison, both of whom cherished Swinburne's poems. Harrison, for instance, includes lines from *Erechtheus* in her essay on *Art and Ritual* (1913) in which she explains the inseparability of art and ritual in the wake of Nietzsche's reflection on the Dionysian pole of Greek art:

> The Panathenaic frieze once decorated the *cella* or innermost shrine of the Parthenon, the temple of the Maiden Goddess Athena. It twined like a ribbon round the brow of the building and thence it was torn by Lord Elgin and brought home to the British Museum as a national trophy, for the price of a few hundred pounds of coffee and yards of scarlet cloth. To realize its meaning we must always think it back into its place. Inside the *cella*, or shrine, dwelt the goddess herself, her great image in gold and ivory; outside the shrine was sculptured her worship by the whole of her people. For the frieze is nothing but a great ritual procession translated into stone, the Panathenaic procession, or procession of *all* the Athenians, of all Athens, in honour of the goddess who was but the city incarnate, Athena.

> > 'A wonder enthroned on the hills and the sea,
> > A maiden crowned with a fourfold glory,
> > That none from the pride of her head may rend;
> > Violet and olive leaf, purple and hoary,
> > Song-wreath and story the fairest of fame,
> > Flowers that the winter can blast not nor bend,
> > A light upon earth as the sun's own flame,
> > A name as his name –
> > Athens, a praise without end.'
> >
> > SWINBURNE: *Erechtheus*, 141

> Sculptural Art, at least in this instance, comes out of ritual, has ritual as its subject, *is* embodied ritual. (Harrison 1913, 172–3)

Interestingly, the quotation from Swinburne's play encourages a derationalising of Greek sculpture in favour of 'embodied ritual', an embodiment suggested by the profusion of colours which adorn the head of the maiden who is not described in terms of marmoreal purity ('Violet and olive leaf, purple . . .'). By insisting on a pre-eminently *visual* culture rather than relying on a purely philological tradition which was still very male-dominated at the time (Evangelista 2011, 519), Harrison is striving to recreate the sensual 'aura' both of the original Panathenaic frieze and of the Elgin Marbles when they were still *in situ*, on the Acropolis. This bringing back to life of the true original colours of the artworks is also very close to Pater's analyses of Hellenic sculpture in *Greek Studies*:

> The whole black and grey world of extant antique sculpture [needs] to be translated back into ivory and gold, if we would feel the excitement which the Greeks seem to have felt in the presence of these objects . . . We must

seek to relieve the air of our galleries and museums of their too intellectual greyness. Greek sculpture could not have been a cold thing ... whatever a colour-blind school may say. (Pater 1910, 7.191)

The use of the expression 'colour-blind' is here extremely ironic as it may refer both to Gladstone's theories about Homer's colour-blindness and to the blindness of some Hellenists and critics who, in their obsessive quest for the marmoreal purity of Dorian art, refused to acknowledge the colours and sensuality of the more Ionian, Eastern, and thus Dionysian trends of Greek artworks. By questioning the centrality of the Olympian gods in favour of the Mystery divinities who 'shift and change' (Harrison 1915, 204–5) in the manner of the strange dyes or the pied animal-skins worn by Dionysian figures in the works of the aesthetes, Jane Ellen Harrison was 'negotiating aestheticism as a powerful new way of reading antiquity' (Evangelista 2011, 515), deliberately siding with Swinburne, Pater, and Symonds against modernists such as Ezra Pound, who later deposed the Victorian poet he had once hailed as the 'High priest of Iacchus' in the poem 'Salve O Pontifex'. Pound was indeed put off by Swinburne's feminine lyricism: 'The real Greek heritage', Pound claimed in his essay 'The Greek Heritage' (1957), 'is neither the Swinburnian swish nor the 18th century formalism but ... laconism' (Pound 1991, 9.179). T. S. Eliot agreed with Pound's conclusions: 'Greek poetry will never have the slightest vitalizing effect upon English poetry if it can only appear masquerading as a vulgar debasement of the eminently personal idiom of Swinburne' (Eliot 1920a, 73).

The question of the purity of Swinburne's Hellenism, constantly raised by his Victorian contemporaries, was therefore still very much an issue among modernist authors who, in spite of a growing interest in the new sciences of archaeology and psychoanalysis, tended to repress some of the stains on the ideal Greek body revealed in the poetry of Swinburne and the works of other aesthetes. By rejecting the 'Swinburnian swish' in favour of a supposedly more Dorian 'laconism' (could Pound have been alluding here to the virile 'Laconian' Spartans?) and by refusing the poet's 'personal idiom', Pound and Eliot were trying to eradicate the 'feminine' romantic but also Dionysian trend they felt in the Hellenic works of their predecessors in favour of 'dry, hard, classical verse' (Hulme 1998, 79), to take up the highly gendered opposition used by T. E. Hulme in his essay 'Romanticism and Classicism' (1912). The Victorian poet's Romantic excesses and disordering of the Greek canon were indeed perceived as a source of gender trouble in an age when the body of the Doric warrior or hero was still very much the locus of ideological projections. In the midst of the masculine epic fantasies fostered by the two world wars, Swinburne's provocative and sensuous Hellenic poetry still offered shocking glimpses of an oxymoronic Hellas, 'un-Greek' because 'too Hellenic' (McGann 1972, 72–3). But where some modernists strove to break away from what Pound, in 'The Caressability of the Greeks' (1914), calls Graeco-Victorian 'sentimentalism' (Pound 1991, 1.230), some female writers saw the breach opened by Swinburne and other aesthetes within the masculine Hellenic bastion as a hidden sensuous path to be explored. Thus H. D., in her 1922 novel entitled *Asphodel*, signifying the flower of Persephone, would deliberately reclaim this aesthetic Victorian filiation: 'We are legitimate children. We are children of the Rossettis, of Burne-Jones, of Swinburne. We are in the thoughts of Wilde . . . They talked of Greeks and flowers. Do people talk that way? None I know' (Doolittle 1992, 53).

4

'A JUGGLER'S TRICK'?
SWINBURNE'S JOURNALISM 1857–75

Laurel Brake

It is something of a juggler's trick to squeeze into reviewing shape all one has to say of a great book. ([Swinburne], *Spectator* 1862b, 694)

These Essays, written at intervals during a space of seven years, are now reissued with no change beyond the correction of an occasional error, the addition of an occasional note, and the excision or modification of an occasional phrase or passage. To omit or to rewrite any part would be to forfeit the one claim which I should care to put up on their behalf; that they give frank and full expression to what were, at the time of writing, my sincere and deliberate opinions ... As I see no reason to suppress what I have no desire to recant, I have not allowed myself to strike out the rare allusions, which might otherwise have been erased, to such obscure and ephemeral names or matters as may be thought unworthy even of so slight a record as the notice here conferred on them ... these diverse waifs of tentative criticism ... [that I have] gathered together. (Swinburne 1875a, vi)

I have told him indeed that I can have nothing to do with a paper which should have anything in common with the Hornets, Tomahawks, Worlds, and Everlasting Cesspools of the period; also how glad I was, when a filthy libel on Jowett appeared in Vanity Fair, that I had turned a persistently deaf ear to its editor's solicitations for my patronage: to which he has replied in an excellent spirit.[1] (14 February 1877 to Theodore Watts; Swinburne 1959–62, 3.278)

SWINBURNE AND JOURNALISM

In the spirit of the current renewal of interest in Swinburne, it is time that we turn to his journalism. How do the discourses of journalism amidst which much of Swinburne's work originally sits contribute to its meaning? In the epigraphs above, he represents his views of journalism variously even within a short period of time: in 1862 he defines its requisite skill; in 1875 he values it, defends its conditions of production, and reproduces it largely as originally published; in 1877 he denounces it to Thomas Purnell, editor of the *Tatler*, while allowing him to publish *A Year's Letters* in his weekly. Swinburne's diverse responses resemble those of other late Victorian writers including Matthew Arnold, Henry James, and Oscar Wilde who valued and denounced the press while persisting in writing for it. Typical too is the belated scholarly attention paid to Swinburne's considerable participation in journalism; just as with these other canonical authors, journalism is a relatively recent focus of research.

Clyde K. Hyder, reflecting the dominant discourse of the English literature of his day, hailed Swinburne the *critic* in 1972. In his introduction to his anthology of Swinburne's 'criticism', he wrote 'Re-reading his prose has strengthened my conviction that Swinburne belongs among the great critics, not merely among the great poets' (Hyder 1972, xi). The 'merely' indicates the enhanced value accorded to literary criticism in a period in which high literary culture was favoured. The subsequent opening of the literary field afforded by cultural studies, with its subsets of popular culture and media history, has facilitated the visibility of journalism and its material culture in conjunction with 'criticism', poetry, the novel, and other forms of literary production. In this context, Swinburne's criticism is also journalism, and his essays articles.

Swinburne's vivid responses to journalism above show him alert to its vicissitudes and engaged with it. They are indicative of the tenor of all of his pronouncements on the subject, which are similarly observant, satiric, and/or expressive. The prodigious variety of his writing practices – as poet, playwright, novelist, political commentator, and critic – combined to make him a professional 'man of letters' involved in many facets of the cultural industries of his day. A significant proportion of this work – prose and poetry – appeared first in the press, in a surprising range and number of titles. However miscellaneous, Swinburne's journalism is a genre of his writing, as may be seen when the pieces are examined in the context of the issues in which they appeared: the meaning of a poem such as 'January' from 'Carols of the Year' (later retitled 'A Year's Carols' in *Astrophel and Other Poems*, 1894) is immediately enhanced by knowing it was published in the January (1893) number of the *Magazine of Art*, framed by a full-page illustration to enhance its Almanac element (Figure 4.1).

Likewise, it is important to the understanding of his bold 'essay' on

Carols of the Year.

Hail, January, that bearest here
On snowbright breasts the babe-faced year
That weeps and trembles to be born.
Hail maid and mother, strong and bright,
Hooded and cloaked and shod with white,
Whose eyes are stars that match the morn,
Thy forehead braves the storm's bent bow,
Thy feet enkindle stars of snow.

W.E.F.Britten

JANUARY.
(Poem by Algernon C Swinburne. Drawing by W. E. F. Britten.)

4.1 Illustration by W. E. F. Britten for A. C. Swinburne, 'Carols of the Year',
Magazine of Art 16 (January 1893), 95.

Baudelaire that the reader knows it was published as an *anonymous* article, and that, like his other contributions to the *Spectator*, it is subject to the norms of reviews in a mid-century weekly. For example, all the *Spectator* pieces are notably shorter than Swinburne's articles in the *Fortnightly*, where generally articles are longer, as might be expected in a monthly review. In the case of Swinburne, with whom the editor John Morley was indulgent, they are particularly long, and consequently present even a greater contrast with the *Spectator* reviews; the pieces in the *Fortnightly* are also signed, which is a significant difference.

Swinburne's earliest foray into periodical publication occurred in 1857–58 in the Oxford-based *Undergraduate Papers*. In the 1860s he wrote on art more than once, as well as publishing poems and reviews of poetry and fiction, French and English; and in 1871 in the *Dark Blue*, another Oxford title, he combined poetry and art, publishing a poem with an illustrator of his choice, and an article on the artist, Simeon Solomon, in a subsequent number (Swinburne 1871b and a). Additionally, Swinburne's ideas and writing are often *provoked* by journalism, and many of his pamphlets, poems, letters, and articles are in dialogue with it. In the early 1860s, Swinburne even considered becoming a periodical editor himself.[2]

It is largely in the first fifteen years of his career, 1860–75, from his first arrival in London after Oxford to the publication of *Essays and Studies*, a collection of journalism, that Swinburne might be said to be among other things a journalist. This route from the universities to writing for the press in London was relatively common in this period for graduates whose religious positions debarred them from a clerical or academic career; Leslie Stephen and John Morley exemplify such a trajectory in London in the 1860s. Similarly others, like Humphry Ward, entered journalism from the university when they married – a result of colleges being slow to accept the idea of married Fellows. These men – and journalism was an overwhelmingly masculine culture – could expect to earn a reasonable living in a print culture which was proliferating after removal of the various newspaper taxes between 1855 and 1861. The *Daily Telegraph* (1855) and the *Saturday Review* (1855), the latter a reformulation of the weekly magazine genre, were the results of the reconsideration and subsequent removal of the newspaper stamp duty in 1855, as was the launch of a new, more popular form, the shilling monthly, in 1859. It gave rise not only to many imitators of the first generation of these – *Macmillan's Magazine* and the *Cornhill* – but also to a new mid-century type of *monthly* review in the *Fortnightly Review* (1865), the *Contemporary Review*

(1866), and the *Nineteenth Century* (1877), which supplanted the older quarterlies. It was into this explosion of print that Swinburne stepped.

He began writing journalism as a twenty-year-old student in the winter and spring of 1857–58 in the (monthly and then weekly) university magazine, *Undergraduate Papers*. He had five articles in this small, thin, short-lived journal of anonymous pieces. The ludic naughtiness of a spoof review and the virulence of a polemical piece on 'Church Imperialism' are matched by other colourful 'papers' in the journal that aim provocatively to critique contemporary figures and institutions of authority such as Matthew Arnold and the *Saturday Review*: Swinburne's 'Modern Hellenism' undermines the Oxford Professor of Poetry's recent lecture on 'Culture and Its Enemies' (7 June 1857) with its retort that the culture of classical Greece is *not* superior to that of Elizabethan England; and the *Saturday Review*'s attack on romantic love and marriage is denounced by another writer as 'accomplished scoff[ing]' and the use of 'wit to cover . . . ignorance' (Anonymous [John Nichol] 1857, 90).[3] In the anonymity that John Nichol's undergraduate journal afforded, Swinburne and the other contributors could assay the scope of journalism – useful experience that Swinburne deployed subsequently, in his professional work as a journalist in the 1860s and in defence of his own work.

From the bibliographical record, it appears that Swinburne had two early bursts of regular employment by single periodicals in the 1860s, separated by a four-year interval; one was a solid weekly, founded in 1828 by an earlier generation of the press that venerated anonymity, and the second was a new monthly review, established in 1865, that insisted on signature.[4] In 1862 he published in rapid succession some twelve or thirteen contributions to the *Spectator*, with the prose anonymous and the poetry signed (Paden 1962, 111), and between 1867 and 1870 he wrote regularly for the *Fortnightly*: starting in January, five poems and two articles appeared in seven of the twelve issues for 1867, the year that a new series of the *Fortnightly* began, signalling a new editor who took Swinburne on.

Five months before his first publication in the *Fortnightly*, Swinburne was the victim of an anonymous review of *Poems and Ballads* in a vituperative weekly. These two events are related, as the editor of the new series of the *Fortnightly*, John Morley, had been the anonymous author of the attack. However, while Morley's review (along with threats of others) had forced Swinburne to find a new publisher when *Poems and Ballads* was withdrawn from sale, the volume reappeared with a new imprint in

September, followed by *Notes on Poems and Reviews*, Swinburne's pamphlet in its defence. By the end of 1866 and before his remarkable employment by his castigator, Swinburne had established a reputation as a brilliant poet in *Atalanta in Calydon* (1865) and *Poems and Ballads*, an eloquent advocate and editor of Byron, and an able defender of his own work. The quality and variety of his achievements in these years were doubtless a factor in Morley's decision to make amends and invite Swinburne to contribute to his new journalistic venture, from the first month of his editorship.

A second factor may have been Morley's distaste for the anonymity that was a condition of his work on the *Saturday Review*, a stint of work that he regretted then and retrospectively:

> instead of thinking out questions independently and exercising their own judgment, [men] habitually find themselves consulting this demigod of an abstraction considering what IT would dictate, reflecting in moods, almost in phrases what they might suppose the demigod using. Writers are not deliberately dishonest who thus give the world, instead of the products of independent judgment, the supposed thoughts of a shadowy abstraction. It is the anonymous system which teaches the journalist to look upon himself as nothing, and his Journal as everything. (Morley quoted in Hirst 1927, 1.59)

This complaint, from an unspecified and undated source, reveals Morley's feelings about his position as an anonymous critic when he slated Swinburne's volume in the *Saturday Review* and, as F. W. Hirst suggests, Morley's subsequent commitment to freedom of expression and signature when he commences life as an editor: 'It was all to Morley's honour and credit that after escaping from thraldom he determined as an editor to grant contributors a freedom he so much prized' (ibid.). Morley also writes to Swinburne directly about his abhorrence for unsigned reviewing (15 September 1867; Swinburne 2004b, 1.107–8), and, earlier in the same month, Morley had gone public on the question and contributed 'Anonymous Journalism' to the *Fortnightly*. In respect to Swinburne then, Morley's restless 'thraldom' under the strictures of his employment at the *Saturday Review*, and his new power as an editor, together explain why in part he hired Swinburne and why in the same letter he patiently persuaded Swinburne to accept edits and cuts as propriety and space demanded.

That Swinburne in turn accepted the invitation from Morley, whom he knew was his denouncer (Hirst 1927, 1.79), indicates, as Edmund Gosse suggests (Gosse 1917, 168), Swinburne's desire to re-enter journalism, and to get his work into the press and past the gatekeeper editors. His strategy of using his affiliation with the press as a platform for ensuring his notice in it may be seen to have worked: in December 1867, while he was writing regularly for the *Fortnightly Review*, Swinburne's original and percipient *William Blake: A Critical Essay* appeared, though dated 1868 (Swinburne 1868a). It was reviewed the following February in the *Fortnightly* by a renowned North American critic, Moncure Conway, who had high praise for Swinburne's work: 'In his hands words blossom again into the flowers from which they were once scattered as seed, and even letters hint the forms of which they were originally copies. This work is a very important contribution to both the poetical and philosophical literature of our time' (Conway 1868, 219–20). In respect of his work, Swinburne seems to go from strength to strength. In the 1860s, then, when he lived in London and worked as a freelance writer who frequently wrote for the press, he might be justly regarded as a jobbing journalist as well as a poet, playwright, critic, novelist, and political activist as his posthumous reputation suggests.

Swinburne's contributions of poems and articles to the *Fortnightly* continued after 1870, regularly but less often, until in 1880 he published another three articles in the same year. Meanwhile from the 1870s his poetry was appearing, repeatedly, in two weeklies, the *Examiner* (in 1873) and over twenty-five years in the *Athenæum*; occasionally in *Belgravia*, the *English Illustrated Magazine* (from 1883), and the *Magazine of Art* (from 1889); and once or twice in the *Academy*, the *Glasgow University Magazine* (February 1878 only), *Once a Week*, and the *Pall Mall Gazette*. He had numerous letters to the editor in a diverse range of titles, from the *Gentleman's Magazine* to the *Examiner*. His novel, *A Year's Letters*, appeared in parts in the *Tatler* (August–December 1877), and his books were regularly and often prominently reviewed and advertised from 1865 onwards. The regular attention by the press to Swinburne in all of its manifestations – the publication of his poetry, prose, and Letters to the Editor, but also the paragraphs of literary gossip, the reviews, and the adverts for successive works and editions – keeps his name and work in circulation, constantly before the eyes of readers of the 'higher journalism'. This record of Swinburne's implication in the press exemplifies that of relations between literature and journalism more generally from the 1860s.[5]

However, even for Swinburne, with his talent for exploiting fully the scope of the press, his consciousness of its limitations may be seen in his

occasional recourse to pamphlets, two of them (Swinburne 1866 and
1872a) especially famous. This form has the advantage of free-standing
publication, with timing and content in the control of the author rather
than hedged in by the constraints of the politics, format, and frequency of
a journal and the gatekeeping and cuts of its editor. That Swinburne's
retort to the hostile notice of *Poems and Ballads* in the *Saturday Review* in
August 1866 was a pamphlet – *Notes on Poems and Reviews* – rather than an
article may be better understood from this perspective; similarly the
energy of its invective reflects that of his *Saturday* reviewer, whose piece is
irascible, even scurrilous:

> He finds that these fleshly things are his strong part, so he sticks to them. Is
> it so wonderful that he should? . . . he deserves credit for the audacious
> courage with which he has revealed to the world a mind all aflame with the
> feverish carnality of a schoolboy over the dirtiest passage in Lemprière. It is
> not every poet who would ask us all to go hear him tuning his lyre in a stye.
> ([Morley], 4 August 1866, 145)

> And no language is too strong to condemn the mixed vileness and childishness
> of depicting the spurious passion of a putrescent imagination, the unnamed
> lusts of sated wants, as if they were the crown of character and their
> enjoyment the great glory of human life. ([Morley], 4 August 1866, 145)

Part of the function of these passages is to warn respectable readers of
the *Spectator* of the unsuitability of Swinburne's volume for women's and
young people's reading. Morley's consciousness of this duty as a reviewer
in the *Saturday Review* is most explicit in the next passage that begins: 'The
only comfort about the present volume is that such a piece as "Anactoria"
will be unintelligible to a great many people, and so will the fevered folly
of "Hermaphroditus," as well as much else that is nameless and abom-
inable' (145).

The dialogue between article and pamphlet is similar in 1872, when
Swinburne published another pamphlet, *Under the Microscope*, to defend
his own and his friends' poetry from an equally shrill attack, Robert
Buchanan's 'The Fleshly School of Poetry'. However, in 1864, he had used
the pamphlet form for a different and more anodyne purpose, to circulate
a short story, 'Dead Love', *after* it had appeared in the date-specific format
of a periodical (Swinburne 1862c), to perpetuate its life beyond the serial
issue. Pamphlets are part of a continuum with serials on the one hand and
books on the other in the nineteenth century. As a *form*, then, pamphlets
generically interact with other forms of print such as the press and books,

to which they are responsive or provocative. In the case of Swinburne and
Morley in 1866, the system that Morley identified in the quotations previ-
ously cited – the weekly *Saturday Review*, with its customary thrusting and
acerbic discourse and its staff journalist's necessarily anonymous review,
spurred by the sexual provocation of Swinburne's poems – resulted in a
fateful and overdetermined match that affected the course of publishing
history. Distribution of Swinburne's volume was halted, followed by a
shift to a new publisher, an indignant pamphlet circulated by Swinburne,
and the departure of the anonymous reviewer from the *Saturday Review*
soon afterward. It was that same reviewer who decided – as the new editor
of the *Fortnightly Review* – to employ Swinburne and regularly publish his
poetry and criticism. Thus Swinburne's pamphlet references Morley's
anonymous review, and Morley responds in his new position as editor of
a different journal by hiring his victim. However, simultaneously with
Swinburne's signed appearances in the *Fortnightly*, attacks on *Poems and
Ballads* and *Notes on Poems and Reviews* continued in 1867, particularly in
the *Contemporary Review*. These are more understandable in the context of
the journalism industry: the *Contemporary* was not only the primary rival
of the *Fortnightly* but its antithesis, pitting its Christian framework against
the *Fortnightly*'s Comteism and liberalism.

Lastly, it is important to note that Swinburne remediates many of his
pieces first published in the press by removing them from the context of
journal columns and the matrix of the contemporary miscellaneous
material in the respective numbers, and regrouping them, normally
generically, with other poems or articles, often from different serial
matrixes, in a *collection* of poems or 'essays' that is branded by the sign of
the author rather than that of respective periodical titles. *Essays and
Studies* (1875), the Preface of which supplies one of my epigraphs, is the
first of several volumes of Swinburne's collected journalism, which
include *Miscellanies* (1886) and *A Study of Ben Jonson* (1889).[6] Like his friend
W. M. Rossetti, Swinburne is minded not to disguise the origins of his
collected pieces in journalism, *except* through selection: the 1875 volume
silently excludes his *Spectator* articles.[7] The other intervention is that, like
Matthew Arnold, Swinburne publishes his *articles* as *essays*, thus moving
them from the discourse of journalism to that of literature and letters.[8]

While the topic of Swinburne and journalism is vast, what follows is
limited to a few of the critical problems arising from his participation in
the journalism economy: first, the difficulty of the 'fit' between journal-
ism and Swinburne's work, and the variety and types of journals to which

he *did* gain access, and why; and secondly, how the shape and effect of work are determined by its *location*, including how work is customised to its respective host, and how work in each location is distinctive.

SWINBURNE'S ACCESS TO THE PRESS: NETWORKS

Looking at the small number of journals that published Swinburne's work between 1857 and 1872 and the pattern of discrete clustering of his appearances in them, the observer might seek an explanation. Swinburne's publication record is not one of regular contributions over a dozen or so years, but (with one exception) of sporadic affiliations. The problem, I suggest, is one of 'fit' between journalism and journalist, in this case on two counts: it is unsurprising that the sexual, religious, and political content of some of Swinburne's work made it unacceptable to some editors and/or unsuitable for some serials; in a period dominated by Mudie's Circulating Library and 'family papers' such as the *Cornhill* and *Temple Bar*, such censorship is not unique to Swinburne, but in his case more titles might reject particular pieces, given their character. In addition to contents, Swinburne's ludic or intransigent behaviour as a journalist could be off-putting to editors: whereas in 1857 his spoof review of an imaginary 'Spasmodic' volume was enjoyed in *Undergraduate Papers* (Swinburne 1858), in 1862 the editor Richard Holt Hutton was angered by his submission of a review of an imaginary and indecent volume of French poetry to the serious *Spectator*. So, not only are there problems in the nexus of journalism and Swinburne but these problems indicate the character and working conditions of both the journalism of the day and this particular would-be journalist.

In this light, it seems significant that Swinburne's entrée to each of the four main titles to which he contributed between 1860 and 1872 was *not* through submission of his work to an unknown editor but through personal access to a network, such as his membership in Old Mortality, an Oxford essay society, which opened up *Undergraduate Papers* (see Monsman 1998); personal introductions by Monckton Milnes and Joseph Knight that secured him access respectively to Holt Hutton of the *Spectator* and to the *Fortnightly*; and personal friendship with George Meredith for *Once a Week*. For the *Dark Blue*, the personal element is less clear, but it may have involved a circular to 'Oxonians' for submissions to the new University-based project, combined with endorsements by his friends John Ruskin, who backed the venture, and William Michael

Rossetti, another contributor. The first issue, in the judgement of the *Publishers' Circular*, was highly thought of, as 'a magazine [which] for the quality of writing and true art as regards illustrations, has hardly been equalled ... the names of the contributors guarantee success' (*Publishers' Circular*, 1 March 1871, 140; qtd in *Wellesley* 1966–89, 4.179). The characteristics of the journal identified by the *Publishers' Circular* are precisely those cultivated by Swinburne in his two contributions: the first, a poem accompanied by an illustration, and the second, a review of an artist's 'vision'.

On Swinburne's part as a would-be contributor, Gosse claims that by 1867 the difficulty of getting past the gatekeeping of editors was proving formidable: he 'was very anxious to find some channel through which to pour the convictions and expose the erudition which he had formed ... He had long fretted at his inability to discover an editor for his critical prose' (Gosse 1917, 168). Publication in pamphlet form proved an effective strategy to avoid the gatekeepers, and in 1866 both Swinburne in *Notes on Poems and Reviews* and William Michael Rossetti in *Swinburne's Poems and Ballads. A Criticism* decided to publish outside of the periodical press in pamphlets issued by John Camden Hotten, Swinburne's new publisher. In his 'Preface' Rossetti even explains the pamphlet format of his work in terms of the *impossibility* of publishing in his intended periodical location – the *North American Review*, which was about to print an unfavourable notice of Swinburne's work. This is a fine example of the conditions of periodical publication that pamphlets and sometimes books circumvent:

> This criticism was written, on my own spontaneous offer, with a view to its publication in the 'North American Review,' the leading Quarterly of the United States. Before I had completed it, I discovered that that Review had already committed itself, in a notice of Mr Swinburne's 'Atalanta in Calydon' and 'Chastelard,' to a view of his poetic powers with which mine is considerably at variance. I therefore deemed it hardly desirable to obtrude upon the deservedly respected Editors a criticism which they might feel embarrassed in inserting, and pained in rejecting, and as I found about the same time that Mr Swinburne's present publisher would willingly take my MS, I have adopted this mode of publication. I have preferred, however, to leave the form of the critique strictly unaltered. (W. M. Rossetti 1866, v)

It is interesting that Rossetti, like Swinburne in his Preface to *Essays and Studies*, acknowledges differences between the discourses of journalism and the pamphlet, *and* opts to retain the immediacy of the article, rather than revising it for the new format.

There are five main titles to which Swinburne contributed in this period – *Undergraduate Papers*, the *Spectator*, *Once a Week*, the *Fortnightly Review*, and the *Dark Blue*. They are located in three different sectors of the press that apparently have little in common. The two university-based titles (*Undergraduate Papers* and the *Dark Blue*) are both short-lived literary magazines, but even they differ significantly: the first (1857–58), the organ of a University Society, Old Mortality, was aimed at and confined to the University community and its articles were anonymous, whereas the *Dark Blue* (1871–72), aiming to avoid collapse from low take-up like an earlier namesake of 1867, characterised itself as a general magazine with a university affiliation. Published well after the debates on signature in the 1860s, the *Dark Blue* articles by Swinburne were signed. While Swinburne's five contributions to *Undergraduate Papers* appeared throughout its publication span (in numbers 1–3), he published only twice in the *Dark Blue* (in numbers 2 and 5, in April and July 1871). The sparsity of his contributions to the latter may be due to financial reasons. According to *Wellesley* (4. 179), by November 1871, it was known that John Freund, editor of the *Dark Blue*, was delaying or simply not paying his contributors, and after September 1871 few Oxford men contributed. By 1871, Swinburne was a well-known and professional writer, so he was unlikely to publish without payment, despite Freund's evident willingness to publish controversial work.

By contrast the *Spectator* was an established, metropolitan weekly of folio format that had been going since 1828. At this period it cost 6d, its weekly numbers were a crisp twenty-eight pages with ruled columns, divided routinely into a political and topical front half commenting on the week's news, and an arts and reviews back, followed by advertisements. In accordance with the newspaper conventions of this period, articles in the *Spectator* were normally anonymous, or signed with pseudonyms, for example 'Amateur' or 'Dry Point' (*Spectator*, 12 April 1862, 410) in the first issue to which Swinburne contributes. We know of twelve or thirteen contributions by Swinburne that are confined to one year, 1862; only the poetry was signed.

The monthly *Fortnightly Review* was a new breed of Review, combining characteristics of the weighty *quarterly* reviews of the early nineteenth century with the frequency and wider variety of the monthly magazines. With pages roughly half the size of the *Spectator*, and five times as many, each monthly issue was fatter and not newspaper-like in appearance and contents. Similarly, its cover price of 2s signalled a different type of serial from the weekly, whose readership had other expectations: not news or instant responses, but more thoughtful, lengthy pieces on topics of historical as well as contemporary relevance. Unlike the *Spectator*, the *Fortnightly* had a cover, and its pages were book-like, without columns or rules. According to its cover, it was to be found in 'Booksellers' rather than 'Booksellers' *and* 'Newsagents' like the *Spectator*, and its imprint was that of a book publisher, Chapman and Hall. Swinburne's contributions to these serials are significantly inscribed by their respective locations: they differ in length, remit, and function and they are perused by readers with different expectations. While there is overlap between readers of the weekly and monthly, the titles fall into different market niches: readers of the *Fortnightly* are among the most serious and intellectual, willing to follow extended arguments, and largely of an advanced liberal persuasion, whereas those of the *Spectator* are news-driven, and desirous of short arts reviews of quality. Although politically liberal rather than Tory, the *Spectator* is more conservative in 1862 than the *Fortnightly* is in 1867.

Although *Once a Week* shared its frequency with the *Spectator*, its readership was from a different demographic group and its origins were relatively recent, dating from 1859–60; it was a family magazine, featuring serial and short fiction, and entertaining feature articles. Conceived by its publisher / printer Bradbury and Evans as a rival to Dickens's weeklies, *Household Words* and *All the Year Round*, it basically resembled them in format, contents, and market niche. However, having lost the contract for *Household Words* after a disagreement with Dickens in 1859, Bradbury and Evans produced a slightly upmarket alternative, with the familiar format of two columns on a small page, but longer and illustrated issues costing fifty per cent more, 3d rather than *Household Words*'s 2d. As with most of the other titles to which Swinburne contributed in these years, he had access to *Once a Week* in 1862, through a network of personal contacts: his close friend George Meredith, a frequent contributor of poetry, short stories, and serial fiction in the first years of the magazine, was favoured for his realism by its first editor, Samuel Lucas, formerly of *The Times* (Savory 1984, 287–91). Swinburne's poem 'The Fratricide' and his (rare) short story, 'Dead Love', appearing in issues of 15 February and 11 October 1862 respectively (Swinburne 1862d and c), coincided with 'The Last Chartist' (9 February 1862), an illustrated poem which was the last of Meredith's contributions, frequent since issue No. 1.[9] As may be surmised from their titles, Swinburne's lugubrious pieces, which involved familial murder and necrophilia, seem at the limits of acceptability for this family

weekly, and similar in that respect to the spoof reviews rejected by the
editor of the *Spectator* in the same year. Even in this early moment in his
journalism career, the tensions of the 'fit' were manifest. The tacit objec-
tions to Meredith's continued affiliation to the weekly might explain the
brevity of Swinburne's contributions as well.

THE LOCATIONS OF CULTURE: JOURNALS, FORMAT, AND CONTENT

The period of Swinburne's contributions to the *Spectator*, which began in
April and concluded in September, barely spanned six months, but it was
an intensive press debut: in that period he published seven signed poems,
four anonymous reviews, and a letter. As already indicated, in the main
Spectator articles at this time are anonymous, or exceptionally signed with
initials or pseudonyms. In the preponderance of anonymity, the weekly
Spectator is following the format of newspapers rather than monthlies.
However, most of Swinburne's poems were anomalous in two respects:
they were the only poem in the issue, and they were the only contribution
of any kind signed with the writer's name. This is particularly noticeable
in the Table of Contents on each front page in which his name appears;
when it does, it is the sole name in what is essentially a list of departments
or article titles such as 'The Week Abroad' or 'New England and the War'
(*Spectator* Table of Contents 1862, 701). Even in the two issues (28 June
and 26 July) in which his poems appeared with others, his are attributed in
full, and the others are not (*Spectator* 1862, 701, 830). Both the frequency
of Swinburne's contributions and the anomaly of signature suggest that
the editors recognised the high quality of their young contributor's work,
and were keen to accommodate him to retain the connection.

Other full names appear beside Swinburne's in *Spectator* issues, but
only as part of the economies of those departments whose discourse
formally accommodates them – Letters to the Editor, the bibliographical
footnotes for reviews in the Books section, and in the adverts that end
each issue. It is interesting for comparison to look at the adverts for peri-
odical contents. Only some – monthlies – use signature at all, and even
those use it irregularly. In the *Spectator* adverts of 31 May for example,
only six out of ten articles in the *Cornhill* are attributed, and in the display
for *Fraser's* Ruskin's name is the only one to appear (*Spectator*
Advertisements 1862, 614). Swinburne's signatures in the weekly *Spectator*
are thus in all probability a result of volition – that is, his desire to make a
name in London, both as a poet and as a journalist.

Swinburne's first four contributions were poems, and it was only after his June letter to the editor that the *Spectator* commenced publishing his reviews. Using the authority in his letter that his signed published poetry had earned, Swinburne took issue with an unfavourable anonymous review of George Meredith's sonnet sequence, *Modern Love*, which had appeared the previous week in the *Spectator,* and obliged readers by providing an appreciative alternative (Swinburne 1862e). It may be inferred, from the Editor's favourable Note following the letter – 'We insert this gladly, from personal respect to our correspondent, whose opinion on any poetical question should be worth more than most men's' ([Hutton] *Spectator* 1862, 633) – and from the quality of criticism in the letter, that Swinburne's strategy of signed poetry and a signed letter resulted a fortnight later in the publication in the *Spectator* of the first of his three reviews of Victor Hugo's novel *Les Misérables*, which was appearing in French in parts at the time. His last piece on Baudelaire (Swinburne 1862a) was also on contemporary French literature, which the *Spectator*'s practice defines as Swinburne's specialism as a critic.[10] *These* were of course anonymous as *Spectator* conventions dictated, but more of his signed poems appeared simultaneously between June and September, when his final contributions, a poem and a review, both appeared in the 6 September issue.

All of Swinburne's prose pieces for the *Spectator* were short reviews. They appeared as did the poetry in the second half of the weekly, among the Arts copy, preceded by the more prominent News and Politics front, and the 'middles' on topics of the day, often by Special Correspondents. While the reviews appeared in the Books department, among four or five other reviews on diverse subjects, the poems were placed just after the Fine Arts column, and before Music and/or Books. The weighty and cosmopolitan contents of the *Spectator*, as well as Swinburne's bravado and integrity, help explain how and why his pieces in the *Spectator,* with and without signature, did not hide his politics (favourable to the Risorgimento), his sensuous sexuality, his morbid interest in death, decay, and necrophilia, and his decadent interests in the perverse. These were visible in his first *Spectator* poems, the last of which was 'Faustine', and they reoccurred in his prose.

It may be noted nevertheless that Swinburne's early and path-breaking 1862 review of Baudelaire's *Les Fleurs du mal* (1857) was unsigned, published as it was under the normal condition of reviewing in the weekly. That Swinburne published none of his anonymous *Spectator*

reviews in his first book of collected journalism in 1875 suggests that he
valued his anonymity. The *Spectator* reviews are also much shorter than
the journalism in *Essays and Studies*, which is preponderantly from the
Fortnightly Review, where longer pieces were the rule. While it may be
argued that anonymity such as the *Spectator*'s *protected* the reviewer, it also
means that such reviews bore the 'signature' of the journal itself, and
were thus carefully overseen. In the autumn of 1862 Swinburne
submitted two spoof reviews for which he had written the louche poetry
attributed to the authors. These were firmly rejected in December by
Hutton in the name of the *journal*: 'Such verses would blow the magazine
off the face of the earth' (quoted in Paden 1962, 99) and 'the subject seems
to me to deserve no more criticism than a Hollywell Street publication
[i.e. a pornographic publication], nor could I speak of it in *The Spectator*
without more real disgust than your article inspires. There is a tone of
raillery about it which I think one should hardly use to pure obscenity'
(quoted in Rooksby 1997, 74). By January 1863, Swinburne was seeking
another journal to publish his work, one that didn't take back its review
copies as he alleges the *Spectator* did, and that sent its authors copies of
their pieces, as the *Spectator* allegedly didn't. While the brevity of
Swinburne's stint on the *Spectator* and the character of its termination
exemplify the problem of 'fit' between Swinburne and journalism, his
contributions also show a serious attempt of the would-be contributor to
meet the conditions of weekly journalism, and to keep his name and
work before the public reliably frequently. It also shows, on the part of the
Spectator, the notable resilience of this public print, which over six months
permitted Swinburne uncensored access to its pages, a freedom that he
embraced in much that he published there.

A four-year interval elapsed before his next regular affiliation with a
journal, but during it he established himself as a poet and dramatist. He
positioned himself as a name ripe for journalism. In addition to the
quality of his poetry, *Atalanta in Calydon* had the added value of associa-
tion with the Pre-Raphaelites, as it was sumptuously bound in boards
designed by Rossetti. *Poems and Ballads* was extensively and prominently
reviewed, fuelled by the brouhaha of the initial attack by the *Saturday
Review* among others, and the resulting shift of publisher from a
respectable firm to a raunchy one. By 1866 the Swinburne list represented
'class' for its new publisher, John Camden Hotten, as well as risk, while
the scandal, sexuality, and atheism of Swinburne's poems suited aspects
of Hotten's profile as a publisher.[11] The publisher's column-length advert

in the *Athenæum* of 3 November 1866 displays his acquisition of Swinburne as a trophy, including as it does three volumes of Swinburne's works – *Chastelard*, *The Queen-Mother and Rosamond*, *Poems and Ballads* – generous quotations from reviews, *Notes on Poems and Reviews* (Swinburne's own defence of *Poems and Ballads*), W. M. Rossetti's 'Criticism' of Swinburne's *Poems*, and most prominently an announcement of a *new* work ('*Essays on the Life and Works of William Blake*'); these are prefaced by a statement: '*The public are respectfully informed that Mr Swinburne's Works will in future be published by Mr Hotten*' (*Athenæum*, 3 November 1866, 580; see Figure 4.2). In the same issue, Hotten managed to get the editor to place an announcement of the Blake and Rossetti titles as the first paragraph in 'Our Weekly Gossip' (ibid., 572). Swinburne was news.

Between 1867 and 1870 Swinburne's *Fortnightly* pieces show certain continuities with the nature and pattern of those in the *Spectator*: he publishes both poetry and prose, some of which exhibits a special expertise in French literature. The frequency of his submissions is also initially high, in the first year particularly – five poems and two long articles. One of Swinburne's finest poems is here (Swinburne 1868b): his grieving tribute to Baudelaire, 'Ave Atque Vale' (January 1868) sits well in the *Fortnightly*, with its pronounced interest in France. A measure of Swinburne's perspicacity about contemporary French literature may be gleaned from a review eighteen months later in the *Athenæum* of some translations of Baudelaire that begins 'The world knows little about M. Baudelaire ... We are not ourselves aware of the French gentleman's having accomplished much in literature' (Anonymous 1869, 237).

However, the range of Swinburne's subjects is far wider than French literature in the *Fortnightly*, which allows him to exhibit an expanded expertise in the press. For example, he is given a trio of major assignments on contemporary *English* poetry by William Morris (July 1867; Swinburne 1867b), Matthew Arnold (October 1867; Swinburne 1867a), and D. G. Rossetti (May 1870; Swinburne 1870a). He also tackles early nineteenth-century poetry by Shelley in May 1869; this follows earlier independent pieces on Byron (1865) and Blake (1868), and coincides with a preface to Coleridge. The *Fortnightly* thus accommodates his extant interest in Romantic poetry. Morley also accepted an art tourism piece on Italian Renaissance pictures in Florence (July 1868), a product of Swinburne's 1864 trip to Italy. His political poems, of which there are many here, chime with the character of the *Fortnightly*, its self-conscious participation

BLACKIE & SON'S PUBLICATIONS.

The IMPERIAL BIBLE-DICTION-ARY, Historical, Biographical, Geographical and Doctrinal. By the Rev. PATRICK FAIRBAIRN, D.D., assisted by numerous Contributors. Illustrated by many hundred Engravings on Wood and Steel. In 2 vols. imperial 8vo. cloth, 3l. 13s. *[Just published.*

The IMPERIAL DICTIONARY, English, Technological, and Scientific. Adapted to the present state of Literature, Science, and Art. By JOHN OGILVIE, LL.D. Above 2,500 Engravings on Wood. 2 large vols. imp. 8vo. cloth, 4l.

The COMPREHENSIVE ENGLISH DICTIONARY, Explanatory, Pronouncing, and Etymological. By JOHN OGILVIE, LL.D. The Pronunciation adapted to the best Modern Usage, by RICHARD CULL, F.S.A. Above 800 Engravings on Wood. Large 8vo. cloth, 12s.

The STUDENT'S ENGLISH DIC-TIONARY. Etymological, Pronouncing, and Explanatory. Prepared specially for the Use of Colleges and Advanced Schools. By JOHN OGILVIE, LL.D. With about 300 Engravings on Wood. Imperial 16mo. cloth, red edges, 10s. 6d.; half morocco, 13s.

The IMPERIAL ATLAS of MO-DERN GEOGRAPHY: a Series of above One Hundred carefully Coloured Maps. Compiled from the most authentic sources, under the supervision of W. G. BLACKIE, Ph.D. F.R.G.S. With an Index to nearly 120,000 Places. Half morocco, gilt edges, 5l. 5s.

The IMPERIAL GAZETTEER: a General Dictionary of Geography, Physical, Political, Statistical, and Descriptive. Edited by W. G. BLACKIE, Ph.D. F.R.G.S. Nearly 750 Engravings on Wood, Views, Costumes, Maps, Plans, &c. 2 large vols. imperial 8vo. cloth, 4l. 4s.

VILLA and COTTAGE ARCHITEC-TURE. Select Examples of Country and Suburban Residences recently erected from the Designs of various Architects of acknowledged position and ability, with descriptive Notices. To be completed in about 14 Monthly Parts, imp. 4to. price 2s. 6d. each. *[Parts I. II. now ready.*

The WORKS of the ETTRICK SHEPHERD. In POETRY and PROSE. New Edition. With a Biographical Memoir by the Rev. THOMAS THOMSON. With 50 Steel Engravings, from Drawings by D. O. Hill, R.S.A., and Keeley Halswelle, A.R.S.A. 2 vols. large 8vo. cloth extra, 25s.; separately—TALES, 15s.; POEMS, 14s.

The WORKS of ROBERT BURNS. COMPLETE ILLUSTRATED EDITION, Literary and Pictorial. With numerous Notes and Annotations; Professor WILSON'S Essay 'On the Genius and Character of Burns'; and Dr. CURRIE'S Memoir of the Poet. 36 Landscape and Portrait Illustrations on Steel. 2 vols. super-royal 8vo. cloth extra, 36s.

The BOOK of SCOTTISH SONG: a Collection of the Best and most Approved Songs of Scotland, with Critical and Historical Notices regarding them and their Authors. Miniature 8vo. cloth, 7s. 6d.

The COMPREHENSIVE HISTORY of ENGLAND, Civil and Military, Religious, Intellectual, and Social. By CHARLES MACFARLANE and the Rev. THOMAS THOMSON. Above Eleven Hundred Engravings on Wood and Steel—Antiquities, Views, Costumes, Portraits, Maps, Plans, &c. &c. 4 vols. large 8vo. cloth, 4l.

A COMPREHENSIVE HISTORY of INDIA, Civil, Military, and Social, from the First Landing of the English to the Suppression of the Sepoy Revolt. By HENRY BEVERIDGE. Above Five Hundred Engravings —Views, Costumes, Portraits, Maps, Plans of Battles, &c. &c. 3 vols. large 8vo. cloth, 3l. 3s.

BLACKIE & SON, 44, Paternoster-row.

BOOKS OF POETRY.

The POEMS of ARTHUR HUGH CLOUGH, sometime Fellow of Oriel College, Oxford. Second Edition. With a Memoir by F. T. PALGRAVE. Fcap. 8vo. cloth, 6s.

"Few, if any, literary men of larger, deeper, and more massive mind have lived in this generation than the author of these few poems; and of this the volume before us bears ample evidence... There is nothing in it that is not in some sense rich either in thought or beauty, or both."—*Spectator.*

MY BEAUTIFUL LADY. By Thomas WOOLNER. With a Vignette Title by Arthur Hughes, engraved by Jeens. Third Edition. Fcap. 8vo. cloth, price 5s.

BROTHER FABIAN'S MANUSCRIPT; and other Poems. By SEBASTIAN EVANS. Fcap. 8vo. cloth, price 6s.

"What the Greeks meant by a poet, and what our forefathers called a poet,—he is a maker. He gives something that has life of its own, and something we never had before."—*Daily Review.*

"Remarkably clever and full of kindly humour."—*Globe.*

The PRINCE'S PROGRESS; and other POEMS. By CHRISTINA G. ROSSETTI. With Two Illustrations, from Designs by D. G. Rossetti. Fcap. 8vo. cloth, price 6s.

GOBLIN MARKET; and other Poems. By CHRISTINA G. ROSSETTI. With Two Illustrations, from Designs by D. G. Rossetti. Second Edition. Fcap. 8vo. cloth, price 5s.

The ANGEL in the HOUSE. By COVENTRY PATMORE. A New and Cheap Edition. In 1 vol. 18mo. beautifully printed on toned paper, price 5s. 6d. Also an Edition, 2 vols. fcap. 8vo. cloth, price 12s.

POEMS. By Richard Chenevix Trench, D.D., Archbishop of Dublin. Collected and arranged anew. Fcap. 8vo. cloth, price 7s. 6d.

SHADOWS of the PAST. In Verse. By Viscount STRATFORD DE REDCLIFFE. Crown 8vo. cloth, price 10s. 6d.

"The vigorous words of one who has acted vigorously, and combines the fervour of politician and poet."—*Guardian.*

The PROMETHEUS BOUND of ÆSCHYLUS. Literally translated into English Verse, by Edward Fitzgerald, M.A., late Fellow of Trinity College, Cambridge. Extra fcap. 8vo. cloth, price 3s. 6d.

DRAMATIC STUDIES. By Augusta WEBSTER. Extra fcap. 8vo. cloth, price 5s.

"Powerful, original, and full of deep and sometimes passionate earnestness. They possess many of the highest attributes of poetry."—*Examiner.*

By the same Author.

BLANCHE LISLE; and other Poems. By CECIL HOME. Fcap. 8vo. cloth, 4s. 6d.

DUKE ERNEST, a Tragedy; and other Poems. By ROSAMOND HERVEY. Fcap. 8vo. cloth, price 6s.

"Conceived in pure taste and true historic feeling, and is pervaded with much dramatic force... Thoroughly original."—*British Quarterly.*

LEONORE: a Tale. By Georgiana Lady CHATTERTON. A New Edition. Beautifully printed on thick toned paper, with Frontispiece and Vignette Title engraved by Jeens. Crown 8vo. cloth, 7s. 6d.

"Her style is graceful and forcible... happily combines freshness with experience, fancy with truth."—*Art-Journal.*

ROMANCES and MINOR POEMS. By HENRY GLASSFORD BELL. Fcap. 8vo. cloth.

CITY POEMS. By Alexander Smith. Cloth, price 5s.

By the same Author,

1. **A Life Drama; and other Poems.** Fourth Edition. Cloth, 2s. 6d.

2. **Edwin of Deira.** Second Edition. Fcap.

BALLADS and SONGS of BRITTANY. By TOM TAYLOR. Translated from the 'Barzaz-Breiz' of Vicomte Hersart de la Villemarqué. With some of the Original Melodies harmonized by Mrs. Tom Taylor. With Illustrations by J. Tissot, J. E. Millais, R.A., J. Tenniel, O. Home, E. Corbould, and H. K. Browne. Small 4to. cloth, 12s.

"A work which will be equally acceptable to the student and the general reader, which is brimful of good and suggestive thought, and which will introduce many English people for the first time to a delightful region of romantic poetry."—*Athenæum.*

MACMILLAN & CO. London.

JOHN CAMDEN HOTTEN'S NEW BOOKS and ANNOUNCEMENTS.

⁂ The Public are respectfully informed that Mr. Swinburne's Works will in future be published by Mr. Hotten.

NEW WORK BY MR. SWINBURNE.

ESSAYS on the LIFE and WORKS of WILLIAM BLAKE, Poet and Artist. In demy 8vo.

RE-ISSUE OF MR. SWINBURNE'S POEMS.

POEMS and BALLADS. By Alger-NON CHARLES SWINBURNE. Fcap. 8vo. pages 360, price 9s.

Recent Opinions of the Press.

"Whenever there is any kind of true genius, we have no right to drive it mad by ridicule or invective. We must deal with it wisely, justly, fairly. Some of the passages which have been selected as evidence of this poet's plain speaking have been wantonly misunderstood... To us this volume, for the first time, conclusively settles that Mr. Swinburne is undoubtedly a poet."—*Punch.*

"The theatre of Mr. Swinburne is co-extensive with his knowledge and experience. It will expand; and there is no fear of his being denied an audience, or crushed by a critique... It is more likely to realize the boast of Nelson, who, finding himself unmentioned in the *Gazette*, declared a day would come when he should have one for himself... The poems have been impregnated by deepening criticism with a prurience and their own."—*Saturday Review.*

"There is enough in this volume to have made the fortune of most members of his craft."—*Spectator.*

"He has been either very blindly or very unfairly dealt with."—*Pall Mall Gazette.*

"The outcry that has been made over his last published volume of 'Poems and Ballads' is not very creditable to his critics. That the book should be thus denounced says little, indeed, for the thoroughness of current criticism."—*Examiner.*

THE AUTHOR OF 'POEMS AND BALLADS' AND HIS CRITICS.

NOTES on POEMS and REVIEWS. By ALGERNON CHARLES SWINBURNE. Demy 8vo. price 1s. *[This day.*

"Mr. Swinburne here speaks for himself without personality of any kind, but with much general expression of scorn, which the small critics have fairly brought down on themselves. It is to be regretted that a young poet, from whom much is to be hoped, should be thus forced into explanations that can only humiliate those by whom they were required."—*Examiner.*

CHASTELARD: a Tragedy. By ALGERNON CHARLES SWINBURNE. Fcap. 8vo. cloth, price 7s.

The QUEEN MOTHER and ROSA-MOND: two Plays. By ALGERNON CHARLES SWINBURNE. Fcap. 8vo. cloth, price 5s.

MR. ROSSETTI'S CRITICISM.

SWINBURNE'S 'POEMS and BAL-LADS': a Criticism. By WILLIAM MICHAEL ROSSETTI. This day, price 2s. 6d. pages 100.

HISTORY of SIGN-BOARDS. By JACOB LARWOOD and JOHN CAMDEN HOTTEN. With 100 Curious Illustrations.

From the Times.

"It is not fair on the part of a reviewer to pick the plums out of an author's book, thus licking away his cream and leaving little but skim milk remaining; but, even if we were ever so maliciously inclined, we could not, in the present instance, pick out all Messrs. Larwood and Hotten's plums, because the good things are so numerous as to defy the most wholesale depredation."—*Times review of these columns.*

'ANGLICAN CHURCH ORNAMENTS.

This day, thick 8vo. with Illustrations, price 21s.

ENGLISH CHURCH FURNITURE, ORNAMENTS, and DECORATIONS, at the Period of the REFORMATION, A.D. 1566. Edited by E. PEACOCK, F.S.A.

"Very curious as showing what articles of Church Furniture were in those days considered to be idolatrous or unnecessary. The work of which only a limited number has been printed is of the highest interest to those who take part in the present Ritual discussions. See Reviews in the Religious Journals."

COMPANION TO 'THE HATCHET-THROWERS.'

This day, 4to. Illustrations, coloured, 7s. 6d.; plain, 5s.

LEGENDS of SAVAGE LIFE. By JAMES GREENWOOD, the famous 'Amateur Casual.' With 36 Intensely Droll Illustrations, drawn on Wood by Ernest Griset, 'The English Gustave Doré.'

"Readers who found amusement in 'The Hatchet-Throwers' will not regret any acquaintance they may form with this comical work. The pictures are among the most surprising which have come from this artist's pencil."

In a few days, sto. on toned paper, price 7s. 6d.

PUNIANA; or, Thoughts Wise and Otherwise. An entirely New Collection of Riddles and Puns. By the Hon. HUGH ROWLEY. With nearly 100 exquisitely beautiful Concerts from his Pencil.

"It contains nearly 3,000 of the very best Riddles, and about twice that number of most outrageous Puns."

"WILL DO FOR WINCHESTER WHAT TOM BROWN DID FOR RUGBY."

This day, crown 8vo., handsomely printed, 7s. 6d.

SCHOOL LIFE at WINCHESTER COLLEGE; or, the Reminiscences of a Winchester Junior. By the Author of 'The Log of the Water-Lily.' With numerous Coloured Illustrations.

London: JOHN CAMDEN HOTTEN, 74 and 75, Piccadilly.

4.2 Advertisement for Swinburne's works published by John Camden Hotten, *Athenæum* (3 November 1866), 580.

in public discourse, and its alignment with progressive politics. The balance between poetry and prose in the *Fortnightly* is more even than in the *Spectator*, with the weight and authority of his prose balancing the poetry. A steady succession of his poems appears on Risorgimento-related themes, beginning with his ode 'On the Insurrection in Candia' and 'The Halt before Rome' in March and November 1867. His sonnets on Louis Napoleon, in 'Intercession' (1869), are dour and uncompromising: the first lines of No. 1 are indicative:

> O Death, a little more, and then the worm;
> A little longer, O Death, a little yet,
> Before the grave gape, and the grave-worm fret . . .
> (Swinburne 1869, 509; 1904, 2.304)

These include vicious sentiments such as the following from No. 3:

> Beats there no brain yet in the poisonous head,
> Throbs there no treason? if no such thing there be,
> If no such thought, surely this is not he.
> (Swinburne 1869, 510; 1904, 2. 306)

According to Morley, they required courage to publish, and 'remonstrances' followed their appearance (Swinburne 1959–62, 2.58–9). Other of the *Fortnightly* poems are bitter-sweet poems of decline, in love and nature, recalling some of the *Spectator* poems without insisting on perversity. All of them offer memorable language.

How did the *Fortnightly* contribute to Swinburne's work and reputation? First, it gave Swinburne a respected platform for regular publication of his poems, endorsing him as one of its 'house' poets. That this weighty and serious journal also vested its critical authority in Swinburne for articles on renowned contemporary poets indicates the respect with which it and its editor viewed both his poetry and his critical expertise. Unlike the *Spectator*, the *Fortnightly* allows Swinburne some latitude for covert jokes: in his review of Arnold, he quotes at great length a French critic in French, which looks like indulgence until, as Arnold correctly detected, it is understood that it was Swinburne himself shifting languages and persona for his own critique. Moreover, he unashamedly spends much of the same article commenting on 'Empedocles on Etna', which is not among Arnold's new poems. The *Fortnightly* pieces also show that both Swinburne and the *Fortnightly* have enough confidence in signature and in the dignity of the journal to allow him to write pieces on his friends Rossetti and Morris that might be read as 'puffs'. They do function as puffs to a degree, and we see Swinburne participating in a journalism economy that none can escape. This *may* account for Morris's next volume of poems, *The Earthly Paradise*, being reviewed by the Editor in brief as a 'Critical Notice' a year later (June 1868), *and* Swinburne's signed review of John Nichol's *Hannibal. A Historical Drama*, again in 'Critical Notices' as the lead review in December 1872.[12] Morley is hedging his bets, both offering an apparently more independent review of Morris's next book, and allowing Swinburne to puff Nichol. By this time, the prominent position of the 'Notice' may be attributed to Swinburne's name as reviewer.

Whereas in the *Spectator*, Swinburne's name stood among the nameless, in the *Fortnightly*, he takes his place among a pantheon of named contributors to John Morley's progressive experiment, which published serial fiction, poetry, and articles on diverse subjects, including politics (domestic and foreign), philosophy, science, religion, classical literature, visual art, and suffrage. Only some of these were reviews. Looking at the covers of the *Fortnightly*, with their informative lists of names, it can be seen that Swinburne is neither the only poet – William Morris and George Meredith also appear frequently in its pages – nor the only prominent critic: fellow writers included Henry Morley, Walter Bagehot, and George Henry Lewes, as well as John Morley himself. From November 1869 Walter Pater, who undoubtedly had absorbed Swinburne's prose over the last two years, joins him as a *Fortnightly* critic. If Pater's first article on Leonardo da Vinci chimed with Swinburne's prose, Swinburne's next contribution invokes Pater. Swinburne's poem 'The Complaint of Monna Lisa', obliquely in dialogue with Pater's article, appeared three months later in February 1870 (Swinburne 1870b), but it was composed in November, just after Pater's piece appeared (Swinburne 1959– 62, 2.57).[13] The *Fortnightly* serves then to circulate Swinburne's work and name in exalted company and, as a power in the land, in dialogue with other poets of his day and other critics. Through his *Fortnightly* pieces he is at a pinnacle of authority and visibility in the public sphere. The *Fortnightly* also circulated Swinburne by reviewing him. In February 1868, prominently displayed on the cover as the first of the 'Critical Notices', is Conway's review of Swinburne's *William Blake*. That it is the lead Critical Notice is indicative rather of how closely affiliated with the *Fortnightly* Morley regarded Swinburne to be. The location of Conway's positive review may be viewed as an expression of pride in the quality of the monthly's writing.

Swinburne was included from the start of the new series under Morley, and he appeared regularly, in Nos 1 (January), 3 (March), 7 (July), and

9–12 (September–December) in that first year, clearly marked as one of Morley's flagship writers. For a while, Swinburne's contributions appear consistently in the number two position in the issue, his first three poems as well as the article on Morris, but the piece on Arnold, a lengthy thirty-two pages and the longest article in the issue, is item three in issue No. 10 in October. It is as though, in this first year, Morley wants to acquaint his readers with Swinburne, and reinforce his visibility by putting his work in a familiar and prominent position in the journal, so that readers know where to look. Morley only occasionally uses poetry as filler, and many of the poems that he takes for the *Fortnightly* are as intellectually ambitious and challenging as the articles around them, and also as long. If Swinburne's poems in the *Fortnightly* are less sensuous than those in the *Spectator,* the prose is far more resplendent and 'worked' to the point that it was suspected by others (and corroborated by Swinburne) as the inspiration for Pater's prose, although Morley pointed to Swinburne's poetry instead (Swinburne 1959–62, 2.58). In July 1870 Swinburne reviewed Rossetti's poems, newly collected after some of the originals were secretly exhumed from Elizabeth Siddal's grave, in what is a highly appreciative review (Swinburne 1870a).

Swinburne's appearances in the *Fortnightly* are less frequent after 1870, although he appears in its pages through 1892. It is interesting that in April and July 1871 he publishes some edgy work not in the *Fortnightly* but in the small Oxford magazine *Dark Blue.* Comparable to his boldness in praising Baudelaire in a review and poem in the *Spectator* and the *Fortnightly* respectively is his authorship of two signed pieces connected with a similarly risky subject – the art and work of Simeon Solomon. Swinburne's poem 'The End of a Month' (Swinburne 1871b), later retitled 'At a Month's End' when collected in *Poems and Ballads, Second Series* (1878), is more sensuous than any of the *Fortnightly* poems, a quality mirrored in Simeon Solomon's illustration (Figure 4.3), which adds a degree of gender ambivalence. The lineaments of the heavy-featured lovers reference Michelangelo and Rossetti, with sexual difference signalled only by length of hair. Swinburne's subsequent article on Solomon's 'Vision of Love Recalled in Sleep' in the July 1871 issue (Swinburne 1871a) is artfully written, but caused considerable unease in Solomon, who feared that it would provoke hostility. The famous attack by Robert Buchanan (writing as 'Thomas Maitland') on Rossetti and 'The Fleshly School of Poetry' duly appeared in the religiously oriented *Contemporary Review* in October that year ('Maitland' 1871, 334–50).

DRAWN BY S. SALAMAN   "THE END OF A MONTH."

4.3 Illustration by Simeon Solomon for A. C. Swinburne, 'The End of a Month',
in the *Dark Blue* 1.5 (April 1871), between pp. 220–1.

Although it is the case that various friends of Swinburne such as
Bulwer-Lytton, W. M. Rossetti, and Watts-Dunton collaborated with him
on publishing strategies, as Lewes did with George Eliot, shared agency
does not detract from the significance of these patterns of publication or
dissemination for meaning, readership, and the economy of authorship.
Swinburne uses serial publication to hone his skills as a critic, puff the
work of his circle, circulate his poetry, and establish his reputation and
literary identity and authority. All of his editors in these years were
likewise convinced of the value to their papers of his contributions: as
long as they could edit his copy, his prose and poetry helped keep their
journals in the literary lead. The writing of an aesthete such as Swinburne
is not only *part* of the press of its day, however counter-intuitive that may
appear, but, as the research here argues, the 'presence' of the press in
Swinburne's writing – its production, contents, distribution, advertising,
and consumption – permeates and shapes it.

NOTES

1 The *Hornet* (1866–1880) and the *Tomahawk* (1867–70) were satiric weeklies, and the *World* (1874–1922) a daily. The phrase 'Everlasting Cesspools' is from Carlyle's *The French Revolution*, and used also in a letter of 9 September 1870 (Swinburne 1859–62, 2.126). 'Jowett' is Professor Benjamin Jowett (1817–93), Swinburne's former undergraduate tutor at Oxford and the Master of Balliol from 1870.

2 According to Welby (1926, 53), Moxon failed to found a literary periodical for Swinburne to edit, after the pages of the *Spectator* closed to him following his first flurry of articles and poetry there in 1862.

3 The authorship of 'Modern Hellenism', a riposte to a lecture by Matthew Arnold, is disputed, although it is now regarded as Swinburne's: according to Hyder (Hyder 1972, 53) and others (Sypher 1974, v; Rooksby 1997, 52), it is by Swinburne; but Wise rejects this in his Bibliography in the Bonchurch edition of Swinburne's Works (Wise in Swinburne 1925–27, 20.7).

4 The *Fortnightly Review* began publication as a fortnightly, but became a monthly after a year, owing to pressure from distributors. Its title was retained despite the changed frequency.

5 After 1875 Swinburne continued to publish in magazines and newspapers frequently, but was not regularly associated with single titles as in the 1860s and early 1870s. Nevertheless, it can be shown that he continues to customise work for specific hosts in his placement of poems and criticism as journalists routinely do, and to interact with his critics and the public through letters to the editor. His press contributions are frequent enough to be theorised as that of a nineteenth-century author *and* journalist, rather than that of a jobbing journalist.

6 *Miscellanies* comprised seventeen articles in total from diverse sources, four each from the *Fortnightly Review* and the *Encyclopaedia Britannica*; three from the *Nineteenth Century*; one each from Ward's *English Poets*, the *Athenæum* (1883), the *Examiner*, the *Academy*, and the *Gentleman's Magazine*; one appeared for the first time in the collection. The book *A Study of Ben Jonson* was organised in three parts, previously published as four articles in different monthly reviews: two in the *Nineteenth Century* (April and May 1888) and two in the *Fortnightly Review* (July and October 1888).

7 Catherine Maxwell argues that, after the arrest of Simeon Solomon in 1873, Swinburne abandons his aesthetic style. She attributes his failure to reprint the Baudelaire article to an increasing sensitivity about the respectability of his reputation (Maxwell 2006, 102–3). On the topic of collecting journalism, Swinburne may have seen the review of W. M. Rossetti's *Fine Arts Chiefly Contemporary* (1867), the full title of which is *Notices Reprinted, with Revisions*. The *Saturday Review* (16 May 1868) devotes over half a column to comment on the topic.

8 See Matthew Arnold's volume of journalism and lectures, *Essays in Criticism*, first published in 1865. In 1873 Walter Pater called his journalism 'studies' in *Studies in the History of the Renaissance*. Swinburne's title might be drawing on Arnold's *and* Pater's. For more on the remediation of journalism to literature in mid-century Britain, see Brake 2010.

9 Meredith's *Modern Love*, published in 1862, was reviewed disapprovingly by the end of May in the *Spectator* and the *Athenæum* ('In "Modern Love" we have disease and nothing else', Anonymous 1862a, 719) and in September in the *London Review* (which begins 'We have several heads of indictment against Mr George Meredith', Anonymous 1862b, 237); the charges, of offences against morality and good taste, may explain why Meredith's work ceased to appear in *Once a Week*, a family-oriented journal.

10 Paden (1962, 115) argues that a *Spectator* piece in October 1862 on Hugo's philosophy is probably not by Swinburne.

11 Hotten probably had an under-the-counter business in pirated or unauthorised books, and pornographic photographs and books. But he also took risks, publishing Balzac in 1860, before *Poems and Ballads*. See Eliot 2004.

12 Only some of the main articles in the *Fortnightly* were reviews; a 'Critical Notices' department at the end of each issue accommodated short reviews in smaller type, four or five of which 'notices' appeared in each issue. Some were signed.

13 In this letter (to D. G. Rossetti) Swinburne mentions Pater's alleged indebtedness to his prose. Did Swinburne decide wittily to reverse the process by taking 'inspiration' from Pater immediately in his poem 'The Complaint of Monna Lisa'? For more on Swinburne's relation to Pater's work, see Østermark-Johansen, 2002b and c.

Part II

FORMS

5

METRICAL DISCIPLINE: ALGERNON SWINBURNE ON 'THE FLOGGING-BLOCK'

Yopie Prins

In 1909 *The Eton College Chronicle* announced the delivery of 'a great wreath of ilex and laurel' to the grave of Algernon Charles Swinburne. Inscribed 'with grateful homage from Eton' and two lines from an ode composed by Swinburne himself as homage to the school, the laurel wreath confirmed his status as England's unofficial poet laureate (Anonymous 1909, 471). Swinburne had been commissioned to write 'Eton: An Ode', celebrating the four hundred and fiftieth anniversary of the foundation of the school and predicting its future fame: 'when four hundred more and fifty years have risen and shone and set, / Bright with names that men remember, loud with names that men forget, / Haply here shall Eton's record be what England finds it yet' (Swinburne 1904, 6.191–3).[1] But if Swinburne was to be numbered among the names that men remember, it would be not only in the official history of 'Eton's record' but also in the unofficial history recorded by Swinburne in 'Eton: Another Ode'.[2] The self-conscious parody of this (unpublished) palinode gives us a glimpse of the other side of Eton – its backside:

Dawn smiles on the fields of Eton, and wakes from slumber her youthful flock,
Lad by lad, whether good or bad: alas for those who at nine o'clock
Seek the room of disgraceful doom, to smart like fun on the flogging block.

Swish, swish, swish! O I wish, I wish I'd not been late for lock-up last night!
Swish, that mill I'm bruised from still (I couldn't help it – I had to fight)
Makes the beast (I suppose at least) who flogs me flog me with all his might.

'Tell me, S—e, does shame within burn as hot (Swish! Swish!) as your stripes my
    lad,
Burn outside, have I tamed your pride? I'm glad to see how it hurts you – glad –
Swish! I wish it may cure you. Swish! Get up.' By Jove, what a dose I've had.

In the 'swish' and 'burn' of the boy's body on Eton's notorious flogging block, the name of Swinburne ('S—e') is made legible in 'stripes' on his posterior, and recorded for posterity as the poet laureate of Victorian flagellomania.

Now that we have arrived at Swinburne's centenary, it may be time to look back at this history from another perspective. Surveying new trends in Swinburne studies, David Riede regrets that 'a Swinburne icon for our times could only be a parodic version of the flamboyant sexual rebel of the 1860s, and is probably not devoutly to be wished for by more "passionate Swinburneans" who are more interested in seeing justice done to his complex and challenging poetry' (Riede 2010, 170). But the extensive corpus of Swinburne's flagellant writing – in poetry, prose, dramas, letters – suggests a more complicated logic that should be of interest even, and especially, to Swinburnians who are passionate about poetic form. As Steven Marcus already observed more than forty years ago in *The Other Victorians*, 'the literature of flagellation is on its surface a much more sophisticated kind of writing than ordinary pornography', because it 'makes use of a wider range of literary forms' (Marcus 1966, 252). To analyse the formal complications and implications of Swinburne's flagellant verse in particular, I propose to read 'on its surface' a manuscript that is still unpublished: a series of flagellation fantasies set in a mock-pastoral school setting reminiscent of Eton, copied out by hand between the years 1862 and 1881, and compiled into a volume entitled 'The Flogging-Block: An Heroic Poem in a Prologue and Twelve Eclogues by Algernon Charles Swinburne, with Illustrations by Simeon Solomon'.[3] These poems are not a secondary by-product of Swinburne's poetics, but a remarkable body of writing that produces a reading of Algernon Swinburne's poetic signature, in reverse.

To preview this backward logic, we may begin by looking at the end of the manuscript (Figure 5.1). Here we find a table of contents that we would normally expect to see at the beginning, with a series of titles for Eclogues (not all of which are actually included in this manuscript). The names that appear in each title are dramatically enumerated in a rhythmic repetition that is visually striking: after Algernon's Flogging in Eclogue I, there is Reginald's Flogging, Percy's Flogging, Willie's Flogging, Charlie's Flogging, Edward's Flogging, Frank's Flogging, Philip's Flogging, Arthur's Flogging, Freddy's Flogging, Leonard's Flogging, Edwin's Flogging. The substitutability of one name for another is evident, as Algernon is increasingly listed in every prelude and epilogue ('Epilogue to

5.1 List of Eclogues (final page of 'The Flogging-Block')

Arthur's Flogging – Algernon's Flogging. Prelude to Freddy's Flogging – Algernon's Flogging. Epilogue to Freddy's Flogging – Algernon's Flogging', and so on in a seemingly infinite regress). Beginning and ending with 'Algernon', the flogging list revolves around his name as the generic name for any boy who has ever been or is about to be flogged. We might even read into, or out of, this name a mock etymology, combining the Greek verb *algeo* (meaning 'to feel pain') and the English preposition 'on': to be Algernon means to feel pain on the flogging block.

Swinburne's algolagnia has been interpreted from multiple perspectives, as a biographical idiosyncrasy or a typical example of 'the English Vice', as a physiological symptom or a psychoanalytic phenomenon, as a pathological perversion or a subversion of sexual mores, as a pornographic performance or a social parody, as a cultural critique or a philosophy of sadomasochism, as a form of (homo)sexuality or a formalised aestheticism; as Rikky Rooksby concludes in his biography of Swinburne, 'whatever the cause, Swinburne's fixation should not be reduced to a simple formula' (Rooksby 1997, 40).[4] Focusing more on the effects than the causes, I approach 'The Flogging-Block' not through a 'deep' reading of the manuscript to discover the interiority of the poet or uncover the inner workings of his poetic psyche but through a reading that calls attention to the surface of his writing. The elaborate versification of Swinburne's flogging poems plays out an allegory of rhythm that is inscribed on the body and made visible, as we shall see, in lines on the page. I further suggest that we read this rhythmic display – the beating of the body incorporated into the beat of the poem, and vice versa – as an initiation into the disciplinary measures of metre. I situate 'The Flogging-Block' within nineteenth-century metrical discourses, and especially debates about classical verse composition during Eton reform, in order to show how the beaten boy becomes an exemplary Eton boy: rather than learning verse by heart, he learns his lesson by having it written on his bottom. My reading of (or on) 'The Flogging-Block' concludes that this metrical discipline works according to a logic of externalisation rather than internalisation, reversing an abstract discourse about metre so that it can materialise, strikingly, in Swinburne's own writing.

ALG – RN – N

To date, 'The Flogging-Block' has been more written about than read. Although much of Swinburne's flagellant writing was suppressed by Edmund Gosse and T. J. Wise in the early twentieth century, this manuscript is mentioned in passing by literary biographers from Lafourcade onward. Jean Overton Fuller dedicates a separate chapter to 'The Flogging-Block', describing in vivid detail how it is hidden in the Manuscripts Department of the British Museum, among papers 'Reserved from Public Use':

> special application is necessary. If the application is successful, the manu-
> script is brought up in a wrapping of thick brown paper ... The parcel is

tied with tape, and the tape is secured by a special seal, in such a manner
that it cannot be untied, but has to be cut with scissors. The cutting can only
be done by a senior official. One may watch. The seal falls with a plop.
Inside the parcel there is, together with the manuscript, a list (to which
one's own name will be added) of previous persons for whom the manu-
script was brought out. (Fuller 1968, 256–7)

As presented by Fuller, the scene of preparing for a reading of the manu-
script anticipates the flogging ritual: although 'one may watch', a senior
official does the unwrapping and cutting of the package, and the skin is
revealed (in this case, a blue leather binding). With Fuller's name added to
the list of previous persons who have seen the manuscript, her voyeuristic
reading corresponds to what she finds in the manuscript, namely 'the
boys' voyeuristic pleasure in watching each other's torment' (258). After
quoting some excerpts from 'these awful pages', Fuller concludes,
'perhaps the British Museum authorities do well to keep the manuscript
out of the public's way' (260). Is she suggesting that 'The Flogging-Block'
should not be read at all? Or is there some other way to read what is
written on these pages?

How to read 'The Flogging-Block' is a question raised by subsequent
critics, including the imaginary dialogue scripted by Jerome McGann in
Swinburne: An Experiment in Criticism. When one of his dramatis personae
('Kernahan') asserts that 'no deep meanings lie concealed at its bottom (so
to speak)' (McGann 1972, 269), another critic ('Murdoch') quotes passages
from the manuscript to emphasise 'the depth of impression Sade's writing
made on him' (272), while a third critic ('Wratislaw') emphasises that
Swinburne 'objected to the gross details in Sade' and wrote his flogging
poems as a highly stylised performance, with 'the mere idea of flagella-
tion repetitively invoked and religiously presented at a high level of
abstraction' (280); a fourth critic ('Mrs. Watts-Dunton') chimes in that
'Swinburne's flagellant verse, precisely because it is so schematic, clarifies
an aesthetic attitude specifically allied to the masochistically inclined
personality' (281). McGann's experiment in criticism ventriloquises
various ways of reading 'The Flogging-Block' – as the literary production
of a parodist, a satirist, a sadist, a masochist – but without coming to one
conclusion: 'these patterns are discernible in all of Swinburne's flagellant
verse, the serious and the humorous alike' (282).

To encourage more reading of a seemingly 'minor' literary corpus that
remains largely unread and unknown (except perhaps among the most
passionate Swinburnians, and connoisseurs of flagellation), the recent

Yale edition of *Swinburne's Major Poems* edited by McGann and Sligh includes a passage from 'Arthur's Flogging' (Swinburne 2004a, 418–20). Published in 1888 for *The Whippingham Papers*, this mock-heroic poem is not one of the 'eclogues' included in 'The Flogging-Block', but it suggests how we might learn to read Swinburne's manuscript. The flogging of Arthur is a Byronic parody (written in ottava rima, like *Don Juan*) that presents the body as a blank page marked by writing:

> And harder still the birch fell on his bottom,
>   And left some fresh red letters there to read;
> Weeks passed before the part inscribed forgot 'em,
>   The fleshy tablets, where the master's creed
> Is written on boy's skin with birchen pen,
> At each re-issue copied fair again.

(lines 115–200)

Written 'with birchen pen' on the skin are 'fresh red letters there to read', marking Arthur's bottom with lines like a poem: both body and poem become legible in letters that are 'red' or 'read' on 'fleshy tablets'. The body is disciplined according to prescribed rules that are strictly enforced by the creed (or screed) of the master, as a form of metrical discipline. In the strict versification of this poem, the beating of the birch is accentuated in the beats of accentual verse: 'and **hard**er **still** the **birch fell** on his **bott**om', or perhaps (shifting the accent to 'on'), 'the **birch** fell **on** his **bott**om'. Through the repetition of the flogging, 'at each re-issue copied fair again', Arthur is made into a lesson-book for other boys to read as well:

> The fair full page of white and warm young flesh
>   Was ruled across with long thick lines of red,
> And lettered on the engraved backside with fresh
>   Large characters, by all boys to be read.

(lines 129–32)

The letters that materialise as 'large characters' on the 'engraved backside' of this boy allow him to be read as an exemplary character for 'all boys', including Swinburne himself (as the 'author' of 'Arthur'). Thus 'Arthur's Flogging' exemplifies a poetic performance, in verse, of a reverse logic that turns the bottom into a surface for the inscription of metre, figured as rhythmic beating of the body and literalised in lines written on the page.

When we look at 'the fair full page' of 'The Flogging-Block' (more than a hundred pages of densely scribbled lines) we see how this poetic logic is repeated over and over with multiple variations in multiple scenes of flogging, 'at each re-issue copied fair again' in Swinburne's own handwriting. In his manuscript, the beating of the body is graphically visualised in letters, lines, stripes, and other marks that are figuratively 'red' and literally 'read' in black ink on white paper. This kind of visual reading is illustrated in a sketch by Simeon Solomon, inserted at the beginning of the manuscript (Figure 5.2). Entitled 'The Eve of the Birching', the sketch features the idealised faces of two boys who are, we assume, about to lose face in a flogging. Between them on a table is a long switch of birch twigs, placed next to a book that is opened, face down, with its back spine exposed. The juxtaposition of the birch and the book anticipates the flogging ritual as a scene of writing and reading, to be played out on the backside of the boys. As the instrument of punishment that will inscribe their bodies with the marks of a rhythmic beating, the birch turns into a writing implement like a pen that will leave its traces on the page.

Taking pleasure in the graphic visualisation of flogging, Solomon and Swinburne liked to exchange flogging fantasies in their personal correspondence. Solomon wrote to Swinburne about 'the marks of many

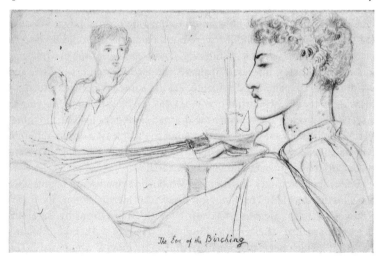

5.2 'The Eve of the Birching,' pencil sketch by Simeon Solomon
(first page of 'The Flogging-Block')

Etonian rods' to illustrate 'the *real* merit and meaning of that instrument of delight' and in response to 'the recital of the boyish agonies you depicted in your last [letter]', Solomon added his own vision to the scene: 'I was doubled up with grief at the idea of so many tender posteriors quivering under the pitiless strokes of the rod' (possibly late September 1869; Swinburne 1959–62, 2.32). In return for Swinburne's writing, Solomon promised, 'I will make you many drawings', including a picture of 'The Queen presenting rods to the Schoolmasters of the United Kingdom' (Swinburne 1959–62, 2.35). They turned poems into pictures and pictures into poems during a period of friendship and artistic collaboration, described in further detail by Thaïs Morgan; she argues that the 'perverse male bodies' in the work of Solomon and Swinburne reflect an emerging discourse about 'perversity' in Victorian England, but also 'reverse' this discourse into 'an ever mobile eroticism, a "perverse" play between fantasy and action, aesthetics and lifestyle' (Morgan 1996, 81).

More than Solomon (who was later arrested for homosexual acts and 'cut off' by Swinburne), Swinburne played out this reversed discourse primarily in his flagellant writing, which circulated among other friends in Swinburne's inner circle as well. When George Powell sent a photograph of the Eton flogging block to Swinburne, Swinburne wrote to him in a letter (5 October 1867): 'I would give anything for a good photograph taken at the right minute – say the tenth cut or so – and doing justice to *all sides* of the question', and he went on to imagine how he might visualise the flogging ritual himself: 'If I were but a painter – ! I would do dozens of different fellows diversely suffering. There *can* be no subject fuller of incident, character, interest – realistic, modern, dramatic, intense, and vividly pictorial, palpitant d'actualité. Do get some fellow with a turn for drawing to try it' (Swinburne 1959–62, 1.265–6). By turning to flogging as a scene for writing and reading, the dramatic eclogues in 'The Flogging-Block' can be seen as Swinburne's attempt to do at least a dozen 'different fellows' in his own versification, all of them 'diversely suffering' in poetry that is 'dramatic, intense, and vividly pictorial'.

Following Solomon's illustration, Swinburne's manuscript begins with a prologue, entitled 'The Flogging-Block: An Heroic Poem, By Rufus Rodworthy Esq. (Algernon Clavering) With Annotations by Barebum Birchingham Esq. (Bertram Bellingham)' (Figure 5.3). Like 'Arthur's Flogging' (which begins, 'I sing of Arthur's Flogging; I, who heard / The boy himself sing out beneath the birch') the prologue is another mock-heroic poem, but this time written in heroic couplets in the style of Pope:

5.3 Page 1, 'The Flogging-Block: An Heroic Poem'
(Prologue to 'The Flogging-Block')

I sing the Flogging-block. Thou, red-cheek'd Muse,
Whose Hand the Blood of smarting Boys imbrues,
Scholastic Dame, revered of State & Church,
Whose Lords to be have writhed beneath the Birch.[5]

This invocation to the Muse is in the epic tradition of *arma virumque cano*
('arms and the man I sing'), with *arma virumque* ironically translated into
the birch and the boy and *cano* translated into the song of the cane; and
again (like 'Arthur's Flogging') all this epic beating takes the form of

writing on the body. Rhyming with 'Muse', the verb 'imbrues' can be read actively or passively, meaning both to 'stain' (as with blood) and to 'pierce' (as with 'a weapon piercing a part', an obsolete use listed in the *OED*), so that it remains ambiguous whether the hand that writes is passively stained with blood or actively piercing the body in order to draw blood. The same ambiguity is written into the epithet, 'red-cheek'd Muse', whose face red with shame is also the bottom red with pain: either way, this reddening is a mark of the flogging that we must learn to read as writing.

The didactic function of the prologue is underscored by a series of annotations that appear in four separate pages inserted into 'The Flogging-Block' (Figure 5.4). The first note, marked number 1 after 'Muse' in line 1, corresponds to remarks written by the fictional editor, the so-called Barebum Birchingham or Bertram Bellingham, who seems to be fixated on the marking of the bottom by the birch (indeed, the doubling of his name seems to call attention to the two butt-cheeks exposed in the letter B).[6] According to B. B., the red-cheek'd Muse is 'The Muse who presides over the ceremony of Flagellation & inspires the Song which attempts to celebrate the Flogging-Block ... so styl'd from the Hue produced by the first Strokes of the Rod on the nether Cheeks of the Boy chastised – "his nether Cheeks full broad & white" when first exposed to the Lash, but after a few good hearty Strokes (well applied with a good smart Rod) all suffused with a glowing Crimson'. In this pseudo-scholarly annotation, the muse that inspires the song is identified as a figure for writing, as she is 'so styl'd from the Hue' of the blood that appears on the bottom: a blank writing surface that is 'full broad & white' at first, but gradually 'suffused with a glowing Crimson' by the strokes of the rod that are also the strokes of the pen. So also the blank page is filled with the strokes of the pen, turning the figure of red blood into black ink, line after line.

From the prologue we learn that the ceremony of flagellation is a necessary initiation rite for Lords and Bishops and Judges, but especially important for budding poets. Starting in line 10, the rhythmic repetition of the birch is applied to the 'Poet's Bum' in particular. Here the word 'birch' is repeated thirteen times, although this emphatic repetition also throws off the scansion of the lines, causing distress in all the right places:

> And ere his Brow be ripe for Bays to come
> Birch, Birch entwine[2)] the beardless Poet's Bum
> Birch, Birch alone embrace his brawnier Part,

Birch, Birch inflame his Flesh with constant Smart,
Birch, daily Birch,[3] ring Music in his Ears,
Birch, hourly Birch,[4] renew his recent Tears,
Birch, Birch, incessant Birch,[5] fill all his Days with Fears.

If we look more closely at the manuscript (figure 5.3), we see additional marks inserted by B. B. in these lines: note (2) after the word 'entwine', note (3) after 'daily Birch', note (4) after 'hourly Birch', and note (5) after 'incessant Birch'. This compulsive counting of the strokes of the birch is further

5.4 Notes to 'The Flogging-Block' (Prologue to 'The Flogging-Block')

recounted by B. B. (see figure 5.4), who writes in note (4) that 'I have known a young Gentleman of good Family & good Parts severely Whipp'd no less than seven Times in one Day, receiving at each Bout eighteen smart Lashes on his bare Breech . . . his fault being, first, that he fail'd of saying his morning Lesson.' His remarks for note (4) go on (and on) for several pages to enumerate all seven floggings in detail, and conclude with a sentence in parentheses: '(This experience occurr'd at School to Mr. A. Clavering (the Author of this Poem) on the Day on which he completed his fifteenth or sixteenth year.)' At this point the annotations end, as even the compulsive annotator to the poem seems to lose count; B. B. never gets to note (5) on 'Birch, Birch, incessant birch', but it has already become clear that the counting is an infinite series, for endless repetition.

The experience of infinite measure, like Kant's formalised account of the mathematical sublime, is a rite of passage into the metrical sublime. This is what young poets must learn from the Muse, if we follow the instructions for whipping on page two of the Prologue:

> Thou that hast whipp'd so many a boyish Bard
> So soundly, & so often, & so hard,
> (For chief the Stripling Songster's Breech invites
> The full Performance of thy frequent Rites,
> And most the Nurslings of the Muse require
> The Lash that sets their lyrick Blood on Fire,
> The Lash that ever when they cry keeps Time,
> When Stroke to Stroke responds in glowing Rhyme,
> And still the humbled Bottom hails the Rod sublime,
> Till Heart & Head the rhythmic Lesson learn
> From Wounds that redden & from Stripes that burn,
> As Twig by Twig imprints the Crimson sign in turn.)
> Till, faint with Fear, bowed Head & trembling Heart
> Learn of the Bottom, of that lowliest Part,
> The lesson learnt & taught at once with Shame & Smart.

In whipping 'so many a boyish Bard / So soundly, so often, & so hard', the Muse seems to rhythmicise their bodies, teaching them lash by lash and stroke by stroke to incorporate this rhythm until 'Heart & Head the rhythmic Lesson learn'. This rite of passage is also a passage into writing: the 'stripes that burn' are imprinted on the bottom as 'a Crimson sign', a graphic figure that turns the rhythmic lesson into metrical marks.

Thus the invocation to the Flogging Muse uses the trope of flogging to proclaim the vocation of poets, who come into writing by being written upon. The prologue's function in 'The Flogging-Block' is not only to proclaim this trope but also to begin performing it, as the poem shifts from the third to the first person, and into the present tense. At this point, the Muse inspires a vision that repeats the primal scene of flogging:

> She hears! She hears! Already on my Eyes
> Scenes once but too familiar seem to rise,
> Again I see, & shudder at my Doom
> The dark high Precinct of the Flogging-Room.

From the general principle of flogging 'so many a boyish bard', the poem now brings into view the flogging of one boy in particular:

> But who is he, the bare-breeched Boy there kneeling? Who?
> With visionary eye reversed I see
> Myself in him, & gaze myself on me.
> I see the Shirt drawn up, the Bottom bared,
> The Bottom daily stripped & never spared;
> I see my Stripes, I see the numerous Weals
> That prove what pain my Bum each morning feels:
> I see my Breeches hanging loose about my Heels.

This moment of vicarious identification, identifying the boy and also identifying with the boy, happens through a backward look ('with visionary eye reversed I see') that places the 'I' in the same posture as the kneeling boy: his 'Bottom daily stripped' turns into a vision of 'my Stripes' on 'my Bum'.

The rhetorical doubling transforms the prologue into a performative utterance, as if experienced in the present moment. The beating of the body is performed in the beat of the poem, in a series of strongly accented iambs:

> I feel once more each Twig, each Knot, each Bud,
> Sting my soft Flesh & fire my fevered Blood:
> I feel the Stripes behind me burn & throb;
> I smart, I writhe, I groan, I moan, I sob,
> I wince, I flinch, I howl, I roar with pain,
> 'And weep the more because I weep in vain.'

In the repetition of verbs beginning with 'I' (a stroke of the pen we could read as a metrical mark), each verb is like another stroke of the birch, lashing the body to make it feel pain, and creating a rhythmic response in turn. To make this rhythm legible, it is literally inscribed in 'Stripes' on the body and figuratively on the page and, vice versa, it is literally inscribed in lines on the page and figuratively on the body: the graphic inscription makes body and poem interchangeable, each a figure for the other.

These lines are visualised not only horizontally in the poem's alineation but vertically in the left margin of this page in the manuscript (Figure 5.5a). Here we see three lines that run perpendicular to the lines of the poem, scribbled in small letters that are barely legible: the first line is 'C.(A.) – that stands for 'Cl – v – r – ng (Alg – rn – n)' and the next two lines are crossed out. This annotation is supposedly provided by 'B. B.' whose earlier explanatory notes have already identified 'Mr. A. Clavering' as 'Author of this Poem.' But of course the handwriting reveals author and annotator to be one and the same, making the authorial signature visible as a function of marking. Simultaneously scored out and underscored by heavy black lines, the name is emphasised by its placement in parentheses and by dashes that strip away the vowels in the name, as if the very name is marked by stripes from the flogging: (Alg – rn – n).

Striking out the vowels, this stripped-down name is repeated further down on the same page of the manuscript, in the body of the poem (Figure 5.5b). As the flagellation allows the poem to visualise the boy who is being beaten, his name becomes legible in the signature left by the strokes of the birch on his bottom. It is Algernon himself, predetermined by his very name to suffer pain on the flogging block:

> His Flagellation is but now begun:
> He'll have enough to cry for ere it's done:
> The Birch itself delights to whip young Alg – rn – n.'
> I hear my Cousin whispering to my Brother –
> 'This was a good tough Rod – but see the other!
> See, Charlie, what a lithe, fresh, sappy one!
> I call your Brother's Flagellation Fun:
> I like to see the Birch-Twigs tickling Alg – rn – n.'

The reiteration of Alg – rn – n in quotation marks makes it possible to read the scene of flogging as a scene of writing, suspended between the first and the third person: what 'I hear' and what 'I see' is both identification of, and identification with, the body being written upon. The reversibility of the third and first person in the name of Algernon produces a vicarious logic that also allows the reader of the poem to enter

I feel once more each Twig, each Knot, each Bud,
Sting my soft Flesh & fire my fevered Blood:
I feel the Stripes behind me burn & throb:
I smart, I writhe, I groan, I moan, I sob,
I wince, I flinch, I howl, I roar with pain, [5]
'And weep the more because I weep in vain'
And still the Birch-Twigs ply my Bum afresh,
And still the Torment rages in my Flesh.
Now, tho' my Cheek the burning Tears besmirch.
My Torturer calls for yet another Birch:
And while my Breech expects another Dozen
I hear my Brother whisper to my Cousin
'Ah! won't the Youngster's Bottom smart, by G–!
Ah! won't it blush & redden from the Rod!

Ah! won't it blush & redden from the Rod!
His Flagellation is but now begun:
He'll have enough to cry for ere 'tis done:
The Birch itself delights to whip young Alg-rn-n. [16]
I hear my Cousin whispering to my Brother –
'This was a good tough Rod – but see the other!
See, Charlie, what a lithe, fresh, sappy one!
I call your Brother's Flagellation Fun:
I like to see the Birch-Twigs tickling Alg-rn-n.

5.5a and b Page 4, 'The Flogging-Block: An Heroic Poem' (Prologue to 'The Flogging-Block') into, and identify with, the scene of flogging as if in the second person: 'I call your Brother's Flagellation Fun.' Algernon's incorporation of this rhythmic lesson thus proves to be anyone's and everyone's initiation into the disciplinary measures of metre, demonstrating how to make 'the Youngster's Bottom smart', painfully but thoroughly educated in metrical discipline.

The flogging of schoolboys was a controversial subject, widely debated but also celebrated within nineteenth-century discourses about educational reform, corporal punishment, and sexual flagellation that Ian Gibson has surveyed in *The English Vice*. Focusing on Eton in particular as an iconic site in the Victorian imagination, Gibson's chapter on 'Eton, the Birch, and Swinburne' reproduces a photograph of the flogging block in 'the Library' at Eton (Gibson 1978: figure 12). With three large birches leaning against the back wall, the flogging block is placed beneath a painting of a classical amphitheatre, and framed by wooden benches on either side. In this highly theatrical setting, countless boys from the best British families lost face by baring their bottoms in a highly formalised ritual, enacted before an audience of pupils, who came to witness an event where every word – stern command, plea for mercy, merciless reply, cry of woe, tearful repentance – was scripted. The performance of subjection to this form of discipline, both real and imagined, was central to the formation of character for Eton boys and the very idea of 'the Eton boy'.

This Etonian scenario was obsessively played out in the popular press, which circulated so-called 'memoirs' of the floggers and the flogged at Eton, alongside newspaper reports, letters to the editor, eye-witness accounts, photographs, pornographic images, and comical cartoons, including a caricature of James Lee Joynes in *Vanity Fair*: the 'Lower Master' of Eton is depicted with a birch in hand, while the flogging block looms in the background (Gibson 1978: figure 14). This cartoon was published on the occasion of his retirement in 1889 along with an ironic tribute to the man who 'handled the birch with an unsparing hand' and thus 'left a lasting impression on many generations of little boys' (quoted by Gibson 1978, 123). One of the boys on whom Joynes seems to have left a lasting impression was Swinburne. At the tender age of twelve, the young Algernon was lodged at Eton with Joynes for his Assistant Master, and later in life Swinburne recalled 'a swishing that I had the marks of for more than a month', delivered by a 'stunning tutor' whose 'pet subject was *metre*'. Gibson speculates that this tutor may have been Joynes, but, if so, the memory is also transformed by Swinburne's metrical imagination: 'I firmly believe that my ear for verses made me rather a favourite', he wrote, boasting that 'of all the swishings I ever had up to seventeen and over, I never had one for a false quantity in my life', but 'I made it up in arithmetic, so my tutor never wanted reasons for making rhymes between his birch and my body' (*c.* 10 February 1863; Swinburne 1959–62, 1.78).

Swinburne's imaginary incorporation of metre reflects, and reflects on, a broader cultural imaginary in which Eton was associated with metrical as well as corporal discipline. As part of their classical education, Eton boys were given weekly assignments in Greek and Latin verse composition, including the translation of English poetry into classical metres; by the sixth form they were composing their own verse in epic hexameters as well as elegiacs, iambics, Alcaics, Sapphics, and so on. But it was a difficult discipline, as Swinburne later remembered, or perhaps imagined, 'a contemporary of mine at Eton, who after two hours' labour ... was safely delivered of a single hexameter – only unhappily it had seven feet instead of six. The consequences in that case were tragic' (20 April 1880; Swinburne 1959–62, 4.136). Pupils were flogged if they did not know the right rhythms, and even if they knew them too well, according to another anecdote recounted by Swinburne about his youthful attempt to write Galliambics. Having learned this metrical scheme from an Eton edition of Catullus, prepared for the 'young mind', Swinburne claimed that 'I *tried* ... to do my week's verses in it once, and my tutor said it was no metre at all ... and the consequences were tragic' (Autumn 1864; Swinburne 1959–62, 1.110). In Swinburne's memory (or fantasy) of this painful episode, his metrical experiment with a 'hard' classical metre led to a hard beating: 'And *then* I showed my verses indignantly (*after* the catastrophe) to another master, and he said they were very good, and there was but one small slip in them, *hard* as the metre was; ... but that did not heal the cuts or close the scars imprinted on the mind and the body', supposedly inducing 'a just horror of strange metres' (Swinburne 1959–62, 1.110). Even more than cuts and scars, what was 'imprinted on the mind and body' by flagellation was an idea of metre itself as a painful pleasure.

Instruction in classical verse at Eton was at the upper end of a widespread pedagogical practice in schools of all levels, where students were compelled to memorise poems for elocution and recitation and punished if they failed. Catherine Robson has argued that 'the affective experience of pedagogical beating' became part of the popular transmission of poetry in Victorian England, where 'the compulsorily memorized poem inserted itself into individuals and established its beat in sympathy with, or in counterpoint to, their bodily rhythms' (Robson 2005, 157). According to this argument, the internalisation of metre depended on literalising the 'beat' of English accentual verse. But this figurative incorporation of rhythm was complicated by the compulsory memorisation of classical metres, since quantitative verse was artificially superimposed on accentual verse. Rather than regulating the rhythms of the body, what was at stake in the rarefied practice of classical verse composition at Eton (and elsewhere) was the regulation of metre itself, as an abstract discipline and an elaborate metrical discourse that was widely circulated and hotly debated in Victorian England. In *Essays on Liberal Education* (1868) for example, F. W. Farrar published his essay, 'On Greek and Latin Verse-Composition as a General Branch of Education', as an extended polemic against 'compulsory verse-making'. He complained about 'the mysteries of the dreadful drill' and asked how any student could possibly benefit from 'the Latin which he endeavours to torture into rhythm' (Farrar 1868, 212–13). As an advocate of educational reform, Farrar maintained that classical verse composition was a useless discipline, without any practical ends to justify the means: 'As for the disciplinary value of verses, is it necessary that discipline should be so purely infructuous?' he asked (217), rejoicing that 'a serious effort is now being made to emancipate English boys from a yoke whose "cruel absurdity" neither they nor their fathers have been able to bear' (216–17).

While some condemned the uses and abuses of this metrical exercise, it was vigorously defended by others, including William Johnson (later known as 'Cory').[7] Like Joynes, Johnson became another legendary Eton figure, but more known for his interest in versification than his insistence on flagellation. He published his own poems in English, Latin, and Greek and also several manuals for students on learning to read and write Latin lyric verses and Greek iambic verses.[8] Johnson had attended Eton as a pupil and, when he later returned as a tutor, he taught classics during Swinburne's years at Eton. In a pamphlet entitled *Hints for Eton Masters*, he maintained that exercises in translating English poetry into Greek and Latin were an important discipline for the educational development of boys at Eton:

I believe every Cambridge man hates the passages which he has to translate, and they are indeed too often ugly and dull; but I trust it is not so at Eton. I may be deceived, but I hope I have very often set verses to be turned or 'reduced' (as they say of engraving) from really attractive and beautiful passages of English poets, which have struck and stirred some boys, and have given them the wish to read the books ... In particular I think it worth while to say that I have had great success in setting passages of English verse for Latin hexameters. (Johnson 1898, 7–8)

The rhythms of English poetry 'which have struck and stirred some boys' were thus transposed by classical verse composition into a metrical abstraction: a disciplinary exercise in the 'reduction' of poetic form that could be used to form and reform the character of the pupil.

During a surge of debates about educational reform in the 1860s, Johnson went to great lengths to explain the purpose of 'formal' education at Eton. In two pamphlets published in 1861, *Eton Reform* and *Eton Reform II*, Johnson addressed critics who had accused the school of catering to 'clever boys' without offering practical instruction for the average pupil. 'It is well known to all who have been at Eton within the last ten years', he replied, 'that boys who are not brilliant versifiers ... take considerable pains, and often with success, to do well' (Johnson 1861, 9–10), although the reason for taking such pains often required some clarification:

As soon as boys are old enough to ask the question, 'Why do we learn these lessons?' – and they do ask it very early in their career – it strains the ingenuity of grown-up people to explain to them the bearing of dead languages upon their after-life, and, as a matter of fact, they are bribed to learn things that they take no interest in, and obstinately believe to be useless, by the great and peculiar social pleasures of school and college, which they would have to forego [sic], if they exchanged Greek and Latin for professional and practical studies. (Johnson 1861, 11)

Not only was the cultivation of classical metres rewarded by the 'social pleasures' of Eton culture, but according to Johnson there was a fundamental 'instinct ... at the bottom of verse-making' that made it a creative pleasure: 'Even the dullest boy has some satisfaction in turning out a verse that will scan and construe. In composition we have the required machinery for eliciting the energies of ordinary minds' (11).

Indeed, in Johnson's mind, the 'required machinery' of such classical discipline was the very foundation of a liberal education, as he went on to argue in his essay, 'On the Education of the Reasoning Faculties' (commissioned by Farrar for inclusion in *Essays on Liberal Education*). Here Johnson defended the traditional method of teaching Greek and Latin verse composition as a form of moral education: 'The classical method, characterized by accuracy, by constraining and chastening discipline, and by some consciousness of progress in the acquirement of craftsman's skill, we would, if possible, apply to what we have called, for the sake of convenience, moral philosophy' (Johnson 1868, 355). By learning to write in classical metres, pupils could discipline the mind and cultivate greater refinement of expression, as Johnson found that 'the Latin verse of young people ... is more honest, more sincere, than their English rhymed verse' (329). Precisely because quantitative metre was learned as an abstract pattern, it could reform both the mind and the body, through an imposition of metrical discipline that was different from accentual metre already incorporated into the body by habit or convention.

Swinburne, who excelled at classical verse composition, turned these various ideas about Eton form and reform into an extravagant performance of his own ideas about poetic form. Looking back on his metrical education at Eton, Swinburne wrote: 'As to my quantities and metre and rule of rhythm and rhyme, I defy castigation. The head master has sent me up for good on that score. Mr. Tennyson tells me in a note that he "envies me" my gift that way. After this approval I will not submit myself to the birch on that account' (c. 20 April; Swinburne 1959–62, 1.121). Nevertheless Swinburne loved to imagine submission to the birch, and his personal correspondence is peppered with so-called memories of pupils who suffered through metrical discipline at Eton. In a letter to Charles Howell (18 November 1870), with whom he liked to exchange flogging fantasies, Swinburne inserted an imaginary letter addressed to himself, concerning the plight of two fictional cousins at Eton:

> My dear Algie – I must tell you about the young un – it's worse than ever this half – He was swished 3 times last Friday, & once every day the week before. ... My tutor told him the other day he'd be turned into a birch some day at this rate – he says he shall give the subject for verses to our division next week – Ovid's Metamorph[oses]: you know – & that style of thing – I wish you'd do some for me. (Swinburne 1959–62, 2.133–4)

Turning this 'urgent' plea to his own pleasure, Swinburne commented to Howell: 'The Ovidian metamorphosis of a boy into a birch-tree is really a sweet subject for Latin verse, I think I shall try it' (2.134). According to a metamorphic logic perhaps more Swinburnian than Ovidian, the perfect subject of this classical verse composition would be the figurative incorporation of its metrical form, as if (by transforming what in classical metrical theory would be called the 'ictus' on the 'arsis') the birching of the boy could turn the beat of English accentual verse into Latin metre.

The person who responded most enthusiastically to Swinburne's version of Etonian discipline was his cousin, Mary Gordon Leith, with whom he shared a keen interest in stories (and a personal history) of flagellation.[9] In their correspondence now published in *Uncollected Letters*, we learn that he sent her a book about Eton and she replied: 'how many changes seem to have been made of late, tho' let us hope that it may never see a change in *one* respect & that it may be said *of* the birch as of the school "Florebit"' (29 January 1892; Swinburne 2004b, 3.47). In contrast to Eton reformers who would do away with corporal punishment, she and Swinburne imagined the practice of birching – the very idea of it, as 'may be said *of* the birch' – as the highest form of aesthetic education. Thus she followed up in another private letter (written in code, transposing initial letters):

> Cow, my nousin do you meally rean to *stand there* & tell me that the time-honoured & traditional pode of nunishment is disused at Eton? I am more upturbed & perset than you can imagine. I fear 'Eton's record' will certainly '*not* be &c' (vide 'An Ode') & that we may expect to see a capid deradence of England's screatest ghool. (2 February 1893; Swinburne 2004b 3.50–1)

Ironically reversing the logic of Swinburne's celebratory ode to Eton, Leith suggests that the 'disuse' of birching as a traditional mode of punishment would erase 'Eton's record' and lead to the decline of England's greatest school. According to a more perverse logic (as Swinburne went on to write in 'Eton: Another Ode', dedicated 'To M.'), continued use of birching would be a better example of Eton reform: a form of metrical discipline that could leave a mark of distinction on the school, and its pupils.

SWISH! OH!

In 'The Flogging-Block' we can see how Swinburne self-consciously plays out, and plays on, different disciplinary regimes in mid-Victorian England. Debates about the uses of metrical education at Eton were closely linked to the discourses documented by Gibson in *The English Vice*, about the use and abuse of corporal punishment in sexual flagellation and juvenile flogging in schools. But in his recent book *In Praise of the Whip*, Niklaus Largier calls into question 'the commonplace that the proverbial predilection of the English for flagellation can be explained by the educational methods of English schools or by Victorian sexual morality', and he argues that 'this cannot be the sole form of explanation, since it misappropriates the genuine productive moment in the history of flagellation' which according to Largier appears as 'the analogue of poetic writing' (Largier 2007, 362). In pursuing a new history of voluntary flagellation, Largier argues that Swinburne's flagellant verse should be read not as 'pathology' but as a 'poetological' reflection:

> Swinburne's rhetorical strategy is more complicated than might be supposed from a first glance at the apparently simple texts, for it always emphasizes the moment of staging. What is described, what is narrated, is not merely punishment with the whip, not merely the sight of the rod that strikes the naked buttocks, but the staging of this action as a ritual on the 'flogging block' in which the same arousal that lies at the basis of poetic creation takes shape and becomes visible. (Largier 2007, 354)

Indeed, Swinburne's rhetorical strategy is more complex than it may first appear. But to go beyond 'a first glance at the apparently simple texts', we may need not to read deeper into the text of 'The Flogging-Block' but rather to look more closely at the surface of the manuscript, as a further poetological reflection on the process by which Swinburne's 'poetic creation takes shape and becomes visible.'

The eclogues in 'The Flogging-Block' are presented as dramatic scripts, the first of which is entitled 'Algernon's Flogging' (Figure 5.6). The words are more difficult to decipher here, as Swinburne disliked writing by hand; indeed, on the copying of passages meted out as punishment at Eton, Swinburne wrote: 'Birching is better than the cursed system of impositions – "poenas" as the Eton phrase is – manlier and wholesomer. The other makes all writing hateful and tedious and gives hours of discomfort instead of minutes of torture' (13 February 1868; Swinburne 1959–62, 1.291). To set the imaginary stage for writing this eclogue, Swinburne copied out directions at the top of the page: the 'scene' is 'the public flogging room' and the cast of characters includes a Schoolmaster, Algernon, a chorus of schoolboys, and The Rod. At the start of the

5.6 Page 1, 'Algernon's Flogging' (Eclogue I from 'The Flogging-Block')

flogging ritual, the Master sternly commands one of the boys to 'take Algernon's breeches down' and announces that he will 'give Master Algy a thorough good flogging':

> A thorough good flogging shall Algernon get,
> His posteriors have never been whipped enough yet,
> So in sight of his equals in age & superiors
> I'll do justice on Algernon's naked posteriors.

The flogging that follows turns out to be poetic justice, with the school-master striking just the right musical response out of the body of Algernon. Here Swinburne's versification turns Algernon's flogging into a perfectly metrical performance:

> O, don't hit so hard, sir! I don't sir – I won't
> O, sir, the birch hurts me so awfully – don't!
> O please, sir, don't always hit just the same part!
> O, sir, you don't know how you're making me smart!

In these lines, the letter o that was struck out of Alg – rn – n in the Prologue reappears in the repetition of O in response to each lash, making Algernon increasingly visible and legible as a body disciplined by metre.

The dramatisation of metrical discipline in this manuscript is even more graphic several pages later, where Algernon is scripted to say 'Oh!' every time the Rod says 'Swish!' (Figure 5.7). The emphasis on the very word 'Swish!' recalls a passage in Swinburne's novel *A Year's Letters* in which a flogging episode is narrated by one schoolboy to another:

Reginald recited this pleasing episode with a dreadful unction. No descrip-tion can express the full fleshy sound of certain words in his mouth; he talked of cuts with quite a lickerish accent, and gave the word swish with a twang in which the hissing sound of a falling birch, or the clear hard ringing noise of a tough stroke on bare flesh, became sharply audible. (Swinburne 1974, 24)[10]

But in moving from a description in prose to this performance in verse, the manuscript of 'The Flogging-Block' makes the words more visible than audible, as we see how Algernon's rhythmic flogging materialises graphically as an effect of metrical writing. Here the flogging is measured out like two hexameter lines that are diagonally placed across the page: in the first diagonal line, the Rod begins with 'Swish' and Algernon follows with 'Oh' (repeated six times), while the second diagonal line marks a reversal, as Algernon begins with 'Oh!' and the Rod follows with 'Swish'. Having memorised the metre, Algernon now anticipates the lash even before it strikes, as if its rhythm has already been incorporated into his body.

Through the example of Algernon, the chorus of schoolboys watching the scene also learns to read his rhythmic lesson as a metrical pattern: 'Oh, isn't his bottom a pattern when stripped?' one observes with relish, while another remarks: 'You can see the rod's marks all down Algernon's back.' And indeed, the marking of his bottom is graphically presented in the

5.7 Page 8, 'Algernon's Flogging' (Eclogue I from 'The Flogging-Block')

manuscript, at the very end of the eclogue (Figure 5.8). After reading in the stage directions that 'the Master gives Algernon's bottom a final cut', we see an emphatically final 'SWISH!' that leaves Algernon 'writhing with pain'. This writhing (and this writing) is made visible in 'Algernon's Flogging', not only in the lines left by the birch on his bottom but in three lines at the bottom of the page, below the very word 'bottom':

Master. Now get up, sir! & look at the clock
And remember the time – & the birch – & the block.
You ought to remember them.
George.   Some have forgot 'em
But Algernon won't: only look at his bottom!

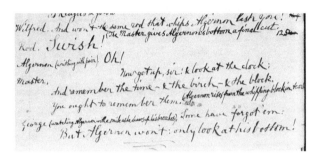

5.8 Bottom of page 12, 'Algernon's Flogging' (Eclogue I from
'The Flogging-Block')

These lines are measured out in a visual pattern, figuratively marked in
red blood on the skin and literally marked in black ink on the page, to
make Algernon into a body disciplined by metre. By counting the stroke
of the birch on the block, like the mechanical ticking of time on the clock,
Algernon's flogging is not an internalisation of rhythm into the body but
an externalisation of metre written on the body, in long and short lines
that look like an abstraction of classical verse. By locating this scene in an
imaginary theatre with other schoolboys watching, 'The Flogging-Block'
allows 'Algernon's Flogging' to be read as an exemplary performance of
the metrical discipline associated with Eton.

The graphic inscription of Algernon's bottom as the primary site (or
primal scene) for metrical instruction is a dramatic reversal of Victorian
ideas about poetry learned 'by heart'. In *Victorian Poetry and the Culture of
the Heart*, for example, Kirstie Blair argues that new theories of rhythm
were emerging in mid-Victorian England, at a time when metaphors of
the heart were increasingly literalised and embodied in literary and
medical discourses: 'as physiologists considered the pulse in relation to
measure, so both poets and poetic theorists in this period can be seen
moving toward a "physiological" view of poetic metre, as opposed to
classical scansion which earlier writers had attempted to impose upon
English' (Blair 2006b, 75). Extending this argument into a reading of
Victorian physiological poetics, Jason Rudy explores in *Electric Meters* how
pulsing rhythms were performed by Spasmodic poets such as Sydney
Dobell, who imagined all rhythmic experience originating in 'the systole
and diastole' of the body (Rudy 2009, 86). Sydney Dobell's *Balder* is

perhaps most famous for its attempt to embody this idea of rhythm in language:

Ah! ah! ah!

Ah! ah! ah! ah! ah! ah! ah! ah! ah! ah!

(Dobell 1875, 260)[11]

Of course the regulation of rhythm by metre in this line of verse already suggests a metrical mediation that produces the figure of rhythm, according to a logic made more explicit in 'Algernon's Flogging', in the reiteration of 'Swish! Oh!' on the page. 'The Flogging-Block' demonstrates an alternative to the expressive reading of rhythm that physiological poetics tried to locate inside the body: we can read Swinburne's manuscript as a parodic inversion of the Spasmodic impulse, not felt 'in' the heart but imposed and exposed 'on' the bottom.

Recent work in historical prosody has begun to analyse and historicise the proliferation of nineteenth-century theories of rhythm and metre, as shifting terms in a complex (and often reversible) interplay between the internalisation and externalisation of poetic form, between rhythmic embodiment of rhythm and metrical abstraction, between the naturalisation and mechanisation of metre, between individual incorporation and the abstract embodiment of metrical culture.[12] While situating 'The Flogging-Block' within these Victorian discourses about metre, my reading 'on' the manuscript also proposes an approach to historical prosody that reflects (as Swinburne did) on the materialisation of metre on the page: here, in the traces of his handwriting, we see Swinburne's subversion, or perversion, of Victorian metrical culture.

Although Swinburne did not articulate a comprehensive theory of metre, Yisrael Levin points out that 'the metrical proficiency of his poems, as well as some of his privately offered remarks on them, shows a poet very much thinking *as prosodist*' (Levin 2011, 179). Proposing (suggestively) that Swinburne was 'a closet prosodist', Levin cites a letter written by Swinburne to a classicist well-versed in classical prosody (11 October 1891); Swinburne claimed that his poetry was 'intended – as far as I remember – "to be set out" if necessary – "in rigid metrical schemes"', even while disclaiming knowledge about 'the technical definition of metrical feet (e.g. I never could remember – if indeed I ever knew – about Pæons or Pyrrhics)' (Swinburne 2004b, 3.30). But notwithstanding Swinburne's rather disingenuous disclaimer that 'Coleridge's "Lesson for a Boy" contains all I ever mastered on the subject', 'The Flogging-Block' is a masterful performance of his own lesson for a boy, or many boys, in rigid metrical schemes.[13] This exercise (like Swinburne's imaginative response to the photograph sent to him, of the flogging block at Eton) was a way of doing poetic justice 'to *all sides* of the question', reversing the sentimental prosody of the beating heart into a perverse prosody for beating the bottom, and dramatising 'dozens of different fellows diversely suffering' in the infinite variations of his verse.

To make the metrical instruction of one boy stand in for many, Algernon's name is repeated as a synonym for flogging throughout 'The Flogging-Block', as we learn in 'Charlie's Flogging' (Figure 5.9):

> Flagellation and Algernon (Swish!) must appear
> Synonymous terms to the younger boys here:
> When they hear but the word flagellation, I guess,
> That word must remind them of Algernon. Yes,
> And when Algernon's name is pronounced, the sensation
> It evokes must recall a good sound flagellation;
> Or rather, considering that youth's daily rations,
> Of birch, a good many good sound flagellations.

Making Algernon 'synonymous' with flagellation, Swinburne turns metrical discipline into the very definition of poetry: with every boy who is beaten, another poem is being written. The seemingly endless production of poems through the reiteration of 'Swish!' (written again, and

5.9 Detail from 'Charlie's Flogging' (Eclogue V from 'The Flogging-Block')

again and again in the pages of his manuscript) gives us another perspective on T. S. Eliot's often-quoted essay, 'Swinburne as Poet': 'It is, in fact, the word that gives him the thrill, not the object. When you take to pieces any verse of Swinburne, you find that the object was not there – only the word' (Eliot 1920a, 148). Or perhaps not even the word is there, only the thrill of (Swish!) in parentheses: an empty mark of metre, enumerating youth's daily rations of metrical discipline so that we may learn to read the sound of a 'good many good sound flagellations', as an effect of metre. If Swinburne was a 'closet prosodist' who transformed Victorian ideas about metre through his own poetic practice, his hyperbolic performance of metrical discipline in 'The Flogging-Block' brings him out of the closet: 'Only look at his bottom!'

NOTES

1 Eton's tribute to Swinburne is published in *The Eton College Chronicle* 1270 (13 May 1909): 471–2. Swinburne's 'Eton: An Ode for the Four Hundred and Fiftieth Anniversary of the Foundation of The College' first appeared in a catalogue of 'Portraits, Views, and other Objects of Interest Connected with the History of Eton' (1891) and was printed in *The Athenæum* (30 May 1891). Correspondence with Eton about Swinburne's ode is included in Swinburne 2004b, 3.24.

2 The manuscript for 'Eton: Another Ode' is at the British Library (Ashley MS 5271) and quoted in Lafourcade (Lafourcade 1932, 47). As noted by Burnett 1969 and Meyers (in Swinburne 2004b, 3.51), this unpublished ode seems to have been dedicated to Mary Gordon Leith.

3 'The Flogging-Block' is held at the British Library (Ashley MS 2526) and has not been published. I am grateful to the British Library for permission to quote and reproduce passages from this manuscript. Additional poems related to 'The Flogging-Block' are in the collection at Worcester College Library, Oxford: 'a large boxful of more than forty sheets' that include 'completed poems and dialogues which describe with obsessive repetitiveness the beating of schoolboys', as well as a draft of 'Eton: Another Ode' (Rooksby 1990, 275). Other flagellant verse by Swinburne was published anonymously in *The Whippingham Papers* and in *The Pearl*, signed 'Etoniensis' (see Rooksby 1997, 34).

4 Following on Edmund Gosse's essay 'Swinburne's Agitation' (Swinburne 1959–62, 6.233–48), scholarly and popular speculations about the 'perverse' side of Swinburne include Bragman 1934, Hughes 1952, Rosenberg 1967, Baird 1971, Henderson 1974, Ober 1979, Dellamora 1990, Barrett 1993, Alexander 1996, Morgan 1996, Vincent 1997, Lane 1999, Maxwell 2003, Largier 2007, Louis 2009a, Lutz 2011.

5 On Swinburne's flogging muse as 'Scholastic Dame' associated with the figure
  of Sappho, see Prins 1999, 152–5. My current argument about metrical disci-
  pline at Eton is a further elaboration of that discussion.

6 In 'Suffering in Style', a paper presented at the Swinburne Centenary
  Conference in 2009 and forthcoming in his book *Exquisite Pain*, Ellis Hanson
  suggested that the capital letter B seemed 'especially protuberant and
  spankable' in the grammatical reversal of Swinburne's 'But' in the middle of a
  stanza. On the spankability of the butt in relation to queer style, see also 'A
  Poem Is Being Written' in Sedgwick 1993.

7 After leaving Eton under the shadow of pedagogical pederasty, Johnson
  renamed himself Cory (the Greek name for 'young boy'). In a letter to
  Swinburne (late November 1872), Simeon Solomon commented on the
  scandal: 'have you heard that Johnson has left and changed his name to Corry
  [*sic*], it is creating a sensation at Eton' (Swinburne 1959–62, 2.202). On Johnson
  as a teacher see Mackenzie 1950; Carter 1959; and Costigan 1972.

8 Johnson's poems were published anonymously at his own expense in *Ionica*
  (1858) and *Ionica II* (1877), and later collected under the name of William
  Johnson Cory (1891). During his years at Eton, Johnson produced books
  designed for exercises in classical metres, including *Lucretilis: An Introduction to
  the Art of Writing Latin Lyric Verses* (1871) and *Iophon: An Introduction to the Art
  of Writing Greek Iambic Verses* (1873). Johnson also wrote 'The Eton Boating
  Song', set to music by Algernon Drummon, and sung by generations of
  Etonians.

9 On Swinburne's relation to his cousin Mary Gordon Leith, see Fuller 1968;
  Wilson 1969; Birchfield 1980; Swinburne 2004b, 3.48; Maxwell 2009; and
  Maxwell 2010a, 128–31.

10 Composed between 1862 and 1863, *A Year's Letters* was published in 1877 under
   the pseudonym 'Mrs. Horace Manners', and reissued in 1905 as *Love's Cross-
   Currents* (with some passages excised) under the name of Swinburne. Sypher's
   1974 edition is based on the original manuscript.

11 On the Spasmodics, see also LaPorte and Rudy (2004) and Cronin, who quotes
   'this remarkable passage from *Balder*' to demonstrate how 'Spasmodic poetry
   aspires to a single pitch of stylistic intensity from which, inevitably, it often
   tumbles into bathos' (Cronin 2002, 299).

12 On historical prosody, see Prins 2000 and 2005, and more recently Martin and
   Levin 2011; Hall 2011a; Hall 2011b; Martin 2012.

13 In his letter to the classicist F. H. Myers, Swinburne refers to Coleridge's poem,
   'Metrical Feet: Lessons for a Boy', and he goes on to mark the metrical feet of
   his own verse, 'with all the weight or stress thrown upon the last syllable'
   (Swinburne 2004b, 3.30–1).

6

WHAT GOES AROUND: SWINBURNE'S
A CENTURY OF ROUNDELS

Herbert F. Tucker

This chapter begins, somewhat like the form of Swinburne's devising that is its subject, at the end, which is to say at the 'Envoi' concluding *A Century of Roundels* (1883) on its last and hundredth page:

> Fly, white butterflies, out to sea,
> Frail pale wings for the winds to try,
> Small white wings that we scarce can see
> 　　Fly.
>
> Here and there may a chance-caught eye
> Note in a score of you twain or three
> Brighter or darker of tinge or dye.
>
> Some fly light as a laugh of glee,
> Some fly soft as a low long sigh:
> All to the haven where each would be
> 　　Fly.
>
> 　　　　　　　　　　　(Swinburne 1904, 5.193)

We see from this example how a roundel is wrought: in the structural terms that distinguish this formal genre, it is a double whorl displaying geometric increase.[1] A first circuit returns after three lines to the verbal point of origin – here the single word 'Fly', though a phrase of two to six words is more usual in Swinburne's *Century*; then a second circuit opens, twice as long, and runs its extended lap back to the same verbal starting line. A glance at the rhyme scheme shows, further, how within the nine long lines an elementary *aba* pattern – or, as little Hans might say, *Da–Fort–Da* (Freud 1961, 8–9) – is resumed at wider gauge by the whole poem: *aba bab aba*, run the lines, recapitulating across the ensemble of three stanzas, at a higher order of magnitude, the same *aba* structure that internally constitutes each one of them. Meanwhile, as this process takes its course, in the hemistich lines 4 and 11 the phrasal origin punctually returns to impose a full stop and clinch the *b* rhyme it quietly initiated back at the start of line 1.

If this last circumstance quickens an ear for ad-hoc internal rhyming, it should. Within the first stanza alone of roundel 100 we find, with some allowance for variation in the poetic licence, 'Fly' and 'butterflies', 'Frail' and 'pale', 'wings' and 'winds', and 'white' with itself two lines later, again in second syllabic position. This exact repetition also highlights the oddity of *rime riche* linking 'sea' to its homonym 'see' as end-rhymes for lines 1 and 3.[2] The mix of sameness with difference that makes a rhyme rhyme is also at play – or at least something very like it is – in the rhythm of this roundel, whose tetrameter one hesitates to specify as either iambic or anapaestic because Swinburne so freely plays duple, triple and spondaic rhythms across the four-foot base. The nine scannable lines yield five distinct scansions, and yet the very diversity among these scansions exhibits pattern at a higher level. Lines 1–3 (call them the 'A' stanza) share an identical prosody (spondee–trochee–iamb–iamb), which in the 'B' stanza lines 5–7 replace with hoppier rhythms but which then returns – just where the rhyme scheme would suggest we look for it – in line 8 as the original *aba* rhyme of the 'A' stanza comes back: 'Some fly light as a laugh of glee'. Line 9 then repeats line 8's syntax, but not its rhythm, not quite, given the final spondee: 'Some fly soft as a low long sigh'. And line 10 then resumes the alternative rhythm (trochee–iamb–anapaest–iamb) that had prevailed in stanza B with lines 6 and 7. This leaves us – always presuming the gentle reader's patience in such matters of detail – one rhythmical singleton, namely line 5. Such singularity always merits a second look in things so small, to see what else there may be special about the nearly stagey pause which that spondee effects at the enjambed threshold of line 6: 'Here and there may a chance-caught eye …' What may a chance-caught eye chance to do? '… Note in a score of you twain or three', that's what: what the chance-caught eye may catch is, in other words, lepidopteral microvariations of the kind that by now it may be conceded are, *mutatis mutandis*, the very life of a roundel well wrought. After all, eyes 'note', but so do ears, especially when nudged as here to do their noting 'in a score', which is to say, by a surely licit Swinburnian pun, in a text marked for acoustic performance.

The reader's indulgence of just a few more closely analytic matters should make the more general reflections shortly to follow feel by contrast like large-motor activity, and should make Swinburne's *Century of Roundels* taken as a whole seem, as with acquaintance they do become, positively roomy. One matter has to do with our seed term or *logos spermatikos*, the upper-cased monosyllable 'Fly'. Each of its three occurrences is a verb: enlisting it as a noun would, I suspect, have struck Swinburne as too cheap a way to purchase the variety he preferred achieving by other means; for at each occurrence the verb 'Fly' appears in a different mood, or mode. Line 1 issues the imperative, as in a conventional envoi it should: 'Go, litel bok', 'Go, dumb-born book', and so forth.[3] 'Fly' in line 4 is a fancier thing, a doubly subordinated infinitive that hangs from the main infinitive 'see' that hangs in turn from the main verb 'can'. Thus the flight of the butterfly flutters at a double remove from power: it's a verb, all right, but one that, as the line above it points out, we scarce can see as such.[4] At last, in line 11, our refrain verb comes back for its curtain call in a role that lines 9 and 10 have rehearsed in lower-case cameo: all Swinburne's footwork comes down to the blunt aplomb of a main verb and the simplicity of the declarative mood. The flashy exhortation of apostrophic command (line 1) and the intricacies of *trompe-l'oeil* perceptual relativity (line 5) give final word to what was always this poet's place of greatest strength: the statement of the case, the unconstrained concession that things are the way they are and not otherwise.

Like so many figures in Swinburne's poetry, the butterflies are questers, souls at risk but not at a loss. Traditional emblems in art and literature for the metamorphic psyche at the threshold of life and death, all are animated by a motive desire, all bound by a destiny to seek 'the haven where each would be'. Where that haven may lie the roundel never gets around to saying. It prefers leaving us to frame some answer – an answer that homes in, I suspect, on a point where birth intersects mortality.[5] For what the roundel doesn't say, *A Century of Roundels* does; the concluding image of flight to a 'haven' is an end that recapitulates a distant textual beginning, sending us back to the roundel entitled 'In Harbour' that appears on page 1. Call that page square 1 and the printed work as such becomes freshly prominent, its gatherings and openings bibliographical figures for the overdetermined hazards of the venture to which a poet commits wingèd words on frail paper for the winds to try. Go, litel bok; fly, white butterflies; scatter, ye leaves, my words among mankind; and take, in the world, the chances your rhyme and rhythm have been in faithful training for.

One thing to love about Swinburne's little book is the modest thrift
whereby it contrives to make page numbers do double duty as poem
numbers, without incurring the Roman-numerical pretension of *In
Memoriam* (1850) or *Sonnets from the Portuguese* (1850) or forfeiting the
pleasure that a collector might take in grouping roundel sequences into
suites like 'A Baby's Death' (36–42), 'In Guernsey' (92–9), or – my favourite
– 'Recollections' (5–7; re-collection being just what the circuitous form of
the roundel, and *a fortiori* an anthology of roundels, does). In another of
these suites, a trio entitled 'A Ninth Birthday' (56–8) sprout from the same
three-word seed-phrase, 'Three times thrice', which phrase of course
turns up – as the formal arithmetic dictates – nine times, or three times
thrice.[6] Not exactly a roundel of roundels; but the ghost of a fractal
analogy is there to tickle the mind. Or consider, again, how the whole
sequence falls macrostructurally into a threefold roundel ratio when
pages 34 and 67 – at four and eight o'clock, as it were, trisecting the book's
modular dial – each display a miniature *ars poetica*.

PLUS INTRA
Soul within sense, immeasurable, obscure,
Insepulchred and deathless, through the dense
Deep elements may scarce be felt as pure
        Soul within sense.

From depth and height by measurers left immense,
Through sound and shape and colour, comes the unsure
Vague utterance, fitful with supreme suspense.

All that may pass, and all that must endure,
Song speaks not, painting shews not: more intense
And keen than these, art wakes with music's lure
        Soul within sense.
                                        (Swinburne 1904, 5.140)

A SINGING LESSON
Far-fetched and dear-bought, as the proverb rehearses,
Is good, or was held so, for ladies: but nought
In a song can be good if the turn of the verse is
        Far-fetched and dear-bought.

As the turn of a wave should it sound, and the thought
Ring smooth, and as light as the spray that disperses
Be the gleam of the words for the garb thereof wrought.

Let the soul in it shine through the sound as it pierces
Men's hearts with possession of music unsought;
For the bounties of song are no jealous god's mercies,
    Far-fetched and dear-bought.

(Swinburne 1904, 5.165)

'Plus Intra' and 'A Singing Lesson' alike celebrate the outstripping of mere meaning by music, alias prosody, alias numbers. 'Art wakes with music's lure / Soul within sense', and verse turns on 'sound as it pierces / Men's hearts with possession of music unsought'. The 'soul' that is in poetry must 'shine through the sound', and 'the thought / Ring smooth', where the primarily auditory image of ringing sound shapes up spatially in the bullseye pattern of concentred, sequentially iterative form that Swinburne's coinage the roundel epitomises. A centripetal involute, the form curls into itself, by an ever-inward (*plus intra*) economy that peculiarly justifies roundel 34's sublime rhetoric of the 'immeasurable' character of what abides 'within'.[7] Hence the paradoxical attribution of dimensions 'by measurers left immense'. Immensity as such is an effect of the baulked endeavour to measure it; the exquisite (like its better known counterpart the enormous) may compass sublimity only when mensuration has lost its way in the infinitesimal (as in its counterpart the infinite).[8] And it is likewise the presence of metrics that makes the arresting central stanza of roundel 67 count: at the head of line 6 the poem's first clear spondee, and at the head of line 7 its first elided iamb, let the turns of anapaestic verse ring changes well worthy 'the turn of a wave'.

'In my beginning is my end'; 'In my end is my beginning'; 'And the end of all our exploring / Will be to arrive where we started / And know the place for the first time.'[9] Thus *Four Quartets*: a title deriving in form, perhaps, from *A Century of Roundels*? That the modernist poet who wrote the lines just quoted from 'East Coker' and 'Little Gidding' did so only after he had first said a lot of unhandsome things about Swinburne is no surprise.[10] Nor is it surprising that Swinburne held in supreme regard the poetry of the Romantic who had written that 'the common end of all *narrative*, nay, of *all*, Poems is to convert a *series* into a *Whole*: to make those events, which in real or imagined History move on in a *strait* Line, assume to our Understandings a *circular* motion – the snake with it's Tail in it's Mouth' (Coleridge 1959, 545). Three major poet-critics – Coleridge, Swinburne, Eliot – all apprehended the workings of imaginative form as metamorphoses of the circle.[11] Bent on curbing the tangent and centrifugal linearity of meaning to the bit of form, they all wreathed iron pokers into true-love knots, and not for the form's sake alone but for the sake of the inwards, *plus-intra* meaning that a rounded form bore about the recurrencies of life, the recursiveness of mental grasp, matter's vast and intimate recycling, the renewal of the spirit.

To this commodious vicus of recirculation none of the three poets ministered as assiduously as Swinburne, and he never with less collaterally distracting razzle-dazzle than in *A Century of Roundels*. Here for once the whole algebra of Swinburne's vision is patently formulated: straight, no chaser, by which of course I mean roundly delivered as the story its form tells. That story plays out the dialectic of sameness with difference whose pet name during the nineteenth century was *change*. For the poetic imagination, the function of this dialectic is to surprise the mind into fresh apprehension of what was thought known already, its ambition less novelty than renewal of acquaintance, its goal a reconnoitring of its origin. 'Though sight be changed for memory', as roundel 92 puts it, such are the returns of Romanticism that memory is 'changed by love to sight' again (Swinburne 1904, 5.188). Such has been modern poetry's programme for over two centuries now, differently canted and stressed by political, psychological, socio-economic, and other designs: a restorative programme for which the roundel's mandate of formal return virtually spells out the code of the operating system. All poems open, run, and close; begin, develop, and conclude; and it is probably fair to say that within the Romantic tradition the default pattern contrives that the third movement shall bend or nod back towards the first. Swinburne's roundel is so short – shorter by half than 'the Italian type of sonnet' to which he compared it, shorter by one-fourth even than the rondeau he stripped it down from – that merely to execute this pattern seems all that can be fairly expected of it (22 June 1883; Swinburne 1959–62, 5.27). Where that is all you expect, that may be all you get: witness the late Thomas Disch's unhappy judgement that, where Swinburne applies the form 'across the entire discursive spectrum of the lyric ... in the echo chamber of his roundels he manages to say virtually nothing at all' (Disch 2002, 281). Swinburne's rangier verses have been so routinely assailed on this score, and for so long, that it may be worth pausing over the indictment when it is pronounced, as here, on the least of his forms. Like others in the chorus of detractors, Disch went looking for Swinburne's soul of sense in all the wrong places. Because he wanted meanings that were ingredient in the poet's themes, all he got out of *A Century of Roundels* was forms.

Egregious formal flagrancy, which is notoriously the dragon in the gate of

Swinburne's oeuvre, draws into ardent focus what more generally seems *the* problem stymieing modern readers who just can't get into poetry – any poetry, though admittedly Swinburne's sets the bar higher than most – no matter how hard they try. More often than not, in my teaching experience at least, the problem is that they are trying too hard, jiggering away at the lock of conceptual meaning while, just a shift of perspective away, the doors of perception stand open wide. The annoyance poetry causes such minds may be epitomised in the pointless loop of the roundel form, which, going nowhere by design, manages to say, even to Disch (a poet himself, who therefore should have known better), 'virtually nothing at all'. If we can refocus expectation so as to read our way not *past* form but *through* it, to grasp meaning as ingredient in verse structure rather than in spite or in lieu of it, we may attune reading more faithfully to the principled mannerism that at once declares and performs itself in phrasal refrains like 'The wind's way' in roundel 3, 'A little way' in roundel 55 or, with minimalist aplomb, 'How' in roundel 19 (Swinburne 1904, 5.117, 155, 128). In poetry *the way* is the truth and the life. *How* is indeed the question – to which right answers entail an embarrassment of thematic riches, all we know on earth and all we need to know. Working out answers to the riddle of a roundel's form lets us, moreover, renew acquaintance with modalities of literary experience that lie hidden in plain sight within some of the oldest writing we know. Witness the bravura explications offered in Mary Douglas' book, *Thinking in Circles* (2007), of the ring composition that alike structures Genesis and Numbers, the *Iliad* and *Tristram Shandy*, and that, we might here add, emerged with some frequency in the nineteenth century as a sort of formally commemorative conscience or book-balancing flywheel within the era's headlong linear- and serial-mindedness.[12] The 'internal organisation of parallel rungs, preferably alternating in character, the two series organised inversely', for which the anthropologist Douglas gives us new literary eyes, is also a pattern for which the roundel provides a template in miniature.[13]

What Disch received within the roundel's delicate quintessence of 'internal organisation' as 'echoes' – passive, mindless or mechanical mirrors of resonance – I propose we listen for instead as *reverberations*, a word whose cognates show up in roundels 7 and 20 (Swinburne 1904, 5.120 and 129), or in other words as performed rediscoveries of the unex-pected, harboured within the insistence of the same. That is what *change* means in Swinburne's book, as we may see from the roundel he titled 'Change' and numbered 35:

But now life's face beholden
Seemed bright as heaven's bare brow
With hope of gifts withholden
But now.

From time's full-flowering bough
Each bud spake bloom to embolden
Love's heart, and seal his vow.

Joy's eyes grew deep with olden
Dreams, born he wist not how;
Thought's meanest garb was golden;
But now!

(Swinburne 1904, 5.141)

Consider here the sequence of changes wrung on the seminal phrase. Like the verb 'Fly' in Swinburne's 'Envoi', 'But now' comes back with a difference at each entrance. First it means 'Just a minute ago', and then in line 4 'Just for the time being' (the hoped-for gifts are withheld only for now, and not for long). The difference in idiom registers a subtle advance in time from recent memory to expectant presence; this forward momentum then, with the final occurrence of the phrase, overflows into future shock: 'But now!' has at last the force of 'Now what?' There is no knowing whether what has transpired during this phrasally calibrated time lapse is a disappointment or the transmutation of once golden hope into absolutely platinum bliss. In either case an unanticipated change has taken place, one that, against the pastel and umber palette that prevails across Swinburne's 1883 book, leaps into stark relief. Yet the semantic shift within 'But now' that has recorded this bit of lyrical melodrama says something else too that matters. It says the sudden change was to have been expected, its anticipation having been ingredient from the verbal outset, hidden all along in plain sight – a sight made plain by the degrees of poetic discourse, foresight becoming hindsight for those with eyes to read, which are eyes that habituation to form tends to plant in the back of the head.

That is what I mean by these poems' *reverberation*: a harboured difference maturing within the iteration of the same. To what the autopoetic roundel 63 entitled 'The Roundel' hauntingly calls 'the ear of thought' a trebled phrase resounds, re-sounds, or, to quote an uncannily telephonic phrase from roundel 27, 'rings back, sonorous with regret' (Swinburne 1904, 5.161, 134). *Plus ça change, plus c'est la même chose*; and vice versa too, it seems: the more a phrase is dwelt on in Swinburne's murmurous rounding runes, the more it changes into a fuller version of itself. Which is why the punster's clever paltering in a double sense – although confessedly it draws my kind as a flame does moths – in fact plays a comparatively small role in *A Century of Roundels.* In Swinburne's hands the roundel is not just another type of ambiguity. It doesn't wobble both or several ways; it dithers not, neither does it flinch. Instead, it unrolls its curriculum between a beginning and an end that coincide but are not therefore identical. Early and late instances of the seed-phrase are not equivalent options: the latter's advantage is precisely the seasoning which the rest of the poem has effected. As the poem runs its course, the phrase-reproducing fruit that it bears ripens away from witticism and towards wisdom. What the phrase names turns in the mind, with increase, more and more into what it always was to begin with.

This is why, for all its topical variegation, Swinburne's book tends to zero in on lyric themes emphasising recognition, realisation, second guesses, and second sight. Epitaphically terse elegies for dead friends, artists, and (rather too dotingly) babies fix each in memory through the form's inherently ritual powers of recall (Swinburne 1904, 5.126–9, 132–4; 5.135–6, 185; 5.142–5, 150). Sequences on recollected moods and revisited landscapes, the two often figuring one another, practise elegy in another key, usually drawing on a dialectic of constancy and change to which we have already sampled the form's hospitality. Anniversary poems, poems about those kissing cousins translation and *ekphrasis*, and one especially apt sequence involving the déjà-vu uncanny likewise thematise the roundel movement of return (Swinburne 1904, 5.156–7, 174–8, 168–9). It's not so clear to me as it was to Harold Nicolson once upon a time that 'the mood of gentle remorse' uniquely awakens the only 'real interest' attaching to a volume that is otherwise 'merely of prosodic interest' (Nicolson 1926, 171 and 19). Talking about *merely prosodic* interest, where Swinburne is concerned, is like talking about *merely dramatic* interest in Shakespeare; but let that pass. Better turn Nicolson's order of explanation around and let form be the magnet to content. Surely the affective structure of remorse may especially be evoked by a prosodic structure that is so bent on revisiting the scene of its verbal first act. Furthermore, such a structure virtually prompts the redoubling of emotional honesty, the ethical deepening of candour at a point where illusions are all one has left to lose, and Had-I-but-known ('"Had I Wist,"' roundel 4; 1904, 118) yields place to And-I-did-know.

Witness this slow conversion of pathos to ethos within roundel 32, identified by its title as a prelude to Wagner's *Tristan und Isolde*, in a generous tribute that falls within a year of Swinburne's own magnum opus on the same material:

> Fate, out of the deep sea's gloom,
> When a man's heart's pride grows great,
> And nought seems now to foredoom
>   Fate,
>
> Fate, laden with fears in wait,
> Draws close through the clouds that loom,
> Till the soul see, all too late,
>
> More dark than a dead world's tomb,
> More high than the sheer dawn's gate,
> More deep than the wide sea's womb,
>   Fate.
>
>   (Swinburne 1883, 32)[14]

Not much wriggle room for equivocation there. Eat your heart out, disambiguators in the line of Empson. Between the fathomless depths of 'the deep sea's gloom' in line 1 and of 'the wide sea's womb' in line 10, what space for the swift mind dividing this way and that in thought? So little does Fate swerve that the poetic problem may be – as if to anticipate Disch and Nicolson – finding anything to say about it at all. Still, here as in his own *Tristram* and indeed across his oeuvre, Swinburne mobilises fate imaginatively by rehearsing the changes that its very immensity prompts within the human endeavour to come to terms with it. 'Fate' in roundel 32 is notional at first, an idea entertained by the mind when young but in truth inaccessible to authentic existential foresight. A name rumoured by others, an abstraction received on authority that in juvenile experience 'nought seems' to verify, 'Fate' to the proud early mind is just, as we say, a word. Thus the poem's first, lesser circuit between one 'Fate' in line 1 and another in line 4. The second, major circuit then makes good on the word through a steady aggravation of syntax, whereby 'Fate' is felt as not an idea but an eventual accumulating force, legible only in hindsight, 'too late' and, I should judge from the last three images, too overwhelming for the soul even to 'see' at all. What the soul can finally know, if only once the last line clinches the syntax the first has opened, is that 'Fate' is both subject and object of its one inexorable sentence of doom, within which the epiphenomena of human consciousness occupy merely subordinate clauses.

This roundel's one real anomaly is the formally non-mandatory reiteration of 'Fate' at the start of line 5, a line that reverberates, into the bargain, the word's every phoneme a second time: 'Fate, laden with fears in wait'. This fourth, gratuitous sowing of the seed-word feels almost like cheating. Perhaps the poet doth insist too much? Perhaps he doth, compassionately solicitous to tip his hand and mitigate with an extra hint the catastrophe his syntax holds in store. The anomaly can at least underscore for us here one peculiar side-effect of the roundel's verbal repetition: the atrophy, across much of the book, of pronouns. In ordinary prose usage at least one of the instances of 'Fate' in this poem surely would have been an 'it' – an observation applicable also to several other roundels that use a noun or noun phrase as the repetend. The rules of Swinburne's invented form of course forbid such pronominal substitution; but the question then becomes why the invention of a form enforcing that prohibition should have appealed to him. The answer probably involves his scepticism about substitution as such, along with its civilised cousins the delegation of political power, the outsourcing of imagination to religious fetishism, and the sublimation of erotic desire.[15] In this as in many other habits of his writing, Swinburne was uncommonly reluctant to take for granted the premise that our usage of pronouns has to take for granted, which is a received consensus about what words name. This poet wanted words to earn their meanings on the job, within the force field of quickening suggestion and due constraint set up by the verbal vicinity they worked in; and the slightly compulsive machinery of the roundel had them do so in an unusually controlled environment, along the learning curve of defamiliarisation and reacquaintance that a well wrought loop of eleven lines might execute.

NOTES

1 Rikky Rooksby aptly likens the form to a seashell, both for its circular enlargement and for certain corollary 'effects of emptiness' (Rooksby 1985, 256).

2 The same trick reappears in roundel 11 (1904, 5.123). *Rime riche* becomes a device for subtle punning in roundel 3, where the noun 'swallow' rhymes with itself as a verb (1904, 5.117); likewise in roundel 7 the verb 'passes' comes back in rhyming place as a plural noun (1904, 5.120); 'still' the adverb rhymes with

'still' the adjective in roundel 61 (1904, 5.159). And in roundel 73 the verb/noun rhyme of 'rose' not only rhymes with the seed word 'Eros' but is also its anagram (1904, 5.170).

3 These are the envois, respectively, from Chaucer's *Troilus and Criseyde* (Chaucer 1974, 479) and from Pound's 'Hugh Selwyn Mauberley' (Pound 1997, 105).

4 Disclosure: I have suppressed (unless under the roundel's aegis endnotes enjoy more cachet than elsewhere) the admittedly valid reading that would construe 'Fly' in line 4 as a main verb predicating that the 'Small white wings' of line 3, nearly invisible though they be, do indeed fly. This possibility strikes me as less interesting, less intuitive, and less euphonious when pronounced than the double-jointed infinitive. Still, a reader who perceives both options may be pleased to interpret the syntactic ambiguity as germane flutter at a different level.

5 Without doubt such a biographical threshold is where Swinburne's roundel originated. As he explained in a letter of 22 June 1883 to A. H. Japp, 'Having begun by writing on the spur of a moment those roundels on the death of a friend's infant child I took a fancy to the form and went on scribbling in it till in two months' time I had a hundred' (Swinburne 1959–62, 5.27). By the editor Cecil Lang's count a full dozen of the *Century* concern the death of one of two infant twins (Swinburne 1959–62, 5.86).

6 These groupings are emphasized typographically, at the sacrifice of the elegance of pagination that graces the 1883 book, in volume 5 of the 1904 *Collected Poems*, where the groups I have singled out occur respectively on pp. 142–5, 188–92, 119–20, 156–7.

7 Susan Stewart's meditations on miniaturisation effects are also pertinent here: 'The more complicated the object, the more intricate, and the more these complications and intricacies are attended to, the "larger" the object is in significance' (Stewart 1984, 89).

8 This parallel or tangency of inner with outer, micro with macro immensities is manifest in the linkage of roundel 34, 'Plus Intra' (1904, 5.140) with roundel 13, 'Plus Ultra' (1904, 5.125), where the refrain 'Far beyond' migrates from a preposition – its object, 'the sunrise and the sunset', vast but still declared – to a free-floating modifier, neither adjective quite nor adverb, a verbal principle of sheer excess. The inside/outside topology of the roundel's ring or torus form is treated, with a twist, in an unpublished paper delivered by Joanna Swafford at the 2010 conference of the Victorians Institute, 'Swinburne and the Möbius Strip: Circumvented Circularity in *A Century of Roundels*' (University of Virginia, 1 October 2010).

9 'East Coker', lines 1, 14, 50, 209; 'Little Gidding', lines 240–2, in Eliot 1943.

10 I have in mind 'Swinburne as Poet' (Eliot 1920a), an essay that did not inaugurate, but did firmly install into the judgement of two critical generations, the conviction that Swinburne was linguistically sonorous but referentially

impaired. In fact Eliot's essay is more analytically appreciative than one can readily tell from the effect it had on later readers. For an extended treatment of Eliot's essay, see Catherine Maxwell, Chapter 11 below.

11 This last phrase belongs to Poulet 1979: see pp. 185ff. on Coleridge as the great circle-obsessed English Romantic. Poulet's discussion of Baudelaire is filled with suggestions that should prove useful to the student of Swinburne: e.g., how sundered subjective and objective worlds may be re-conjugated in the shuddering ('frisson') or vibration of verse (Poulet 1979, 409–10). The French connection in which Swinburne's formal adaptation of roundel from rondeau originated persists into Mallarmé's proposing 'a similarity between the circle perpetually opened and closed by rhyme and the circles, in the grass, of the fairy or magician' (quoted in Landy 2009, 112).

12 The Brownings, to instance just two Victorian poets important to Swinburne, made conspicuous use of circular form. On Barrett Browning's adaptation of Homeric ring structure, see Tucker 1993, 63–5. Browning's structural plan for *The Ring and the Book* is bespoken in its title, while the practice is inventoried across his lyric output with impressive comprehensiveness by Bright 1996.

13 My quotation from Douglas 2007, 74, omits her criterion of a 'strongly marked central place' because this criterion evidently interested Swinburne only inter-mittently. What Douglas calls 'central loading' (p. 37) does appear, e.g., in the metapoetic roundel 63 ('The Roundel'), where the medial sixth line – 'Love, laughter, or mourning – remembrance of rapture or fear' (1904, 5.161) – uniquely articulates a burden of content charging the form to which the five symmetrically paralleled lines on either side are devoted instead. Parallels of sound and image are also prominent in the corresponding rungs of 'Tristan und Isolde', roundel 32 (1904, 5.137–8), quoted and discussed below. But ordi-narily Swinburne obviates emphasis on the poetic centre, probably because in so condensed a form the structural balance is immediately perspicuous.

14 The 1883 text ends the first stanza with a comma while the 1904 (137–8) ends it with a full stop. The texts in the 1904 edition were corrected by Swinburne, who was very particular about their accuracy.

15 Of these perennial topics, *A Century of Roundels* directly addresses only the last, but that one arises often. 'Eros' appears three-times-thrice as the seed term for roundels 73–5 (1904, 5.170–1), and roundel 88, 'Aperotos Eros' (1904, 5.184) drives the genre into a classic severity reminiscent of *Atalanta in Calydon* at its starkest. Even roundels 68–9, 'Love Lies Bleeding' and 'Love in a Mist', paired 'flower-pieces' (1904, 5.166–7) of an apparent slightness, acknowledge erotic asperities continuous with the puzzling 'Wasted Love' (roundel 65; 1904, 5.163) and the ponderous 'Dead Love' (roundel 84; 1904, 5.180).

7

DESIRE LINES: SWINBURNE AND LYRIC CRISIS

Marion Thain

The lines of Swinburne's poetry delineate the poetically perverse, the metrically masochistic, and the sensuously sadistic. Yet it is not the sexual intensity of his poetry that I explore in this chapter, although the pun in my title deliberately evokes these aspects of Swinburne's poetry to tease from them a perversely chaste account of lyric community. 'Desire lines' is a term taken from urban geography, and denotes those paths worn away by erosion as people choose to walk across grass, for example, rather than use the designated tarmac path. I use this term poetically, to signify a set of things crucial to the nature of the lyric genre: the power of poetic conventions that are established not through edict but through consensus, and the linking of desire and community. As Swinburne says himself, 'Law, not lawlessness, is the natural condition of poetic life; but the law must itself be poetic and not pedantic, natural and not conventional' (Swinburne 1904, 1.xvi). The purpose of this chapter is ultimately to suggest that Swinburne's work might be located in relation to a period in the history of the lyric genre when poetry confronts modernity, and vice versa. I begin with a reading of a central genre 'problem' of *Poems and Ballads, First Series* (1866), but then turn to Swinburne's much later collection *A Century of Roundels* (1883) to argue that what Swinburne develops here as 'desire lines' of lyric community needs to be read back into our understanding of his earlier work if we are to understand better the nature and effect of some of the complexities of genre experimentation found there.

Swinburne inevitably represents a turning point, poetically, from the mid-nineteenth century to the late. He is best-known for his long 'dramatic monologues' but was also credited with the beginnings of English Parnassianism and a return to the brief and strict French forms that typified aestheticism. It is the 'dramatic' rather than the 'lyric' that has received most attention in Swinburne's poetry in recent years, but *Poems and Ballads, First Series* is a volume of many poetic types and forms; in the poet's own words in his 'Dedicatory Epistle' in the *Collected Poetical Works*, it contains poetry, 'lyrical and dramatic and elegiac and generally heterogeneous' (Swinburne 1904, 1.vi). Swinburne is particularly interested, in fact, in classifying poetry in terms of poetic type, admitting to liking the idea of seeing a poet's 'lyrical and elegiac works ranged and registered apart, each kind in a class of its own, such as is usually reserved ... for sonnets only' (Swinburne 1904, 1.xiv). It is interesting then, that the major problem of reception of *Poems and Ballads, First Series*, both now and at the time of its publication, has resided precisely in a problem of poetic classification. As Nicholas Shrimpton says, 'Swinburne writes dramatic lyrics, monodrama, mask lyrics, and dramatic monologues, and mixes them without warning' (Shrimpton 1993, 61). My purpose here is not a survey of the lyric impulses throughout the book, but to argue that his best-known 'dramatic' poem is principally a meditation on the nature of lyric subjectivity. Camille Paglia called 'Anactoria' 'the most sensuously finished and intellectually developed of Swinburne's poems' (Paglia 2001, 477); and it appeals to us chiefly as a poem that speaks about poetry.

What type of a poem is 'Anactoria'? Critics call it a dramatic monologue because its poetic 'I' is named as Sappho and it incorporates quotations from her work; but this categorisation raises crucial problems of poetic subjectivity that have continuously troubled interpretations of the poem. Shrimpton understands 'Anactoria' not as a dramatic monologue but as the greatest example of 'mask lyric' in the volume, and quotes Rader's definition of a form in which 'the poet speaks through an actor who is registered almost overtly as an artificial self'; he sees Swinburne here as speaking as a woman and inhabiting a female sexuality specifically (Shrimpton 1993, 63, 64; Rader 1976–77, 150). More recently, Catherine Maxwell devoted a few pages of her 2006 book on Swinburne to a useful summation of the problems involved in thinking about Swinburne's use of 'dramatic' speakers, noting the 'lack of actual dramatic action' in some of the monologues and the seeming lack of distance between Swinburne and his personae: 'the dramatic becomes apparently more "personal", but, by the same token, . . . personal experience becomes more "dramatic" and generic and less individual and circumstantial' (Maxwell 2006, 17, 18). Yet most critics still tend to identify these poems as dramatic monologues. Perhaps we should let those questions about exactly who *is* speaking loom a little larger. By unsettling

preconceptions and attending more closely to question of poetic genre in
Poems and Ballads, First Series it is possible to reflect on 'Anactoria''s
discourse on lyric subjectivity.

To be sure, 'Anactoria' (Swinburne 1904, 1. 57–66; 2000, 47–55) is a long
poem, narrated by the persona of Sappho and written in couplets – a form
rarely associated with concentrated lyrical effusion and, particularly at
this time, more usually found with the controlled language of longer
narrative and dramatic works. Yet, sitting oddly within these bounds, the
content of the poem is entirely about lyric song, and is couched within
lyric's condensed and highly wrought style. It is this hybridity, this generic
disjunction between narrative or dramatic form and lyric content, that
must be recognised as lying at the heart of the problems of genre the
poem poses, and that should prevent us from reading it as a dramatic
monologue – albeit an odd one. The dramatic monologue itself has been
read as a 'hybrid' form, combining aspects of the poetic and the narrative
in a turn away from the problems of 'lyric' subjectivity, but the hybridity I
identify in 'Anactoria' is one which is a further supervention on the
questions of genre raised by the dramatic monologue. What I posit in this
chapter is not the mid-century turn to the dramatic monologue discussed
so eloquently by Herbert Tucker, amongst others, who sees Tennyson and
Browning tuning away from lyric as a rejection of a form 'heard
overmuch, overdone, and thus in need of being done over in fresh forms'
(Tucker 1985, 227). What I find in Swinburne is a subsequent reconsider-
ation of lyric, from within those more 'objective' narrative or dramatic
poetic forms.

The poem's central conceit of Sappho as metaphor ('metaphors of
me'; line 214) should alert us not only to Sappho as metrical rhythm or
Sappho as lesbian but, more centrally, Sappho *as* lyric. Anactoria herself
becomes, as Yopie Prins has discussed at length, an emblem of lyric song
(Prins 1999, 126–31). She is not a woman in her own right but Sappho's
song: the lyre Sappho fashions out of her body ('Take thy limbs living, and
new-mould with these / A lyre of many faultless agonies'; lines 139–40).
Yet surely this allegory must point up a further allegory: that Sappho in
this poem is similarly not a persona, not a mask, but lyric itself, placing the
genre as the central object of the poem.

The poem's central concern with identity and difference (the very basis
of metaphor) is worked out through a long, and much studied, tussle
between the separateness and co-mingling of Sappho and Anactoria.
Lexical repetition in and between many of the early lines of the poem

speaks of an identity within difference or separation: 'blood against my blood: my pain / Pains thee' (lines 11–12). The poem imagines the absorption of 'you' into 'I': 'Thy body were abolished and consumed, / And in my flesh thy very flesh entombed!' (lines 113–14); 'Mixed with thy blood and molten into thee!' (line 132). This merging between Sappho and Anactoria has often been read as metaphorical of the poetic relationship between Swinburne and Sappho. Jennifer Wagner-Lawlor, for example, writes that this enables Swinburne to speak not only as Sappho but also as himself: 'This double-voicing, which maintains simultaneously the figures of Sappho and Swinburne, allows the two poets to become, each to the other, "metaphors of me" – Sappho as Swinburne, and Swinburne as Sappho' (Wagner-Lawlor 1996, 930). Camille Paglia later read the poem as enacting a different merging, seeing Swinburne's identification with Anactoria, not Sappho: Anactoria's absence in the poem is Swinburne's imaginative projection of himself as the lyric body abused by Sappho's mastery (Paglia 2001, 478). Both of these must surely be true; as Maxwell argues, this is 'a contradictory poem' of constantly shifting and merging identities between Anactoria, Sappho, and Swinburne (Maxwell 2001, 39–40). Maxwell goes on to offer a scenario in which 'Anactoria is Swinburne, but by virtue of being Anactoria he is also Sappho' (Maxwell 2001, 40). That all these different critical narratives of the poem seem valid should perhaps lead us to see the importance of the poem as ultimately not in any narratable drama of egos on the stage of a dramatic monologue, but in a dramatisation of the process of mutual formation of poetic voice itself. I suggest here that the poem is about lyric community: the idea that the lyric poet is always a multiple subject; never the single isolated lyric voice of the Romantic sublime. In this poem Sappho becomes more of a metaphor for lyric than an individual who narrates the poem. When Swinburne speaks through Sappho he speaks through lyric, through a genre, not through a narrator or a persona. In other words, 'Anactoria' is not a dramatic monologue but a dramatisation of lyric itself, a self-conscious speaking through the lyric genre.

Yet if this poem is essentially 'about' lyric, why does Swinburne house his Sappho, his lyric, in forms that are appropriate for more 'objective' narrative-driven content? Within *Poems and Ballads, First Series*, I suggest, this generic hybridity played a role in the volume's construction of an erotics of excess. The obscenity of this poem comes as much from genre perversion as sexual perversion. If the indeterminacy of the sexual content has played a large role in the offence caused by this poem, as

Richard Sieburth has argued (Sieburth 1984), then its indeterminacy of genre is an extension of this: an effusion of lyric transgressing the orderly couplet form, frothing and desecrating the narrative space. There is surely something obscene about encountering the non-narrative sensuality of lyrical writing within such a form? It is this genre 'problem' that must be seen lurking behind the charge most often levelled against Swinburne by critics, both contemporary and contemporaneous, that he prizes language more for its musical qualities than for its communicative ones. Oscar Wilde's 1889 review which accuses Swinburne of a surrendering 'of his own personality' to the mastery of language over him – 'words seem to dominate him' (Wilde 1968, 148, 146) – and T. S. Eliot's charge of 'uproot[ing]' language and offering 'merely the hallucination of meaning' (Eliot 1920a, 149) are well known, but the issues of genre embedded within these criticisms merit further exploration.

Moreover, this is an approach that is guided by, and furthered by, an examination of some of the less well-known contemporaneous responses, which dwell on the problem of lyric more fully, and which clarify the hybridity of *Poems and Ballads* to be not that which is standardly now recognised as intrinsic to the dramatic monologue form in mid-century formations, but an experiment in re-exploring lyric subjectivity from within that form. A substantial piece in *Fraser's Magazine for Town and Country* comments that 'These poems are, as Mr. Browning says of a volume of his own, "though lyric in expression, always dramatic in principle ..."'. For this reviewer, this hybridity is clearly identified as one between content and form: 'lyrical faculty' is wedded to 'dramatic form'. Indeed, it is the length of poetic form that he or she finds particularly inimical to the compression of lyric, remarking on Swinburne's habit of seizing of 'bright, sudden, characteristic moments', which are 'the moments which lyric poetry should seize', but noting that 'Mr. Swinburne neglects this rule', allowing his lyric moments to run and run. While identifying this poetry as not wholly lyric, the reviewer also questions whether it is dramatic in the usual sense. Comparing his work to other dramatic monologues, the reviewer notes that Swinburne doesn't so much borrow a mask, dramatically, as rather inhabit a body outside of his own. In this sense Swinburne is still a *personal*, lyric, poet, and not a writer of dramatic monologues. This review comes to the conclusion that Swinburne knows how to achieve an intriguing union between the lyric and the dramatic monologue, but urges us to think of him as a writer of lyric poetry first and foremost: 'For in his lyrical faculty lies, after all, his characteristic strength, and we urge him to use the dramatic form only in so far as needful to give variety and modulation to the passion of the lyrist' (Anonymous 1866, 643–4).

Interestingly, the identification of *Poems and Ballads, First Series* as primarily a lyric, rather than dramatic, work is the basis of the author's defence of Swinburne against the charge of profanity: 'We believe that Mr. Swinburne is a true lyric singer, and so believing, we should think it madness and worse to gag him':

> He does not *compose* poetic sentiment and painfully adapt it to appropriate metres; the song *wells* from him, if one may so speak, as water from a perennial spring; the strong light of true passion, however disastrously clouded at times, shines upon it; in all its movements it keeps the harmony and the rhythm of life. (Anonymous 1866, 644)

It seems that Swinburne's defence is his spontaneous outburst of lyric song. Lyric should, it is suggested, be accepted purely on the criterion of whether it '*ring[s] true*' – whether it is genuine, and from the heart. The responsibility of the lyric poet is only to himself or herself and cannot be judged in social terms (Anonymous 1866, 644). The dramatic monologue is usually defended with the claim that the views expressed are not necessarily those of the author. Following the precedent of Baudelaire, Swinburne argued, rather formulaically, in *Notes on Poems and Reviews* (1866) that much of the obscenity found in his verse could be traced back to the ancient poets whose texts he drew on so profoundly in his own work (Swinburne 1866, 9; 2000, 407). Yet this reviewer defends the poems not as dramatic monologues but as lyrics.

Another interesting review titled 'Mr Swinburne's Lyrics', which appeared in the *Edinburgh Review* in 1890, opens its examination of *Poems and Ballads, First Series* by dwelling for several pages on what 'lyrical poetry' is, and drawing out its key features. The definition of the lyric genre here is much the same as that we know today: formally bearing its musical heritage in its complexity and 'beauty' of patterning; subjective in content, and, above all, 'concentrated' in length: 'Few, indeed, are the long lyrical poems which have met with any general acceptance from the world' (Anonymous 1890, 429–30). The reviewer does entertain the idea of a separate sub-species of lyric, the 'objective' type of which the ballad is an example, and which 'will bear, and even demand, greater length of development than the subjective lyric' (Anonymous 1890, 430), but as the review progresses it becomes clear that this is much less central to both this reviewer's overall definition of lyric and to his or her assessment of 'Mr Swinburne's special qualities as a lyric poet' (Anonymous 1890, 443). Measured against the yardstick of the true, 'subjective', lyric, the reviewer finds that the problems of genre in *Poems and Ballads, First Series* ultimately rest on 'want of concentration': the poems are 'full of repetition and amplification of verse with little amplification of sense' (Anonymous 1890, 434). The review argues that not only do individual poems go on at length but they also run into one another, sharing the same themes and tone, so that the whole book becomes one long lyrical effusion (Anonymous 1890, 451).

Both of these substantial reviews see notions of genre as crucial for reading, interpreting, and evaluating *Poems and Ballads, First Series*. They both agree that the poetry is essentially lyric, rather than dramatic, in style and content; but also they both make a case for it being problematically hybrid, identifying particularly the more characteristically dramatic or narrative length of the poetic forms Swinburne uses. To find out why questions of lyric feature so prominently in the reception of *Poems and Ballads, First Series*, we have to look further to the wider context of Victorian modernity's suspicion of lyric interiority (Christ 1984, 2–6). As I briefly noted earlier, this resulted in the turn away from the lyric subject in search of more objective voices that have themselves been termed 'hybrid' – the dramatic monologue, the narrative poem or lyric sequence that anchored itself in objective events, and large-scale narrative structures (see Morgan 2007). *Poems and Ballads, First Series*, however, entertains a return to lyric, and one that, in the meta-poetical 'Anactoria' at least, self-consciously raises crucial questions as to what the lyric subject is, and can be, in modernity.

In 'Lyric Poetry and Society' (1957) Theodor Adorno traces an inheritance from Hegel that saw the lyric defined by universalisation through introspection, and argues that this left the lyric divorced from society and in danger of seeming irrelevant to the modern world. Adorno meets this criticism by claiming the form's distance from the social world is intrinsically a critique of it (Adorno 1991). Adorno is immersed here in a European tradition of poetry and philosophy that takes Baudelaire as its poetic touchstone, arguing that Baudelaire was the first to choose the modern itself ('the antilyrical pure and simple') as his lyric subject matter (Adorno 1991, 44). According to Adorno, what Baudelaire confronts is the role of language in anchoring the lyric in society while simultaneously marking its distance from 'mere functioning within a wholly socialized society' – in other words, from mere communicative language (Adorno 1991, 44). Yet one might also say that this linguistic balance of the lyric that simultaneously connects with society while distancing from it is also a major concern of Swinburne. Swinburne reviewed *Les Fleurs du mal* in 1862, and *Poems and Ballads, First Series* is partly a reflection on this volume, both through the figure of Sappho and in other ways. What we see in the generic hybridity of a poem such as 'Anactoria' is, I suggest, precisely a return to lyric to confront its relationship with modernity. Swinburne couches his lyric, a form clearly associated by this point with personal, alienated individualism, in forms that embrace and embed a lyric 'collective', ensuring a generic balance of (to echo Adorno's terms) the poetic and communicative. Of course this leads to a frustration of expectation for the reader as non-narrative poetic effusion, rather than being compressed into meaning through a short, contained form that would force out the patterning and repetition of linguistic form, flows freely through the couplets of a long form.

For example, the poem begins with the very tight patterning more usually found in the short lyric: the linking of each couplet through the end rhyme is echoed by a lexical patterning within each line, such as the balancing of 'my' and 'thy' in line 1, and the repeated similarly balancing, 'me, thy' in line 2, or the repeated negative in line 5. Such density of formal patterning serves within a short lyric form to create meaning but, within a long form such as this, it easily turns into verbal excess: a linguistic intensity that threatens to override the forward momentum (needed to sustain the long form) with a circular motion that keeps directing the movement of the poem inwards towards its own echoes and its own internal linguistic point of reference. This is also the effect of the Petrarchan rhymes that abound within the first page or so of the poem: 'eyes'/'sighs', 'breath'/'death', 'fire'/'desire', 'cleaves'/ 'leaves', 'pain'/'vein', 'flower'/'hour', 'thine'/'mine', 'dove'/'love'. Over a fairly short space, such rhymes foreground a very conventional language of love that marks the intensity of feeling and the close allegiance of strong desire with destructive forces (fire, pain, death), and of both with the transience (flower, hour) that is their corollary. Indeed, the transience of a short poetic form itself is necessary to this language of love, and crucial to the depiction of intensity, as well as providing tight formal control on the emotion. Yet when sustained over a longer form the focus placed on the Petrarchan language through these end-rhymes causes the sentiment to seem not just powerful but excessive: a piling up of weighted signifiers that risks not self-parody but certainly intoxication and a sickening. The end-rhyme 'hour[s]'/'flower[s]' is repeated three times in fairly quick succession (lines 13–14, 39–40, 51–2), with the result not only of exacerbating this sense of content overspilling the form but also, ironically, of stressing the brevity to which great passion is necessarily allied. Yet in spite of the repeated stress on images of impermanence, Swinburne's form here doesn't provide the short formal structure that would enable the contrast of intensity and brevity, excess and control, to interplay. Lines 47 to 58 mirror exactly the end-rhyme words of lines 35 to 46 but, again, this tight formal patterning rather highlights the expanse of the poem. This is what McGann writes about as 'poetry aspiring to the condition of music': 'even the poem's semantic features – the idea of being sickened with love, for instance – get subordinated to the logic of musical and sensuous transformation' (McGann 2009, 628). It is as if Swinburne wants to draw attention to the free rein he gives to passion in this poem. The result is that the reader is made to experience the overflow of Sappho's desire; the couplets of the poem, rather than being given narrative momentum and direction, break repeatedly over the reader in incessant waves.

Many critics' and readers' objections to Swinburne's poetry over the years can be explained by this forced mismatch of poetic genres between content and form: a drama between the individual and the collective that highlights the contemporary crisis in the lyric subject. But while I've begun to explore the lyrical quality of the expression of desire in 'Anactoria', more investigation is necessary to substantiate my claim that this is fused with a form that attempts a more collective or communitarian spirit. What might this mean, and how might it happen? I will first look at this idea in Swinburne's much later collection *A Century of Roundels*, where he explores a conception of the 'desire lines' of lyric community more self-consciously and more formally.

The roundel form that Swinburne adapts from the French 'rondeau' has, in addition to a tight rhyme scheme, a refrain which is set at the start of the first line and repeats in lines four and eleven of the eleven-line form. The form itself stresses vocal repetition and its layering of the refrain suggests the form of the sung round in which different voices sing the same words at overlapping intervals in a 'follow the leader' form. It is a form then whose very essence draws attention to the subject as a multi-layered, multi-vocal one whose repetition gives the echo of different voices singing the same song – not in unison, but in (harmonious) turn. Swinburne dedicates the collection to Christina Rossetti, setting up from the outset the sense of a chain song that is passed from one poetic voice to another: a repetition that is identical but multi-voiced. The roundel form inscribes, through its central refrain, the image of the poet retreading the paths of previous poetic feet.

Swinburne's 'The Roundel' is a poem about the form itself and sets the parameters for the volume's commentary on poetic voice. This poem likens the roundel to a 'ring', 'a starbright sphere', 'round as a pearl or tear' (Swinburne 1904, 5.161). Here the metaphysical influence is clearly seen, and the refrain 'A roundel is wrought' sets up the making of the poem as its own refrain – the assonance between 'round' and 'wrought' further spiralling the refrain in on itself. Identifying the roundel here as a 'jewel of music' 'carven of all or of aught' speaks to the Parnassian influence which, again, pushes the poem in on itself and its own multiple refractions. Most significantly for my purposes the refrain of the roundel is imagined in this poem 'As a bird's quick song runs round, and the hearts in us hear / Pause answer to pause, and again the same strain caught'. Here the image is of the repeated 'round' of a bird's song, but the echoes within that single voice are described in terms of a dialogue – 'pause answer to pause' – as if the bird is singing in response to some unheard and unseen audience. This image encapsulates the fascination of the roundel, in which repetition creates its own dialectic.

It is with this in mind that I turn to the two roundels that appear under the title 'On an Old Roundel (Translated by D. G. Rossetti from the French of Villon)':

I

Death, from thy rigour a voice appealed,
And men still hear what the sweet cry saith,
Crying aloud in thine ears fast sealed,
        Death.

As a voice in a vision that vanisheth,
Through the grave's gate barred and the portal steeled
The sound of the wail of it travelleth.

Wailing aloud from a heart unhealed,
It woke response of melodious breath
From lips now too by thy kiss congealed,
        Death.

II

Ages ago, from the lips of a sad glad poet
Whose soul was a wild dove lost in the whirling snow,
The soft keen plaint of his pain took voice to show it
    Ages ago.

So clear, so deep, the divine drear accents flow,
No soul that listens may choose but thrill to know it,
Pierced and wrung by the passionate music's throe.

For us there murmurs a nearer voice below it,
Known once of ears that never again shall know,
Now mute as the mouth which felt death's wave o'erflow it
    Ages ago.

                      (Swinburne 1904, 5.174–5)

This poem plays with all the elements identified above as central to the purpose and meaning of Swinburne's new form. The first roundel is an answering strain to Rossetti's 'To Death, of His Lady (François Villon)', a close translation of Villon's 'Le Testament', lines 978–89, in French rondeau form.[1] The translation was made in 1869 and published in Rossetti's 1870 *Poems*. Rossetti's poem, like Villon's, is a complaint to Death about the recent demise of his beloved lady – a grief which, he claims, saps his own life:

Death, of thee do I make my moan,
    Who hadst my lady away from me,
    Nor wilt assuage thine enmity
Till with her life thou hast mine own;
For since that hour my strength has flown.
    Lo! what wrong was her life to thee,
    Death?

Two we were, and the heart was one;
    Which now being dead, dead I must be,
    Or seem alive as lifelessly
As in the choir the painted stone,
    Death!

                  (D.G. Rossetti 1881, 281)

The love that united them in life must now unite them in death.

Yet Swinburne's poem is rather a meta-commentary on the process of Rossetti's translation than another straight repetition of the poem. His verse makes no mention of the beloved lady, but takes as its subject matter Villon's appeal to Death and its continuing echo through Rossetti's translation. Like Rossetti, Swinburne uses the one word 'Death' as his thrice-repeated refrain, but in Swinburne's poem it takes on a special significance because of the three voices that he is aware of representing. This refrain should represent the three different, but layered, invocations to the dead beloved 'lady' (Villon's, Rossetti's, and Swinburne's), yet it comes instead to direct attention away from the supposed female object of the poem toward a now more important threesome: the three male poets who write in community. In this way, the three 'deaths' in Swinburne's poem are Villon's death, Rossetti's very recent death (in 1882: 'lips now too by thy kiss congealed, / Death'), and a reflection on Swinburne's own mortality. This poem is about the significance of the lover's complaint, rather than the dead beloved; the beloved lady's death simply cements bonds between the three male poets and Swinburne writes about the immortality of poetic voice as it is passed and shared between them. He is able to gesture towards his own death in that repetition of three refrains because his connection with these other poets means that they live through his poem and he dies a living death in sympathy with their voices. Their poetic voices are bound, living and dead, through this form whose repetition makes both the dead return to life and what is living find community in death. This community of lyric voices is the living death that Rossetti writes of in his poem, but also a bringing back to life of the voices of the dead so that 'men still hear what the sweet cry saith'. Swinburne is writing here about Villon's voice being preserved through Rossetti's, and his own voice preserving both by writing in community with them.

Terms signifying vocalisation occur in nearly every line: 'voice', 'what the sweet cry saith', 'crying aloud', 'voice', 'wail', 'wailing aloud', 'melodious breath', 'lips'. Villon's cry evoked 'response of melodious breath' from Rossetti (who now too is dead), which in turn has been joined by Swinburne's own voice. This poem is an elegiac cry to Death to imagine the speaker's own living death upon that of his beloved, but also an ode to the immortality of the poetic voice that claims this living death, even after the actual death of the speaker. This process of mourning is a sung round started by Villon, with the burden taken up by Rossetti, and then repeated by Swinburne, in an overlapping sequence of voices that, crucially, awake answering 'response[s]' in each other. Such vocal layering is depicted in the poem not only by the repetition of the refrain but also by the layering of language in other ways that invites us to find voices within voices. For example, the first line – 'Death, from thy rigour a voice appealed' – plays on the nesting of 'peal' (yet another term for vocalisation, or the ringing out of the voice) within 'appeal': a voice that pleads with Death to take him as he has taken his beloved, but whose plea for a living death is simultaneously a more positive act – like a peal of celebratory bells – that precisely ensures the immortality of his voice.

The second roundel in the poem reflects at a further level of remove on this round of lyric voices, answering the first with a distancing refrain of 'ages ago' – a term imprecise and casual as if to acknowledge the huge temporal gap between the voices whilst also being quite dismissive of it. In this roundel he traces the mediation from Villon (the 'sad glad poet') to Rossetti:

> For us there murmurs a nearer voice below it,
> Known once of ears that never again shall know,
> Now mute as the mouth which felt death's wave o'erflow it
>   Ages ago.

Although a much 'nearer' voice, Rossetti is somehow already encompassed within the same imprecise historical plane as Villon: 'ages ago'. Both are merged within an immortal collective lyric consciousness that is a part of every lyric subject. It is no coincidence that both Villon's and Rossetti's deaths are imagined in terms of drowning. Just as 'Anactoria' ended with Sappho merging into the sea – 'around and over and under me / Thick darkness and the insuperable sea' (lines 303–4) – these later poets merge with the collective lyric consciousness that Sappho symbolises for Swinburne.

Indeed in his essay 'The Poems of Dante Gabriel Rossetti' when he writes about Rossetti's 'A Young Fir-Wood', he picks out, in particular, the imagery of the sea, commenting on its use to express 'a living thing with an echo beyond reach of the sense, its chord of sound one part of the multiform unity of mutual inclusion in which all things rest and mix' (Swinburne 1870a, 557; 1875a, 70). As much Swinburne's own sense of the sea as Rossetti's, this description forms a useful gloss on the sea that overtakes Sappho, Villon, Rossetti, and, in some strange projection throughout Swinburne's poetry, eventually himself too. It is in this 'multiform unity of mutual inclusion' where the souls of lyric poets merge that Swinburne finds his lyric community – the lines of desire that he too will follow – and it is, ironically, through this process of mourning that he avoids lyric isolation.

So, to reread 'Anactoria'. The review already cited from the *Edinburgh Review* notes just how many verses in *Poems and Ballads, First Series* write 'in celebration or derogation of persons, dead or living', peopling Swinburne's poetry with a sociable hum of voices (Anonymous 1890, 447). I have already argued for 'Anactoria' as a multilayered composition, with Swinburne's lyric troped through the dramatised metaphors of both Sappho and Anactoria (and a discourse on identity and difference). But of course he writes too in community with Catullus, who had produced a poetic translation of the same Sapphic fragment (Fragment 31) that Swinburne refers to, in *Notes on Poems and Reviews*, as 'The Ode to Anactoria' (commonly known as 'To a Beloved Girl', the 'Second Ode', or *Phanetai moi*). When Swinburne incorporates Sappho's words into his poem he cannot help but also write in light of Catullus's translation. Indeed, in his roundel 'To Catullus' we find the refrain 'my brother' clearly asserting a lyrical kinship with the poet whose voice is such an important part of his multilayered subject in 'Anactoria'. In this roundel Catullus's voice lives through Swinburne: 'How should I living fear to call thee dead, / My brother?' (Swinburne 1904, 5.185).

In *Notes on Poems and Reviews*, Swinburne is critical of Catullus's translation of the 'Second Ode' and distances himself from it: 'Where Catullus failed I could not hope to succeed; I tried instead to reproduce in a diluted and dilated form the spirit of a poem which could not be reproduced in the body' (Swinburne 1866, 9; 2000, 406). He claims to turn from Catullus's attempt to capture the body of the text, to a desire to go more directly to the spirit of Sappho (although ironically he reaches the spirit by playing the body, or corpus, of Sappho like a lyre – just as Sappho does in 'Anactoria'). This contrasts sharply with the positive comments Swinburne makes in 'The Poems of Dante Gabriel Rossetti' on the process of translation within Rossetti's work that he follows in 'On an Old Roundel': 'All Mr. Rossetti's translations bear the same evidence of a power not merely beyond reach but beyond attempt of other artists in language' (Swinburne 1870a, 560; 1875a, 76–7). Yet, even in marking his distance from Catullus's translation, he writes with him, recognising him as another voice in the train of voices around the fragment of 'Anactoria', a train in which he consciously takes his place – just as he writes with Rossetti in 'On an Old Roundel'. Swinburne situates himself similarly in both poems: he writes in relation to two other poets (one ancient and the other a translator of the ancient verse), following in each case not with another translation but with a meta-commentary, aiming (as he said of 'Anactoria', but this is equally true of 'On an Old Roundel') to 'represent not the poem but the poet' (Swinburne 1866, 10; 2000, 407). In turning to the poet rather than the poem, Swinburne chooses to comment first and foremost on the operation of the lyric subject, figuring a collective lyric subjectivity that projects both backwards and forwards in time.

Swinburne's personification of lyric in 'Anactoria' enables a double-faced poem that is both a love song and an exploration of the poetic genre; it also enables him to turn the lyric subject from a marginalised, interiorised, voice into a lyric polyphony. In other words, the personification of lyric enables him to make explicit a belief that writing lyrics inevitably involves the author entering into a community. It is no accident that his personification of lyric is Sappho, the archetypal alienated, individualised, sexually perverse, and fragmented figure. He embraces this quintessentially marginalised lyric voice to find through it a mode of poetry that emphasises the commonality of lyric subjectivity that is the twin to its individuality. Indeed, Sappho stresses in this poem the passing of voice from Anactoria, to Sappho, and on into an immortal chorus that will not die with her death:

> but thou – thy body is the song,
> Thy mouth the music; thou art more than I,
> Though my voice die not till the whole world die . . .
>
> (lines 74–6)

This notion of singing in timeless chorus is reiterated throughout the poem:

> Violently singing till the whole world sings –
> I Sappho shall be one with all these things . . .
>
> (lines 275–6)

> Yea, though thou diest, I say I shall not die . . .
>
> (line 290)

This immortal unification with the broader song of the world is possible because Sappho is a personification of the lyric genre; half real individual, half mythical identification with poetry itself. The fragments

of Sappho – for many Victorians the original lyric poet – laid down a track
in which others walked their own walk but in her company. In this way,
Swinburne resolves the contemporary crisis in lyric subjectivity into an
exploration of the paradox inherent in the Romantic lyric subject that is
both highly individual and yet expressed within long-established
paradigms, and thus recuperates lyric from assumptions of its irrelevance
to society. It is in this sense that I read the poem not as a dramatic
monologue voiced by Sappho but as Swinburne's orchestration of a poly-
phonic lyric chorus showing the lyric subject as one which, far from
irrelevant to the social world, actually occupies a unique position for
holding together the individual and a collective voice.

The 'desire lines' concept, elaborated through a reading of the
roundels, gives us a model for how Swinburne finds in sexual desire a
trope for the community of the lyric subject. This can be used to reread
'Anactoria' in a way that changes our understanding of desire in this
poem. The focus on Swinburne's metrical masochism has rather obscured
the importance of sexual desire as a means of dramatising the lyric
subject as simultaneously individual and blended into a collective generic
voice. In 'Anactoria' the imagery of merging bodies that are 'mixed',
'molten', and mutually consuming speaks not just of a masochistic dyad
of pain and pleasure but also of a lyric community. The lines of desire in
this poem mark the coincidence of sexual merging with a sense of a
group of individuals who are collectively marking out a lyric route:
Anactoria, Sappho, Catullus, Swinburne. This is the process of sublima-
tion of the self into a lyric society that is hidden within the tropes of
masochistic submission; and Swinburne plays relentlessly on the fine line
between the disintegration of self and the finding of community that is
attendant on the merging of bodies he depicts in Anactoria.

Wilde's notion of Swinburne relinquishing control to Sappho and to
language becomes odd when one considers how absolutely and unmis-
takably 'Swinburnian' such poems as 'Anactoria' are. Ironically, it is
Wilde's own lyric poems that are more open to this charge of the surren-
dering of individuality; Wilde's *Poems* (1881) contains works, often
translations of existing poems, that are strangely annihilating of the
author, whose distinctive voice is barely discernible behind the lines of
others or of pure lyric itself. Wilde's own poetry highlights the challenges
of the lyric: both the need for individual introspection and the profound
connections with others that it demands. In 'Anactoria' Swinburne may
use the masochistic and sadomasochistic relationship between Sappho

and Anactoria to think about the merging of bodies in lyrical 'desire lines' – and he may dramatise his lyric in the persona of Sappho – but it is through his examination of the necessity to the lyric of the pull between individuality and authorial control, on the one hand, and collectivity and polyvocality, on the other, that he becomes present in his poetry. And it is through his awareness of the social nature of lyric subjectivity that he responds to Victorian modernity's suspicion of the isolation and introspection of lyric voice. Swinburne may have been caricatured in 1866 as a 'melodious twanger of another man's lyre' (Anonymous 1866, 637), but in dramatising the desire lines of a collective lyric subjectivity he makes a crucial statement on the cultural crisis in and formation of the genre.

NOTES

1 McGann's online 'Rossetti Archive' cites Paull F. Baum as observing that this is a close translation, although he 'introduces a different image in the last line' (Baum 1937, 177n); www.rossettiarchive.org/docs/39–1869.raw.html, last accessed on 9 November 2011.

Part III

INFLUENCE

8

'GOOD SATAN': THE UNLIKELY POETIC AFFINITY OF SWINBURNE AND CHRISTINA ROSSETTI

Dinah Roe

Christina Rossetti's relationship to Algernon Swinburne is best remembered for an act of censorship. According to her brother, William, Rossetti pasted strips of paper over the atheistic lines in her 1865 presentation copy of *Atalanta in Calydon*: 'The supreme evil, God. / Yea, with thine hate, O God, thou has covered us' (Swinburne 1904, 4.287–8; 2000, 283, lines 1151–2). William also speculates that 'she never looked at all' at Swinburne's poems, which fell 'outside the range of her approval as a Christian devotee' (W. M. Rossetti 1906, 1.292). Less reported is William's comment that his sister 'regarded Atalanta as ... a stupendous masterpiece' (W. M. Rossetti 1904, lxx). The story of Rossetti's 'cover-up' has been so often repeated that modern readers would be forgiven for imagining that Rossetti's copies of Swinburne would be practically unreadable. Indeed David Riede has written recently: 'Despite mutual admiration and influence on one another in technique and tone ... Swinburne's eroticism was poles apart from Christina Rossetti's piety, and she was able to enjoy his poetry only by deleting the most offensive verses' (Riede 2002, 317).

Recounted far less often than the Rossetti 'cover-up' is Coulson Kernahan's account of Swinburne's first reaction to reading Rossetti's 'Death of a First-born':

Down went the knife and fork as he half rose from his chair to stretch a hand across the table for the manuscript.

'She is as a god to mortals when compared to most other living women poets,' he exclaimed in a burst of Swinburnian hyperbole.

Then in his thin, high-pitched but exquisitely modulated and musical voice he half read, half chanted two verses of the poem in question ...

Then he stopped abruptly.

'I won't read the third and last verse,' he said. 'One glance at it is suffi-
cient to show that it is unequal, and that the poem would be stronger and
finer by its omission. But for the happy folk who are able to think as she
thinks, who believe as she believes on religious matters, the poem is of its
kind perfect.' (Kernahan 1917, 7)[1]

Like Rossetti, Swinburne obscures the lines he finds offensive and, like
her, he is reluctant to even *look* at the offending stanza, needing only 'one
glance' to determine 'that the poem would be stronger and finer by its
omission'.

Leaving aside their narrators' motives, these stories helpfully illustrate
the ambivalence that characterises Swinburne's and Rossetti's relation-
ship. Both poets express praise for poems from which they must also avert
their gaze. While we do not have to search very thoroughly to locate
potential points of conflict between a radical anti-theist and a devout
Christian, the source of their mutual admiration is less obvious. One clue
is David Riede's observation about their 'influence on one another in
technique and tone' (Riede 2002, 317). This comparison has been drawn
repeatedly since the publication of Swinburne's first volume of *Poems and
Ballads* (1866). In his defence of Swinburne, William Rossetti suggested
that Swinburne was a 'not unsympathetic reader' of Christina Rossetti,
citing similarities between her work and the 'cadence of ... "Rococo"',
the 'lyrical structure of "Madonna Mia"' and the 'lyrical tone of "The
Garden of Proserpine"' (W. M. Rossetti 1866, 51–2).

Thirty years later, Edmund Gosse reinforces this point, identifying
Rossetti as the contemporary poet who 'has left the strongest mark on the
metrical nature of that miraculous artificer of verse, Mr. Swinburne'.
Gosse identifies Swinburne's *Poems and Ballads* as the volume in which
'several of Miss Rossetti's discoveries were transferred to his more scien-
tific and elaborate system of harmonies, and adapted to more brilliant
effects', going on to claim that, along with Edward FitzGerald, Rossetti
'influenced [Swinburne's] style the most' (Gosse 1896, 153).

But neither William Rossetti nor Gosse remarks on what these formal
echoes reveal about the poems themselves. Are they a tribute? A critique?
A little of both? On the basis purely of what we know about Swinburne's
and Rossetti's radically different perspectives on faith, it is tempting to
assume that Swinburne simply recasts Rossettian forms and tropes in his
own image, using them to radically challenge or subvert her views. Yet as
Kathy Psomiades points out in her discussion of *Poems and Ballads, First*

Series, Swinburne takes from Rossetti 'not just a series of formal effects . . . but also a series of ideas about . . . the centrality of dream and sleep as tropes for poetic inspiration' (Psomiades 1997, 63).

Just as their mutual appreciation seems to have been predicated on occasional aversions of the literary gaze, their poems often concern a withdrawal or a turning away from direct, unmediated experience. Both Swinburne and Rossetti are interested in experience shaped, filtered through, or mediated by sleep and dream. Unsurprisingly, they are admirers of Keats, a poet rehabilitated and popularised in the Victorian era not only by Tennyson and the Cambridge Apostles but also by the Pre-Raphaelite poets and painters within whose orbit Rossetti and Swinburne moved.

If William Rossetti found Swinburne's 'The Garden of Proserpine' (Swinburne 1904, 1.169–72; 2000, 136–9) similar to his sister's poems in terms of 'lyrical tone', this is partly because both poets during this period were heavily influenced by Keats. Swinburne's 'Garden of Proserpine' echoes both the metre and the mournful tone of Keats's 'In a Drear-Nighted December' (1817). A different Keats poem, 'Ode to a Nightingale' (1819), influences Rossetti's 'Dream-Land' (C. Rossetti 2001, 21) with its melancholy landscape presided over by a sadly singing nightingale. In a watery land of shadows lies a woman deep in a state of 'charmèd sleep' (line 3). Her senses have been numbed: 'She cannot see the grain' or 'feel the rain / Upon her hand' (lines 21, 23–4). Even what she can perceive is mediated.

> Thro' sleep, as thro' a veil,
> She sees the sky look pale,
> And hears the nightingale
> That sadly sings.
>
> (C. Rossetti 2001, 21, lines 13–16).

Through willed detachment from the natural world, she will remain in this limbo 'Till joy shall overtake / Her perfect peace' (lines 31–2). The 'joy' which she awaits is quite possibly Judgement Day, and thus her 'perfect peace' combines the Christian concept of patient expectation with Romantic sensuous trance. The idea of patience is reinforced in the version of the poem which was first published in *The Germ* (1850), where the third line of the last stanza reads, 'Rest, rest, that shall endure': the word 'endure' suggesting the ascetic trial which must be undergone before peace can be achieved (C. Rossetti 1850, 20).

The poem also recalls the conclusion of Rossetti's sonnet 'Rest' (1862), in which an unnamed, dead female figure awaits 'Eternity' in a suspended state which is neither death nor sleep: 'Her rest shall not begin nor end, but be; / And when she wakes she will not think it long' (C. Rossetti 2001, 54, lines 12, 13–14). While 'Rest' has long been credited as the first Rossetti poem Swinburne ever read, Psomiades argues persuasively that in fact it was 'Dream-Land' (Psomiades 1997, 60). Swinburne was fascinated by the poem's exploration of an ambiguous state between sleeping and death, although this fascination was aesthetic rather than religious. He intended 'The Garden of Proserpine' to express 'that brief total pause of passion and of thought, when the spirit, without fear or hope of good things or evil, hungers and thirsts only after the perfect sleep' (Swinburne 1866, 13). Although the metre of Swinburne's poem is borrowed from Keats's 'In a Drear-nighted December', his garden's 'sleepy world of streams' (Swinburne 1904, 1.169; 2000, 136, line 8) is taken from Rossetti's 'Dream-Land': 'Where sunless rivers weep / Their waves into the deep' (lines 1–2).

Swinburne's poem recasts Rossetti's mysterious female figure as Proserpine, goddess of the underworld. In Proserpine's garden, forgetting is not sweet because it signifies disillusionment and resignation: Love 'Sighs, and with eyes forgetful / Weeps that no loves endure' (lines 79–80). The garden is a deadened and infertile place where Proserpine 'Forgets the earth her mother, / The life of fruits and corn' (lines 59–60). 'Dream-Land''s female figure inhabits a similarly barren landscape: having 'left the fields of corn' of 'the purple land' (lines 10, 20) she 'cannot see the grain / ripening on hill and plain' (lines 21–2). Swinburne's poem has no faith in the redemptive 'joy' anticipated by Rossetti's 'Dream-Land'. Disregarding Proserpine's association with the return of spring, it concludes that, just as 'dead men rise up never' (line 86), there will be neither 'wintry leaves nor vernal' (line 93) but 'Only the sleep eternal / In an eternal night' (lines 95–6).

Whereas Rossetti introduces a religious element into Keatsian tropes and landscapes, and to the poetics of death, sleeping, and dreaming, Swinburne rejects such Christian associations. As Margot K. Louis points out, Swinburne's Proserpine poems '[set] the agenda, demonstrating (and applauding) the threat to Christianity (and to any stable system of meaning)' (Louis 1999, 317). Given this 'agenda', it seems at first curious that Christina Rossetti would have any influence on these poems. But Rossetti's early meditations on mortality such as 'Dream-Land', 'An End' (1850), and 'Song' ('She sat and sang alway') (1862) embody a kind of pessimism that would have intrigued Swinburne, a poet whom John Morley dubbed 'the vindictive apostle of a crushing and ironshod despair' (Morley 1866, 39).

Swinburne continues to employ Rossettian forms and imagery in a manner which is at once provocative and admiring. He returns to the themes of 'The Garden of Proserpine' in 'A Forsaken Garden' (Swinburne 1904, 3.22–5) where 'The ghost of a garden fronts the sea' (3.22). The rocky, thorny landscape is barren: even 'the weeds that grew green from the graves of its roses / Now lie dead'. We are told that 'Years ago' lovers walked in the garden together, wondering '"men that love lightly may die – but we?"' (3.23) The passage of time means even their love dies:

> And the same wind sang and the same waves whitened,
>   And or ever the garden's last petals were shed,
> In the lips that had whispered, the eyes that had lightened,
>   Love was dead.
>
> (Swinburne 1904, 3.23)

As well as ironising Browning's final line in 'Love Among the Ruins' ('Love is best'), 'Love was dead' also evokes the comfortless first line of Rossetti's 'An End': 'Love, strong as Death, is dead' (C. Rossetti 2001, 32).[2] Rossetti's speaker invites us to 'make [Death's] bed / Among the dying flowers: / A green turf at his head; / And a stone at his feet' (lines 2–5). This allusion to Ophelia's song is strengthened in the third stanza, where we are asked to sing 'To few chords and sad and low' with 'our eyes fixed on the grass / Shadow-veiled as the years pass, / While we think of all that was / In the long ago' (lines 15, 17–20).[3] Somewhat unusually for Rossetti, no mention is made of eternity, heaven, or resurrection. Rossetti's image of buried love reappears in Swinburne's 'A Forsaken Garden': 'Shall the dead take thought for the dead to love them? / What love was ever as deep as a grave? / They are loveless now as the grass above them' (Swinburne 1904, 3.24).

Like 'The Garden of Proserpine', 'A Forsaken Garden' does not offer its lovers the comforts of reunion in a Christian heaven: 'they loved their life through, and then went whither?' The lovers may have been 'one to the end – but what end who knows?' Resurrection is also explicitly rejected: 'From the graves they have made they shall rise up never'. Oblivion, rather than salvation, is offered: 'When as they that are free now of weeping and laughter / We shall sleep' (Swinburne 1904, 3.24). This recalls the 'perfect sleep' Swinburne strove to evoke in 'The Garden of Proserpine', just as it rejects Rossetti's notion of the Christian 'joy' that will 'overtake' this 'perfect peace' in her poem 'Dream-Land'.

In the same volume, Swinburne returns to Rossetti's 'Dream-Land' in his 'A Ballad of Dreamland' (Swinburne 1904, 3.85–6), a poem densely packed with allusions to Rossetti poems, which casts the poet herself as a Proserpine figure. Published in *Belgravia Magazine* in September 1876, the poem alludes to several poems from Rossetti's collection *Goblin Market, The Prince's Progress and Other Poems* published the year before.[4] Swinburne's ballad concerns a speaker who has hidden his heart 'Under the roses'. Each of its stanzas concludes with 'the song of a secret bird' which threatens to wake this sleeping heart. Rossetti's poems are known for their secrecy, and Swinburne plays Rossettian games with mysterious symbols and allusions. For example, 'under the rose' in Latin is 'sub rosa', meaning 'in secret', and was also a euphemism for a child born out of wedlock. It was also the working title of Rossetti's poem on this subject, '"The Iniquity of the Fathers Upon the Children"' (1866), which begins, 'Oh the rose of keenest thorn! / One hidden summer morn / Under the rose I was born' (C. Rossetti 2001, 158, lines 1–3). Roses are also emblems of love, making them an appropriate hiding-place for the heart of Swinburne's speaker. In the first stanza, though 'never a leaf of the rose-tree stirred' the hidden heart is awakened by the 'song of a secret bird'. This recalls the first line of Rossetti's 'A Birthday' (1862): 'My heart is like a singing bird' (C. Rossetti 2001, 30).

Swinburne's question in line 14 of 'A Ballad of Dreamland' – 'Does the fang still fret thee of hope deferred?' – contains a biblical quotation heavily favoured by Rossetti and used in at least sixteen of her poems.[5] The complete King James quotation suggests heartsickness as one reason the speaker has hidden her heart: 'Hope deferred maketh the heart sick, but when the desire cometh, it is a tree of life' (Proverbs 13:12).

The 'green land's name that a charm encloses' which 'never was writ in the traveller's chart' again evokes 'Dream-Land''s 'charmèd sleep' (line 3), while its trees whose 'fruit' 'never was sold in the merchant's mart' allude to the magical fruit of *Goblin Market*. The 'swallows of dreams' which 'dart' through Swinburne's 'dim fields' recall the 'gathering swallows' which 'twitter in the skies' in Keats's 'To Autumn' (1820). There is also another Rossettian image of heartbreak, taken from 'Songs in a Cornfield' (C. Rossetti 2001, 120–3), a particular favourite of Swinburne.[6] The poem's first stanza mentions Marian, a reaper who has been abandoned by her lover, but she is silent until line 94. Inspired by a swallow's flight, she sings 'Like one who hopes and grieves' (line 93). We are told that, if Marian's lover arrives tomorrow, 'He will find her sleeping' (line 113), while, if he returns the next day, 'He'll not find her at all' (line 115). All of Swinburne's references to Rossetti in 'A Ballad of Dreamland' allude to images of broken hearts, lost things, enchantment, love, and the singers and sleepers which fascinate both poets. By alluding to the mysteries of Rossetti's secretive poems, Swinburne shows an intimate engagement with her content as well as her forms. In identifying the many allusions to Rossetti, we do not emerge with solutions to the questions 'A Ballad of Dreamland' poses: exactly why has the speaker hidden her heart? Why is it sleeping? What is the song that can wake the sleeping heart? The ballad's envoi deepens the mystery.

> In the world of dreams I have chosen my part
>   To sleep for a season and hear no word
> Of true love's truth or of light love's art,
>   Only the song of a secret bird.
>
> (Swinburne 1904, 3.86)

Although there is no direct reference, as a whole 'A Ballad of Dreamland' might be compared to Rossetti's 'Winter: My Secret' (1862), whose defining feature is its half-playful, half-aggressive refusal to divulge what its secret is (C. Rossetti 2001, 41). This is not to say that Swinburne's poem resists interpretation; only that he shares with Rossetti an interest in ambiguities and dreamscapes. Like Rossetti, Swinburne withholds as much as he divulges in order to plunge readers into an atmosphere not unlike the dreamland his poem explores. 'A Ballad of Dreamland' is unmistakably a poem about poetry: it explores how poetry thrives in a self-created and self-generating world of allusion. Swinburne's poetic self-consciousness found expression in the ballad form. Just as ballads are famous shape-shifters, changing with each singer's interpretation, so can the words and music of poetry be inherited and reshaped by individual poets. The musical qualities, the very *sound* of poetry as well as its verbal language, are also passed on like 'the song of a secret bird'. This happens, for example, in the first stanza's unusual rhyme of 'roses' with 'snow's is', which echoes Rossetti's 'ice is' and 'spices' in 'Amen' (C. Rossetti 2001, 85, lines 13, 17).

Attuned to the feminine and the foreign in Swinburne's rhymes, contemporary critics pricked up their ears. Alexander Hay Japp, writing as H. A. Page, observes that

Mr. Swinburne in his various experiments with exotic forms has given a specimen of the French *Ballade*, which would be very perfect were it not for one or two awkwardnesses in the feminine-rhymes – such as 'snow's is' and 'grows is,' which would hardly be deemed happy rhymes in any ordinary English form; while another point is that he gets over a difficulty by the expedient of such words as 'part,' 'apart,' 'dispart,' – hardly rhymes in strictness, but identical words – an expedient, as we know, not uncommon in French poetry, and sanctioned even by Dante in Italian. (Japp 1878, 190)

Swinburne's 'Ballad of Dreamland' was ripe for parody on these grounds; Japp includes the poem 'A Ballad of After Dinner', about an ordinary man enjoying a nap, which gleefully rhymes 'presupposes' with 'toes, is'.[7]

Such 'awkwardnesses' in Christina Rossetti's verses were excused on the grounds of her gender, while her Anglo-Italian heritage and Church of England conservatism permitted her the freedom to 'experiment' with European verse traditions. As Lona Mosk Packer points out, comparisons between the two poets originated with William Rossetti's attempt to invest Swinburne's 'controversial volume with some of the respectable lustre of his sister's impeccable reputation' (Packer 1963, 35), a strategy which Jan Marsh thinks may have backfired. She observes that William's linking of the 'womanly' virtues of Rossetti's poems with Swinburne's verses in his *Swinburne's Poems and Ballads. A Criticism* (1866) may have had the unintended consequence of supporting the view that Swinburne's work was 'unmanly' (Marsh 1994, 356). Edmund Gosse tried to rectify this situation in his 1893 article for *The Century*. He contrasts Swinburne's 'more scientific and elaborate system of harmonies' with Rossetti's 'delicate' and 'naïve' technique, defending Swinburne's masculinity along with his poetic talent by distinguishing it from Rossetti's more feminine approach (Gosse 1893, 215).

It is Rossetti's investment in the primacy of rhyme, rhythm, and melody that is particularly attractive to Swinburne, regardless of her poems' sometimes disagreeable religious subject matter. In 'A Ballad of Dreamland', poetry is more than the 'word' of 'true love's truth or of light love's art'; it is also the 'song' that transmits it. Traditionally, the envoi is addressed to a prince or patron. Is it fanciful here to imagine Swinburne addressing his envoi to Rossetti? She certainly seems to be in his thoughts: the phrase 'light love' alludes to a Rossetti poem of that name (C. Rossetti 2001, 130). Here, Swinburne's admiration requires a kind of selective hearing which values the melody of the verse over the content.

Although 1881 saw the release of Rossetti's *A Pageant and Other Poems*, Rossetti's attention was increasingly directed towards the devotional poetry and prose which would dominate her later work. It was also in 1881 that Rossetti realised she had never sent a presentation copy of her verses to Swinburne, although he had been paying her this honour for some years. She told her brother William that she had tentatively offered Swinburne the devotional work *Called to be Saints*, 'merely however drawing his attention to the verses'. She also reassured William, 'I do not think he is at all offended by my offering him the book' (26 July 1882; C. Rossetti 1997–2004, 3.52). The next year, Swinburne dedicated *A Century of Roundels* to her, sending her a presentation copy. Their next exchange took place in 1884 when he sent her a copy of *A Midsummer Holiday* with its 'A Ballad of Appeal to Christina Rossetti' (Swinburne 1904, 6.71–2), a poem which asked her for 'Sweet water from the well of song', or, to put it more bluntly, more poems. Rossetti was well aware that she was less productive than before, as she wrote to Swinburne: 'dumbness is not my *choice*; nor will I attempt to justify it with the parrot who screamed "But I think the more"' (19 November 1884; C. Rossetti 1997–2004, 3.231).

This 'Ballad of Appeal' is no ordinary ballade; with three ten-line stanzas and a five-line envoi, this is a ballade supreme. Still built around only three rhymes, the ballade supreme (a predominantly French verse form) presents a greater challenge to the English poet's rhyming abilities, adding an ostentatious flourish to Swinburne's tribute. 'A Ballad of Appeal' begins its campaign with its title's Keatsian pun, 'a peal' intended to 'toll' Rossetti back to her sole poetic self, evoking the nightingale that 'sadly sings' in Rossetti's own 'Dream-Land'. The poem recycles many motifs of 'The Garden of Proserpine', 'A Forsaken Garden', and 'A Ballad of Dreamland', including sleep, birds, fertility, flowers, and poetry. Again Swinburne casts Rossetti (and her heart like a singing bird) as a Proserpine figure in the poem's first four lines: 'Song wakes with every wakening year / From hearts of birds that only feel / Brief spring's deciduous flower-time near / And song more strong to help or heal'. This parallel with the Proserpine myth carries an implicit criticism: Swinburne accuses Rossetti of sacrificing her poetic productivity to her religious obligations.

'A Ballad of Appeal' takes seriously the threat that concludes Rossetti's 1881 sonnet sequence *Monna Innominata* – 'Silence of love that cannot sing again' (C. Rossetti 2001, 301) – asking, 'Shall silence worse than winter seal?' Spring here does double duty as a season and the watery source of poetic inspiration, welling up in 'thought's remurmuring cave / The notes that rippled, wave on wave' to produce 'Sweet water from the well of song' (Swinburne 1904, 6.71). This watery cave recalls the 'charmèd sleep' of Rossetti's 'Dream-Land' 'Where sunless rivers weep / Their waves into the deep' (lines 1–2) and 'A Ballad of Dreamland''s dozing 'wind of the warm seas', as well as the 'ghost of a garden' that 'fronts the sea' in 'A Forsaken Garden'.

But here the water is fertile and nourishing, as 'All hearts bore fruit of joy to hear' from the well of song. This song can be 'loud as marriage-bells that peal, / Or flutelike soft, or keen like steel', while its 'sheer music' can be punningly 'sharp or grave'. The 'grave' image is reinforced by the 'ghosts in throng' who recall the ghosts and graves of 'A Forsaken Garden'. Swinburne even manages to cast a biblical reference into this cascade of imagery, as his song bird becomes Moses-like: 'Dark rocks, that yielded, where they clave / Sweet water'.

The water imagery drenches the final stanza, with its 'rains that cleanse and lave' and 'dewfall on an April grave' nourishing 'orchards' and 'corn-fields' reminiscent of Keats's 'To Autumn' as well as Rossetti's 'Dream-Land' and 'Songs in a Cornfield'. Rossetti's poems for children are alluded to in 'the smiles of babbling babes', and even her devotional verse is given a nod of approval in line 23: 'Prayer's perfect heart spake here'.

As in 'A Ballad of Dreamland', the envoi still craves 'the song of a secret bird', but this time it is addressed to the ballad itself. The very 'stave' is instructed to 'Ask nought beside thy pardon, save / Sweet water from the well of song', the double meaning of the word 'save' (rescue and excepting), lending urgency to this plea.

This ballade supreme offers a measured, public version of Swinburne's private thoughts about Rossetti's devotional prose. He was aware that his tribute might be taken in the wrong spirit. 'I hope you will not think I have taken a liberty in addressing you publicly without so much as a "*with* your leave" or "*by* your leave"', he wrote. Although in 1883 he had approached her brother William to seek permission to dedicate his *A Century of Roundels* to Christina, this time Swinburne seems to have felt that the matter was too urgent for such protocols. In fact, her earlier acceptance of the dedication 'emboldened me to express a wish which all your readers must share, and to which I trust you will not always turn a deaf ear – long as it seems since you have given us any fresh cause to thank you for a fresh gift of such verse as only you can give'. He drew her attention to the 'Ballad of Appeal', hoping its 'sincerity and earnestness' would 'atone for its brevity and inadequacy' (17 November 1884; Swinburne 1959–62, 5.88).

His 'appeal' to Rossetti, both in his poem and in the letter which accompanied it, did not, as he feared, fall on 'deaf' ears; in fact, his poetry helped her find her poetic voice again, as her next publication proved. In 1885, she published a devotional work, *Time Flies: A Reading Diary*, in which passages of prose were interspersed with poems. Many of these poems took the shape of Swinburnian roundels, 'understood' at the time 'as an extreme instance of a sound-driven form' (Weiner 2010, 23). Whatever their philosophical differences, the two poets had a common interest in the 'music' of poetry. Rossetti's was a conscious appropriation. Beside the poem for 5 May, a marginal note in Rossetti's handwriting in her own copy of *Time Flies* reads, 'My first roundel'.[8]

Twentieth-century hindsight helped reveal the full extent of Swinburne's influence on Rossetti. Jan Marsh writes that 'it is difficult to reconcile Swinburne's confessed amorality and anti-Christian stance' with 'Rossetti's highly moral and confessedly Christian writing', but she notes that 'in terms of technique, there are similarities', and that 'Both writers ... are undeniably Aesthetic in the musicality of their versification' (Marsh 1996, 23). Valeria Tinkler-Villani picks up on this point, linking it to Pater's 'The School of Giorgione' (1877):

> musicality, in poets such as Swinburne and Christina Rossetti, should be seen as the attempt to take poetry not only closer to painting, but also close to music, moving it, that is to say, away from reality and imitation, and taking it out of time and place – into a religious dimension, inherent in Aestheticism's fundamental belief that 'all art constantly aspires towards the condition of music'. (Tinkler-Villani 1999, 333)

In contemporary Victorian criticism poetic influence was perceived to flow from Rossetti to Swinburne, but there was some reverse traffic as well. Before Swinburne sought Rossetti's permission to dedicate his *A Century of Roundels* to her, he asked William Rossetti to 'sound her', offering a preview roundel, 'A Baby's Death', which memorialised William's baby son, Michael, who had died the month before. William reassured him that a dedication to his sister was appropriate as long as 'all the poems in your proposed volume are to be as innocuous – and indeed, to a Christian reader as edifying' (13 February 1883; W. M. Rossetti 1990, 443).

Swinburne's dedicatory roundel with its tentative refrain, 'Songs light as these' and its anxiety that his songs may not 'please / Ears tuned to strains of loftier thoughts' with their 'too rash reverence', shows that he kept William's advice in mind. At the same time, the roundel indicates the strength of this deceptively 'light' form, cautioning readers not to mistake lightness and musicality for a lack of substance:

> Songs light as these may sound, though deep and strong
> The heart spake through them, scarce should hope to please
> Ears tuned to strains of loftier thoughts than throng
>   Songs light as these.
>
> Yet grace may set their sometime doubt at ease,
> Nor need their too rash reverence fear to wrong
> The shrine it serves at and the hope it sees.
>
> For childlike loves and laughters thence prolong
> Notes that bid enter, fearless as the breeze,
> Even to the shrine of holiest-hearted song.
>   Songs light as these.
>
>   (Swinburne 1904, 5.113)

The double meaning of 'sound' in the first line draws attention to what is 'deep and strong' about the roundel. Although these songs 'may sound' 'light', they are weighty enough to 'sound' unexpected depths of 'The heart'. That sound itself will be the key-note of this poem is made clear not only in the first stanza's end-rhymes ('strong' / 'throng', 'please' / 'these') but also in its internal rhyme ('throng' / 'Songs') and sibilance ('songs', 'these', 'sound', 'strong' / 'spake', 'scarce', 'please' / 'Ears', 'strains', 'thoughts' / 'Songs', 'these'). Our attention is drawn to the way sounds circulate in this roundel; 'prolong' not only finds its echo in 'song' but prolongs itself across the line break. Even the poem's hopes to 'please / Ears' enacts the pleasure of sound by evoking the French word *plaisir*.

In the second stanza, the poem worries the 'rash reverence' of this kind of playfulness will undercut the roundel's claims to depth and strength. However, it counts on the 'grace' of both the poem and its listeners to 'ease' such 'doubt'. The third stanza defends the roundel form, in part by completing its formal circle, arguing that lightness is its virtue. A roundel's 'childlike loves' and 'laughter' are light enough to float on the 'breeze' into the 'shrine' of 'holiest-hearted song'.

When Swinburne sent copies of *A Century of Roundels* to Rossetti and her mother in June 1883, Rossetti wrote a polite note of thanks. A writer of children's verse herself, Rossetti praised the baby poems. Although not effusive, neither was she offended by a volume which one critic recognised as 'stronger and more chastened ... entirely free from that supersensuousness which, at the outset of the poet's career, gave offence in many quarters' (Anonymous 1883, 3). For the more conservative Victorian reader, it seems Swinburne's excesses could be tamed by form. Edmund Gosse declared that Swinburne's roundels were written 'for the sake of self-discipline, to abandon for a time his broad and sweeping measures, and to curb his Pegasus with a rigidly determined fixed form' (Gosse 1917, 266–7).[9]

Rossetti recognised that the formal qualities of Swinburne's roundels were easily adaptable to her own devotional concerns, as her own experiments with the form proved. Based on the French 'rondeau', Swinburne's variant eleven-line form is built around two rhymes, three stanzas, and a repeated refrain which is determined by a part of the first line. Rikky Rooksby notes that

> Swinburne's change from the rondeau was to trim one line from each of the five-line stanzas to produce a structure eleven lines long and to move the refrain from line eight to line four. The chiming quality, created by the use of two rhymes only and the thrice-stated refrain ... gives the roundel its immediately apparent major formal distinction: its circularity. (Rooksby 1985, 251)

Her biographer Georgina Battiscombe notes that Rossetti used roundels 'frequently in her religious verse', adding that 'the formal scheme with its repetition of rhyme and phrase seems ill adapted to such [religious] themes' (Battiscombe 1981, 16). Rossetti herself didn't see things this way; she used this very 'circularity' to evoke the idea of prayer, ritual, and call-and-response central to religious thought and practice.

For instance, in the first roundel in *Time Flies* (1885) 'Love understands the mystery', Rossetti uses the form to enact structurally her poem's sense of weight and measure, while the refrain contributes to the poem's reassuring tone.

> Love understands the mystery, whereof
>   We can but spell a surface history:
> Love knows, remembers: let us trust in Love:
>   Love understands the mystery.
>
> Love weighs the event, the long pre-history,
>   Measures the depth beneath, the height above,
> The mystery, with the ante-mystery.

To love and to be grieved befits a dove
Silently telling her bead-history:
Trust all to Love, be patient and approve:
Love understands the mystery.

(C. Rossetti 2001, 503)

Here, Rossetti uses the 'light' form of Swinburne's roundel to carry a
weighty emotion. The first stanza's confidence in what love is and what
love does is maintained by the roundel's regular iambic pentameter and
comforting rhyme scheme (abab). The lulling rhythm is continued in the
internal rhymes of the first and third lines ('Love ... whereof', 'us trust'),
and the repetition of the word 'Love'. The impression of balance and
symmetry conveyed formally in the first stanza is made explicit in the
second, where 'Love weighs' and 'Measures', balancing 'the mystery with
the ante-mystery'.

The deviations from metrical regularity in the second stanza, as well as
its three lines as opposed to four, and different rhyme scheme (bab) struc-
turally enact the process of weighing and measuring, as the stanza
considers present and past, depth and height, mystery and ante-mystery.
The poem is brought back into balance in the third stanza, as the rhyme,
metre, internal rhyme ('love'/'dove', 'Love'/'approve'), and number of
lines parallel that of the first stanza. The dove telling 'her bead-history'
also refers to human love's expression, the act of prayer, and to the
comforts available in memory and ritual which this poem offers.

Swinburne was correct in guessing that his roundel form would appeal
to Rossetti. The sound of a poem was always very important to her; she
was often praised for the beauty of her lyric poems and her mastery of the
complex rhyme-scheme of the Petrarchan sonnet. Rossetti never
dedicated a volume to Swinburne, nor is it likely that he would have
wished her to, as every work from the period of his dedication to her was
explicitly devotional. William refused the dedication of his sister's 1893
Verses on the grounds of his own agnosticism, and it is likely Swinburne
would have done the same. It was William who rectified the situation after
his sister's death; he dedicated his 1896 edition of Christina's New Poems to
Swinburne, claiming that she had 'hailed his genius and prized himself the
greatest of living British poets' (W. M. Rossetti in C. Rossetti 1896,
Dedication page). This seems an exaggeration of Christina's admiration,
and critics of the time took William to task for this liberty. Even if the
dedication overstates the case, evidence of Christina Rossetti's and

Swinburne's uneasy affinity survives in their poetry, a less restricted space where their relationship could evolve in ways prohibited in life. This détente endured even after Rossetti's death in 1894. When Swinburne received her posthumously collected poems, he wrote: 'Good Satan! what a fearful warning against the criminal lunacy of theolatry! It is horrible to think of such a woman ... spiritually infected and envenomed by the infernal and putrefying virus of the Galilean serpent!' (29 January 1904; Swinburne 1959–62, 6.176). Yet this private denunciation of Rossetti's Christianity should be considered in conjunction with his public memorial poem, 'A New Year's Eve' (Swinburne 1904, 6.321–3). William told Swinburne of her death on 29 December 1894 on the very day it happened; two days later, Swinburne wrote his poem, which first appeared in the *Nineteenth Century* in February 1895, and later in *A Channel Passage and Other Poems* (1904).

Given that the pair communed over the melody of verse, it is appropriate that Swinburne evokes Rossetti's death through an absence of sound: 'silence deeper than time or space'. The 'carol of joy' is 'Not here, not here' because 'There is none to sing as she sang upon earth, not one'. This time Rossetti's songs are not earthly 'water from the well', but heavenly 'waves of light on a starry shore'. The silence in 'The Garden of Proserpine' is eternal: 'the world is quiet', and there is no 'sound of waters shaken / Nor any sound'. But the 'silence' in this 'sunless place' is 'not all everlasting' because of the 'Hope' and 'comfort' derived from 'the sweet song's grace'. In a neat reversal, Rossetti redeems heaven, rather than the other way around. This could be a *sotto voce* moment of blasphemy: Swinburne turning Rossetti's beliefs against her. But in contrast with the pessimism of 'The Garden of Proserpine', this poem presents a hopeful vision of the afterlife, ending with a startling concession to Rossetti's beliefs:

> Who knows? We know not. Afar, if the dead be far,
> Alive, if the dead be alive as the soul's works are,
>   The soul whose breath was among us a heavenward song
> Sings, loves, and shines as it shines for us here a star.
>   (Swinburne 1904, 6.323)

In figuring Rossetti's spirit as 'a star', he may have had in mind the opening pages of *Time Flies*, where 'Christians are called to be like stars, luminous, steadfast, majestic, attractive' (C. Rossetti 1885, 2). This final stanza, which asks, 'Who knows?', can be read as a polite way of agreeing to disagree with Rossetti's Christianity. At the same time, it is a far cry from condemning 'the criminal lunacy of theolatry', a sentiment Swinburne expressed in the same year that he republished 'A New Year's Eve'.

Like Rossetti, Swinburne continued writing and publishing until the end of his life. The consequent layering, deepening, and complication of his beliefs caused him, if not to radically revise his position on Christianity, then at least to imagine how that belief served to inspire a poet he respected. As Rooksby points out, while F. L. Lucas thought '"the nightingale in [Swinburne] died of too much midnight oil"' in his later years, 'the more one reads the later poetry the more one sees that the nightingale did not die, he simply changed his tune' (Rooksby 1988, 413). Rossetti herself went through something similar in her later years, publicly acknowledging the ways in which overzealous, 'Scrupulous Christians' might be trying to others: 'They run the risk of figuring as truthful offensively, conscientious unkindly, firm feebly, in the right ridiculously. Common sense has forsaken them: and what gift or grace can quite supply the lack of common sense?' (C. Rossetti 1885, 2).

To go back to the beginning of this chapter, Swinburne's scrupulous refusal to recite a Christian stanza from Rossetti's 'A Death of a First-born' bears comparison with Rossetti's pasting paper strips over heretical lines of *Atalanta in Calydon*. At the same time, both gestures are partial, biographical moments: truthful but unrepresentative of the whole. A cursory glance at the work of Swinburne and Rossetti shows that these poets spent at least as much time reading each other's work as they did averting their eyes. If their work is consulted, common interests emerge despite the radical differences in their personal beliefs. Just as we might weigh Rossetti's fifty-plus roundels in the balance for her good opinion of Swinburne, so we can consider adding Swinburne's poetic tributes to the scale.

NOTES

1 The third verse reads: 'Stoop to console us, Christ, Sole Consolation, / While dust returns to dust; / Until that blessed day when all Thy Nation / Shall rise up of the Just' (C. Rossetti 2001, 586, lines 9–12).
2 This line alludes to the Song of Solomon 8:6: 'Set me as a seal upon thine heart, as a seal upon thine arm: for love is strong as death; jealousy is cruel as the grave.'

3 'He is dead and gone, lady, / He is dead and gone; / At his head a grass-green turf, / At his heels a stone' (Shakespeare 2003, *Hamlet* 4.5.29–32).

4 This edition collected verses from Rossetti's previously published volumes, and also included new poems.

5 This count is according to Betty S. Flowers's introduction to C. Rossetti 2001, xl.

6 Christina Rossetti wrote to Dante Gabriel on 11 March, 1865: '"Songs in a Cornfield" is one of my own favourites, so I am specially gratified by your and Mr. Swinburne's praise' (C. Rossetti 1997–2004, 1.232).

7 See the parody's first stanza: 'I hid my head in a rug from Moses, / From the clatter of moving dishes apart, / And curled up my feet for forty dozes, / Just for to soothe my beating heart' (Japp 1878, 191).

8 See title note for '"Now They Desire a Better Country"' (C. Rossetti 2001, 1056).

9 This probably alludes to lines 184–7 of Keats's 'Sleep and Poetry' (1817): 'Men were thought wise who could not understand / His glories: with a puling infant's force / They sway'd about upon a rocking horse / And thought it Pegasus' (Keats 1982, 42).

9

PARLEYING WITH ROBERT BROWNING:
SWINBURNE'S AESTHETICISM, BLASPHEMY,
AND THE DRAMATIC MONOLOGUE

Sara Lyons

As an undergraduate at Oxford, Swinburne fantasised about reviewing his own poetry and identifying his 'models' as 'i.e. blasphemy and sensuality' – an arresting formulation that seems to posit transgression itself as a celebrated literary form or precursor poet (qtd in Hyder 1970, xiii). When Swinburne's fantasy of literary scandal was in a sense spectacularly fulfilled in the 'trial-by-review'[1] of his first collection of poetry, *Poems and Ballads, First Series* (1866), he apparently minded the imputations of 'blasphem[y]' far less than he did those of sexual 'indecen[cy]' (Swinburne 1866, 6; 2000, 404). In *Notes on Poems and Reviews* (1866), the pamphlet he composed in response to the controversy that followed the publication of *Poems and Ballads*, Swinburne retaliated energetically against the critical ire that had been directed at erotic poems such as 'Hermaphroditus', but he defended the volume's anti-Christian content only in relation to a single poem ('Anactoria'), and he buried his sharpest riposte to the 'blasphemy' charge in a footnote:

> As I shall not return to this charge of 'blasphemy', I will here cite a notable instance of what does seem permissible in that line to the English reader ... After many alternate curses and denials of God, a great poet talks of Christ 'veiling his horrible Godhead', of his 'malignant soul', his 'godlike malice'. Shelley outlived all this and much more; but Shelley wrote all this and much more. Will no Society for the Suppression of Common Sense – no Committee for the Propagation of Cant – see to it a little? Or have they not already tried their hands at it and broken down? For the poem which contains the words above quoted continues to this day to bring credit and profit to its publishers – Mssrs. Moxon and Co. (Swinburne 1866, 11; 2000, 407)

This gibe at Moxon & Co. – the reputable firm that initially published *Poems and Ballads* and then, afraid prosecution would follow the damning reviews, withdrew the volume – is more charged than it appears. As Swinburne surely knew, *Queen Mab* (1813), the Shelley poem to which he alludes, had in fact procured Moxon & Co. a blasphemy conviction. In 1841, the Chartist and freethinker Henry Hetherington sued Edward Moxon for blasphemous libel in order to dramatise the injustice of the fact that the blasphemy law was enforced only in the cases of 'unrespectable' and politically radical writers and publishers like Hetherington himself.[2] As Swinburne insinuates, Moxon & Co. quailed at the reviews of *Poems and Ballads* in part because Edward Moxon's successors at the firm remembered the *Queen Mab* case (Thomas 1979, 127–8).

Joss Marsh has argued that the *Queen Mab* case was pivotal in what she calls the 'literary redefinition' of blasphemy in the nineteenth century (Marsh 1998, 91). As critiques of traditional religion became more commonplace and socially acceptable, 'blasphemy' increasingly came to signify not a verbal offence against religion as such but the unsavoury twin of polite agnosticism and doubt. Marsh argues that the Victorian concept of blasphemy was class-coded and profoundly political in so far as it hinged less on the actual claims of a given critique of religion than on the felt manner and sensibility of the critique; as it was enshrined in law, 'blasphemy' essentially constituted a crime against literary decorum or aesthetic taste (Marsh 1998, 90–109). Although Marsh's book focuses on the working-class secularists who fell victim to this distinction between sanctioned and unsanctioned styles of religious critique, it also has implications for the study of an aristocratic poet like Swinburne, whose aestheticism was in part a bid to preserve the transgressive potential of atheism at a moment when polite doubt had accrued a considerable measure of cultural legitimacy.

Swinburne reflected more candidly on the blasphemies of *Poems and Ballads* in a letter to William Michael Rossetti:

> As to the anti-theism of 'Félise' I know of course that *you* know that the verses represent a mood of mind and phase of thought not unfamiliar to me; but I nonetheless maintain that no reader ... has a right (whatever he may conjecture) to assert that this is *my* faith and that the faith expressed in such things as the 'Litany' or 'Carol' or 'Dorothy' is not ... it is not the less formally dramatic than the others; and this is the point on which it seems to me necessary to insist ... I for see I shall soon have to defend myself from the charge of being a moralist – a deist – even (chi lo sa?) a Galilean. It is

really very odd that people (friendly or unfriendly) will not let one be an
artist, but must needs make one out a parson or a pimp. I suppose it is part
of the fetid and fecund spawn of the 'Galilean serpent.' (9 October 1866;
Swinburne 1959–62, 1.193)

While Swinburne here claims that the tendency to evaluate art as an
index to the beliefs of its creator is one of the pernicious legacies of
Christianity, he immediately betrays his own Romantic investment in the
idea of art as a testament of (rebellious) authorial intentions: his delin-
eation of his ideal of the disaffiliated aesthete, free to venture across the
terrain of belief and unbelief without commitment to any public identity,
culminates abruptly in an invocation of Shelley as a Romantic infidel and
revolutionary ('Galilean serpent' alludes to Shelley's 'Ode to Liberty'
(1820): 'the Galilean serpent forth did creep, / And made thy world an
undistinguishable heap'; Shelley 2009, 470; lines 119–20). This letter also
suggests that Swinburne's espousal of an art-for-art's sake position –
which here seems essentially a rhetorical feint, a means of asserting and
disavowing radical convictions, perhaps especially anti-Christian ones, in
the same gesture – was shaped by his sense of the prestige of the dramatic
form, a poetic genre associated with Browning and, to a lesser degree,
with Tennyson, the age's two great poets of religious doubt.

Swinburne also defends his poems on the grounds that they are
'formally dramatic' in *Notes on Poems and Reviews*: here he declares that his
poetry is 'dramatic, many-faced, multifarious; and no utterance of
enjoyment or despair, belief or unbelief, can properly be assumed as the
assertion of its author's personal feeling or faith' (Swinburne 1866, 6;
2000, 404). He claims that his use of the dramatic form is actually a mark
of his respect for propriety: where Byron and Shelley used the confes-
sional Romantic lyric to engage in full-dress assaults on the pieties of their
culture, he adopts the 'dramatic method', a mode of indirection and
authorial self-effacement. Yet he adds a teasing double negative to this
protestation: 'I do not say that, if I chose [to attack social conventions], I
would not do so to the best of my power' (Swinburne 1866, 18; 2000, 404).
We can appreciate the archness of Swinburne's self-positioning here only
when we examine the monologues in question, for Swinburne uses the
freedom of subject matter and the appearance of ideological neutrality
afforded by the 'dramatic method' to reinvigorate a tradition of Romantic
iconoclasm he associated with Byron and Shelley (as well as with Blake).[3]
Moreover, Swinburne uses the form to engage in an *agon* with Browning
– specifically, to interrogate Browning's representations of religious

doubt, and to propose an alternative vision of the relationship between religion and art. This chapter argues that two dramatic monologues from *Poems and Ballads, First Series* – 'Hymn to Proserpine' and 'The Leper' – seek respectively to revise two of Browning's best-known examples of the form, 'Cleon' (1855) and 'Porphyria's Lover' (1836). My larger claim is that Swinburne's aestheticism was in part an effect of the complexities he confronted when he sought to define himself against the conventions of Victorian religious doubt and to cast atheism as a mode of Romantic transgression.

'HYMN TO PROSERPINE' AND 'CLEON'

In 1875, Swinburne included in his essay on the Elizabethan dramatist and translator George Chapman a lengthy excursus in which he defended Browning against the charge of obscurity that had dogged his career (Swinburne 1875b, 25). While Swinburne is generous in his praise of Browning, he displays marked ambivalence toward Browning's rhetorical virtuosity, which he compares to that of a 'greater debater or an eminent leading counsel' (Swinburne 1875b, 23), and toward the forensic character of the dramatic monologue form more generally:

> the reader's apprehension takes fire from the writer's, and he catches from a subtler and more active mind the infection of spiritual interest; so that any candid and clear-headed student finds himself able to follow for the time in fancy the lead of such a thinker with equal satisfaction on any course of thought or argument; when he sets himself to refute Renan through the dying lips of St. John or to try conclusions with Strauss in his own person, and when he flashes at once the whole force of his illumination full upon the inmost thought and mind of the most infamous criminal, a Guido Franceschini or a Louis Bonaparte, compelling in the black and obscene abyss of such a spirit to yield up at last the secret of its profoundest sophistries. (Swinburne 1875b, 19–20)

Tellingly, when Swinburne praises Browning for his capacity to induce readers to interpret against the grain of their ordinary feelings, he remarks first upon Browning's suasive power in relation to Christian apologetics and only secondly upon the psychological depth Browning grants dictators and criminals. Swinburne insinuates that Browning not only represents but also specialises in 'profoundest sophistries': what is most remarkable about his poetry is the way it lures readers into agreeing with 'equal satisfaction' to 'any course of thought or argument'.

Swinburne's intention here was probably not to pay Browning a spiked compliment but to express an earnest fascination with the 'secret' of Browning's persuasive gift and, in particular, Browning's capacity to convey to readers the 'infection of a spiritual interest'. That Swinburne read Browning distrustfully, struggling to quarantine aesthetic admiration from any concession to Browning's Christian commitments, is also discernible in his 1870 essay on D. G. Rossetti's poetry, later collected in *Essays and Studies* (1875):

> There are two living and leading writers of high and diverse genius whom any student of work – utterly apart as their ways of work lie – may and must, without prejudice or presumption, assume to hold fast, with a force of personal passion, the radical tenet of Christian faith. It is as difficult for a reasonable reader to doubt the actual and positive adherence to Christian doctrine of the Protestant thinker as of the Catholic priest; to doubt that faith in Christ as God – a tough, hard, vital faith which can bear at need hard stress of weather and hard-thought – dictated 'A Death in the Desert' or 'Christmas Eve and Easter Day', as to doubt that it dictated the 'Apologia' or 'Dream of Gerontius': though neither in the personal creed set forth by Mr. Browning nor in the clerical creed delivered by Dr. Newman do we find apparent or flagrant – however they may lurk, tacit and latent, in the last logical expression of either man's theories – the viler forms and more hideous outcomes of Christianity, its more brutal aspects and deadlier consequences; a happy default due rather to nobility of instinct than to ingenuity of evasion. (Swinburne 1870a, 562–3; 1875a, 80)

Swinburne's display of critical disinterestedness here enables him to cast Christianity as a 'radical' ideology that a 'reasonable' reader will want to sift out of any aesthetic appreciation of Browning's genius. At the same time, Swinburne comes close to suggesting that Browning is too good for his professed creed anyway: Browning's 'noble' willingness to subject his faith to 'hard thought' and contend with the demythologisation of the Christian scriptures performed by Renan and Strauss only confirms his incapacity to recognise the ugly truths of Christianity. Swinburne's own dramatic monologues aim to make manifest what he considered the repressed content of Browning's religious monologues: namely, the 'viler forms and more hideous outcomes of Christianity, its more brutal aspects and deadlier consequences', which he felt 'lurk[ed], tacit and latent' in Christianity's modern and liberal guises.

As Nicholas Shrimpton observes, though poems like 'The Leper' and 'Hymn to Proserpine' fulfil the genre's basic technical requirements, there has been a tendency to dismiss Swinburne's claim to be working within the dramatic genre as 'a mere subterfuge, or convenient mask, for the expression of inconveniently controversial impulses or opinions' (Shrimpton 1993, 52–3). Where Shrimpton defends Swinburne against the charge that his monologues are simply mouthpieces for his own preoccupations and lack Browningesque historicism and irony (60–71), I would suggest that 'Hymn to Proserpine' and 'The Leper' in fact parody the tendentiousness often submerged in Browning's use of the form. More precisely, Swinburne parodies the way in which Browning used the form as a vehicle for Christian apologetics by instead pressing it into the service of his own anti-Christian agenda. In this, Swinburne's dramatic monologues exemplify his delight in pushing the established literary paradigms of religious doubt to their limits and exploiting them to glorify the very threat of atheism which, in the hands of other writers, they had been used to sublimate or contain.

In poems such as 'Cleon' (1855), 'A Death in the Desert' (1864), and 'An Epistle Containing the Strange Medical Experience of the Physician of Karshish' (1855), Browning dramatised moments in early Christian history in order to address the predicament of the modern Christian unsettled by a sceptical historical awareness (Browning 2005, 269–78; 186–94; 311–28). Although these poems are designed to pose hermeneutic problems for the reader in a way that approximates the perplexities faced by a modern exegete of the scriptures in the wake of the German Higher Criticism, their polemical thrust is decipherable. All three poems feature speakers whose failure to apprehend the divinity of Christ or to trust in a divine miracle reveals their spiritual limitations as much as the mitigating complexities of their historical contexts (though in the case of 'A Death in the Desert', the voices of scepticism are only filtered through the speech of the poem's main protagonist, St John). In each poem, this strategy works to relativise Victorian religious scepticism, which is made to seem less prestigiously modern and more like a manifestation of a basic human resistance to mystery that has always made faith a difficult achievement. More broadly, Browning aims to recuperate religious doubt for Christianity by revealing that it was always already woven into the fabric of faith.

Of these religious monologues, Browning's 'Cleon' is the crucial intertext for 'Hymn to Proserpine' (Swinburne 1904, 1.67–73; 2000, 55–61). That 'Cleon' is a response to Arnold's *Empedocles on Etna* (1852), a poem that Browning admired as much as Swinburne did, has long been

recognised (see Harrison 1990, 47–68), and I would suggest that
Empedocles also stands behind 'Hymn to Proserpine'. All three poems
displace a Victorian perception of spiritual malaise on to a classical and/or
early Christian context, and take world-weary, cultured, rhetorically
commanding men for their speakers. At stake in all three poems is the
question of whether the evanescent pleasures of the here and now – iden-
tified with sexuality and with art or aesthetic contemplation – are
sufficient unto themselves and can compensate for the wretchedness of
old age and the fact of mortality.

The protagonist of 'Cleon' is a fictional first century AD Greek
polymath who, over the course of the poem (which takes the form of an
epistle from Cleon to his patron, King Protus), unwittingly exposes the
depths of his spiritual sterility. An ageing sensualist and aesthete who has
'loved his life over-much' (line 322), Cleon can neither believe in anything
'more' than his 'animal life' (line 215) nor reconcile himself to mortality.
He considers his reputation as an artist meagre solace for the fact that his
appetite for life exceeds his 'bounded physical recipiency' (line 246), and
this makes him wistful about the possibility of an afterlife, though the
intractability of his essentially secular and materialist imagination is
indicated by the fact that his concept of an afterlife is really only a fantasy
about the prolongation of worldly pleasure (lines 320–35). The
throwaway final lines of his epistle are a famous instance of
Browningesque irony:

> Thou canst not think a mere barbarian Jew
> As Paulus proves to be, one circumcised,
> Hath access to a secret shut from us?
> . . .
> Oh, the Jew findeth scholars! certain slaves
> Who touched on this same isle, preached him and Christ;
> And (as I gathered from a bystander)
> Their doctrine could be held by no sane man.
>
> (lines 343–5; 350–3)

Browning uses the figure of Cleon to critique the Victorian age's
narcissism about its own modernity and a growing tendency among intel-
lectuals to treat Christianity as primitive superstition, or as a 'doctrine that
could be held by no sane man'. Cleon's complacent belief that he lives in
a super-civilised, 'composite' age (line 65) – that is, a decadent phase of
culture defined by a sense of historical relativism – as opposed to an

originary and 'heroic' one (line 70) necessarily seems myopic to the Victorian reader, who grasps the significance of what looks trivial to Cleon: the advent of Christianity. Browning's gift for capturing the dissonances of colloquial speech is striking here: after Cleon's grandiloquent ruminations on mortality and art, his slur against Christ (whom he confuses with St Paul) is jarring, and unmasks the ugliness of his intellectual chauvinism at a stroke. In turn, this works to awaken the reader to the limitations of her own historical perspective, and to unmask the overweening character of modern scepticism, particularly the assumption that it constitutes the *telos* of human enlightenment.

Like 'Cleon', 'Hymn to Proserpine' returns to a moment of Christian historical rupture and chooses a vantage point from which Christianity looks like a new and alien ideology. However, where Browning casts Christianity as the sympathetic underdog despised by sophisticates like Cleon, Swinburne seizes upon a moment where Christianity symbolically gains hegemonic status, as his subtitle, 'After the Proclamation of the Christian Faith in Rome', makes explicit. We might interpret this difference as Swinburne's allegorical correction of Browning: while modern Christianity might appear embattled to Browning, it still looks monolithic to Swinburne. Likewise, Swinburne inverts the Christian irony of 'Cleon' by revising Browning's use of the classical decadence *topos*. We are meant to recognise Cleon's jaded sophistication, his preoccupation with worldly success and with the life of the senses, as well as his contempt for Christianity, as symptomatic of the spiritual exhaustion of the Roman empire and, by analogy, of Victorian England. 'Hymn to Proserpine' also exploits the Roman decadence analogy, but instead plays with the idea – familiar to Victorian readers from Edward Gibbon's *Decline and Fall of the Roman Empire* (1776–89) – that Christianity tended toward Roman decadence rather than constituting its cure.[4] Notoriously, Swinburne's Roman disdains Christianity as an etiolated offshoot of the paganism it displaced: 'Thou hast conquered, O pale Galilean; the world has grown grey from thy breath' (line 35). A rehabilitated Cleon, Swinburne's Roman is not an arid sophisticate but a vatic figure whose antipathy to the new Christian dispensation reveals his pagan fullness of being. Where Cleon fails to foresee the triumph of Christianity, Swinburne's Roman prophesies its eventual decline (in the Victorian age, we are surely meant to infer). The speaker's sense of the transience of all things radically defamiliarises the figure of Christ, who is imagined as a kind of Ozymandias figure whose claims to omnipotence will seem worse than void to future generations. Swinburne compounds this sense of defamiliarisation by making his Roman sound anachronistically like a Victorian doubter lamenting the retreat of the 'sea of faith':[5]

> I am sick of singing: the bays burn deep and chafe: I am fain
> To rest a little from praise and grievous pleasure and pain
> ...
> O Gods dethroned and deceased, cast forth, wiped out in a day!
>
> (lines 9–10; 13)

By simple inversion, Swinburne parodies alarmist Victorian responses to the rise of secularism: to his Roman sage, the rise of Christianity is a comparably precipitous descent into decadence and nihilism. In particular, Swinburne is parodying the elegiac sage posture that many intellectuals assumed in relation to a perceived crisis of faith: his Roman is in possession of the grandly dolorous, apocalyptic rhetoric of an Arnold, a Carlyle, or a Tennyson, yet what he mourns is the triumph rather than the withering away of Christianity. The poem is designed to make such melancholia over lost faith look narrow and sentimental, for his pagan laments not the loss of a consolation, as Christianity was often constructed within the discourse of Victorian doubt, but a belief system at once more 'bitter' and 'beautiful' (line 8) than Christianity.

As Margot Louis observes, 'Hymn to Proserpine', like many of Swinburne's anti-Christian poems, seeks to 'undermine the yearning for immortality' (Louis 2009b, 56). Louis characterises this poem as radically pessimistic and suggestive of Swinburne's affinities with de Sade and Schopenhauer: 'his Proserpine poems repudiate not only the transcendent but also the deeper, more widespread assumption that life *per se* has value – an assumption that is the very basis of the yearning for immortality' (Louis 2009b, 57–8). Conversely, I read the poem as a critique of the Christian perception that the value of life turns upon the promise of an afterlife, an idea that is an unmistakable subtext of Browning's 'Cleon' and arguably of Arnold's *Empedocles* as well. Rather than celebrating pessimism, Swinburne indicts Christianity for its pessimism, for its denigration of 'all the joy before death' (line 101), and, in a characteristic move, elevates above it a quasi-pagan atheism that heroically embraces life's dialectic of 'grievous pleasure and pain' (line 10). Louis suggests that the speaker's 'yearning for death' epitomises Swinburne's pessimistic strain, yet this yearning is presented quite specifically as the speaker's despairing response to the triumph of Christianity. Within the poem's imaginative economy, the pagan religions were emotionally complete because they honoured life's ambivalence, its 'mutable wings' (line 30) and bracing mix of joy and suffering. Christian monotheism, by contrast, is tantamount to worshipping solely Proserpine, here posited as the goddess of death and the underworld, at the expense of Apollo and Venus, the deities of art and love respectively. Louis's insight that the poem 'turn[s] a Christian trope against itself [and] exposes Christianity as a delusory way station on the road to nihilism and the worship of death' is exact (Louis 2009b, 61); yet her suggestion that Swinburne simply endorses this nihilism renders the poem's critique of Christianity incoherent. One of the poem's Browningesque ironies is that Christianity has partially 'conquered' the imagination of the speaker: he has become a morbid monotheist, worshipping Proserpine at the expense of the other gods in the pantheon. In other words, Swinburne's Roman has 'fed on the fullness of death' (line 36) and partially succumbed to the logic of the Christianity he reviles as a death-cult – an irony more piquant for the fact that his speech sounds like a passionate *non serviam* in the face of an official fiat. In this respect, Shrimpton is right to argue that 'Hymn to Proserpine' is less straightforwardly 'polemical' than is generally thought (Shrimpton 1993, 67–8); it does not simply ventriloquise Swinburne's hostility to Christianity, but imagines its way into a liminal historical figure, one who embodies the ethos of the old pagan religions even as he shows symptoms of having fallen under the spell of the new Christian orthodoxy. 'Hymn to Proserpine', then, is a classically Browningesque dramatic monologue: its speaker is a heroic individualist whose rhetoric recoils upon him, creating an ironic gap between what he means to express and what he actually discloses to the reader.

Swinburne is sometimes caricatured as an unreflective rebel, blithely *épatant le bourgeois*; yet 'Hymn to Proserpine', one of his most famous poems, is about the difficulties of formulating, even inwardly, a coherent opposition to a dominant ideology. While Swinburne's Roman asserts that the Christian attempt to supplant Venus with the Virgin Mary and restrain 'the world's desire' is futile, like an effort to 'chasten the high sea with rods' (line 65), he also wonders plaintively at Christianity's power to divest him of his pagan deities: 'Ye are fallen, our lords, by what token? We wist that ye should not fall' (line 89). Thaïs Morgan interprets the poem as a triumphant affirmation of the fact that 'Christ will never truly oust Venus, for we will never prefer death over life' (Morgan 1984, 193), yet this preference is actually in question throughout the poem; the pessimistic undertow of the speaker's imagery and argument is always dragging against the swell of his rhetoric, and his ultimate embrace of death, or Proserpine, underscores the insidious allure not simply of Christianity's romance of death but of its newly minted official status: 'Yea, once we had sight of another: but now [the Virgin Mary] is queen, say these' (line 77).

The fact that Swinburne's Roman has been fatally seduced by the new orthodoxy is crucial to understanding Swinburne's sense of Christianity as a paradoxical force, mighty and oppressive in its very 'pale' doctrines of compassion, asceticism, and eternal life. This contradiction, manifest also in the mix of triumphalism and defeatism in the speaker's tone, often fissures Swinburne's anti-religious polemics; we are persistently asked to imagine Christianity as at once frail and tyrannical, moribund and all-pervasive. Noting this tension, Louis remarks, 'Even the sympathetic reader must suspect that, if God is dead, we need not rage at him' (Louis 1990, 106). Yet we might understand this less as a simple failure of logic than Swinburne's engagement with the equivocal status and meaning of religious scepticism in mid to late Victorian England. Even at his most vituperatively anti-Christian, Swinburne is highly self-conscious about the extent to which religious doubt had been uncoupled from its traditional associations with sin and heresy, had grown conventional as a literary theme, and had become available as a common language for both committed Christians and unbelievers.[6] Swinburne's anti-Christian poems labour to negotiate the fact that more moderate, decorous critiques of Christianity as well as explicitly Christian explorations of doubt were ubiquitous in the work of an older generation of Victorian writers, including Browning. As a parody of Browning's religious monologues, 'Hymn to Proserpine' calls attention at once to the kinds of formal conventions that had made religious scepticism speakable in Victorian England and to the more radical possibilities those conventions repressed.

'THE LEPER' AND 'PORPHYRIA'S LOVER'

As is often remarked, Swinburne's 'The Leper' (Swinburne 1904, 1.119–24; 2000, 95–100) is a homage to Browning's 'Porphyria's Lover'. It is also an instance of poetic one-upmanship: as Catherine Maxwell points out, it hyperbolises Browning's penchant for the grotesque by transform-ing the 'slight hint of necrophilia in the conclusion of Browning's poem [into ...] the six-months dead body adored by Swinburne's speaker'

(Maxwell 2001, 181). Swinburne appropriates the Gothic romance premise of Browning's monologue and escalates it into an experiment in the decadent aesthetics he had absorbed from Baudelaire's *Les Fleurs du mal* (1857). John Rosenberg rightly connects 'The Leper' to an observation Swinburne made in a rhapsodic review of *Les Fleurs du mal* that he wrote while in the process of revising 'The Leper': 'Even of the loathsomest bodily putrescence and decay he can make some noble use; pluck out its meaning and secret, even its beauty, in a certain way, from actual carrion' (qtd in Rosenberg 2005, 165; Swinburne 1862a, 999; 1972, 30).[7] Swinburne's construction of necrophilic passion for a leper as the *nec plus ultra* of romantic love recalls several poems from *Les Fleurs du mal*: 'A Carcass', 'Danse Macabre', and 'A Martyr' all have thematic affinities (Baudelaire 1993, 59–63, 197–201, 229–33). Yet 'The Leper' does more than ratchet up the shock value of 'Porphyria's Lover' by infusing it with the Baudelairean perfume of 'beauty in carrion': it uses decadent aesthetics to critique the equation between atheism, madness, and evil implied by Browning's poem, and to articulate a provocative vision of art as a mode of sacred transgression, or 'holy insurrection' (Swinburne 1868a, 157).

Browning's monologuists – who are typically male – are famous for the intricate ways they manage to betray themselves while caught up in a process of self-vindication. 'Porphyria's Lover' is traditionally read alongside 'My Last Duchess' (1842) as a study in the murderous extremes of male narcissism and sexual possessiveness. Yet 'Porphyria's Lover' might also be paired with 'Cleon', for, like that poem, the speaker's unwitting self-betrayal pivots on an apparently incidental impiety in the final lines: 'And all night long we have not stirred / And yet God has not said a word!' (Browning 2005, 122–4, lines 59–60). Here Browning gives an ambiguous clue to the logic behind the baffling act at the centre of the poem. The speaker strangles his higher-born beloved in a remote cottage, ostensibly so that he might possess her more completely and render their love immutable. However, even before the final line, there are a number of indications that the speaker does not really imagine the murder as the romantic *liebestod* that he makes it out to be. The fact that the speaker 'debated what to do' (line 35) before committing the act emphasises that, for all his rhetoric of passion, he murders his lover in cold blood. The act itself seems to be undertaken in a spirit of childlike curiosity: the fact that the speaker winds his lover's hair around her throat as if it were 'one long yellow string' (line 39) makes him sound as though he is playing with a doll or with a ball of yarn, while the fact that he afterwards pushes open her eyelids, which he notes were each 'shut like a bud that holds a bee' (line 43), makes him sound as if he were hunting for insects in a flowerbed, or, again, absorbed in oddly clinical play with a doll. That strangling his lover with her own hair seems to him merely 'a thing to do' (line 38), suggesting an arbitrary choice, one idle diversion among others that might be 'found' (line 37), also gives an impression of bizarre nonchalance. The final line suggests that his perception of God's absence from the world has neutralised within his imagination the categories of life and death, sex and violence: passionate love may just as easily inspire murder as 'joy', while a corpse inspires romantic sentiment just as well as a living woman. In effect, the poem dramatises the famous dictum often attributed to Fyodor Dostoevsky: 'If God is dead, everything is permitted'.[8]

Yet Browning complicates this equation between atheism and moral insanity even as he proposes it, and in such a way as to position the poem as an oblique commentary on Victorian religious scepticism. As Terry Eagleton observes, the final exclamation can make the speaker sound either exultant or aggrieved that his crime has met with cosmic silence (Eagleton 2007, 103). Either reading suggests that the speaker has transgressed in order to bait God into showing his face. In this light, the woman is little more than a pawn in a cosmic experiment, and the speaker a kind of psychopathic counterpart to the respectable Victorian doubter, yearning for concrete proof of God's existence. This analogy cuts both ways: Browning implies that the quest for such proof is psychologically akin to strangling a lover so as to achieve total possession; both desires emerge from a remorseless literalism, a need to reduce a sacred mystery (God, a beautiful female other) to something one can squeeze between one's hands. Both desires are also self-consuming in their violence: they destroy the faith or love they strive perfectly to consummate. For its early readers, the religious subtext of 'Porphyria's Lover' was reinforced by its placement beside 'Johannes Agricola in Meditation' (1836) under the title 'Madhouse Cells': this companion monologue uses the medieval Antinomian heresy to dramatise the psychology of religious fanaticism and the wickedness of presuming to know God's will.[9] Read together, these monologues imply that atheism and religious fanaticism are two sides of the same coin – an insight in keeping with Browning's allegiance to a liberalised Christianity, and his resistance to the polarisation of faith and scepticism.

'The Leper' reprises the stock romance motif of 'Porphyria's Lover' – a humble man loves an elusive higher-born woman – but Swinburne renders his setting explicitly medieval, and his speaker is not a murderer but a clerk who tends his lady through the ravages of leprosy. As Rosenberg suggests, Swinburne uses 'clerk' in the archaic sense, that is, a cleric in holy orders (Rosenberg 2005, 166), although, in the medieval period, 'clerk' was also used more loosely as a synonym for a scholar, secretary, or man of letters (*OED*). The fact that Swinburne's 'clerk' – who, by the end of the poem, becomes a figure for his ideal of the artist as a heroic anti-theist and *poète maudit* – occupies an uncertain place on the medieval continuum between the ecclesiastical and the literary reflects Swinburne's desire to destabilise a common Victorian faith in an age-old entente between religion and literature. Swinburne appends in a post-script a concocted French medieval source for the story that spells out the poem's status as a fable about the benightedness of Christian morality. In a pastiche of archaic French, Swinburne invokes the medieval superstition that constructed leprosy as God's punishment for carnality: the poem is supposedly inspired by the story of an adulterous noblewoman named Yolande de Sallières who contracted leprosy and was cast out by her family as a 'thing cursed of God, stinking and abominable to all men', while her former lovers reviled her as a 'detestable sinner' (Swinburne 1904, 1.124; trans. Haynes in Swinburne 2000, 345). Swinburne stresses the hegemonic authority behind her ostracism by noting that King Philip was also 'greatly displeased' by the presence of lepers in his country, which he interpreted as a sign of God's wrath (Swinburne 1904, 1.124; 2000, 345). As Clyde K. Hyder observes, Swinburne is most likely thinking of Philip V, notorious for burning lepers at the stake and expelling Jews from his country for their supposed collaboration in a plot to contaminate wells with leprosy (Hyder 1931, 1283). (Though Hyder does not note this, the reference to 'well-water' that is 'not so delicate to drink' in the opening stanza seems to confirm that Swinburne indeed had this horrify-ing episode in mind (lines 2–3).) Like the noblewoman herself, the clerk is condemned in morally absolute terms: he is 'wicked' and 'cursed' for tending a leper 'gently', as if she were his lover (we are also told that the clerk ultimately succumbs to the disease) (Swinburne 1904, 1.124; 2000, 345–6). The imaginative labour of Swinburne's poem is to dismantle the moral absolutes he ascribes to medieval Christianity in his bogus 'source', and to suggest that the figure of the leper has profound truths to impart about the pitilessness with which Christian societies maintain distinctions between the morally pure and impure.

By turning Browning's murderous speaker into a ministering clerk,

Swinburne renders his speaker a more sympathetic and humane figure –
yet only queasily so, since the clerk's ministrations seem lecherous, and
persist after his lady dies and her corpse begins to decay. Like 'Porphyria's
Lover', 'The Leper' encourages us to understand male sexual perversion
as a longing for ultimate knowledge, yet Swinburne renders unmistakable
what is only insinuated by the final line of Browning's poem: the sugges-
tion of an equivalence between the desire to fathom the relationship
between sex and death via a woman's corpse and the desire to fathom the
nature of God. Where in 'Porphyria's Lover' a madman's strangulation of
his lover seems to allegorise the reductiveness of sceptics who demand
tangible evidence for the reality of God, 'The Leper' grants moral
heroism to its speaker's necrophilia, which is cast as a Promethean bid to
sustain an ideal of romantic love in the face of a malignant God who
afflicts his creatures with disease and death. Yet the poem's crowning
irony is that the clerk has been drawn into his morbid passion by an
almost saintly commitment to the spirit, if not the letter, of Christianity;
he is a paragon of humility and charity, prepared to risk infection so that
he may tend a despised outcast. Owing to the example of Christ, whose
curing of lepers (Mark 1:41) illustrates the miracle of his compassion, the
figure of the leper constitutes a 'sanctified outcast' within the Christian
tradition (Bond 1992, 444). The fact that the clerk's lady is also a sexual
sinner means she symbolically doubles as a fallen woman or Mary
Magdalene type, another archetypal recipient of Christian charity. The
speaker's eagerness to tend a leper or fallen woman – which, as we learn
from Swinburne's 'source', costs him his life – thus perversely resembles
the feats of charity and martyrdom for which medieval Christian saints
are venerated.

The clerk's love is also ironically Christian in its metaphysical aspira-
tions. His necrophilia pursues to its logical extremity the privileging of
spirit over flesh in the Christian–Platonic ideal of love: the disintegration
of his beloved's body and even her death do not curdle his carnal interest
in her because sex only expresses a transcendental love, impervious to
gross materialities. As one Victorian commentator quipped, the speaker's
love is a 'triumph of mind over matter' (qtd in Hyder 1931, 1280). This
irony is compounded by the fact that the speaker's description of his lady
is a travesty of a Petrarchan blazon, the courtly tradition of idealising an
unattainable lady by cataloguing her physical attributes, often via hyper-
bolic conceits. Here the conceit is obviously the fact that the lady's
reduction to beautiful parts is a peculiarly gruesome organic process.

Swinburne means us to notice that his speaker's fetishisation of the necrotic 'fragments' (line 98) perversely literalises the rarefied fragmentation of an ideal woman that is standard within the courtly love tradition. 'The Leper' hinges upon the malevolent deity *topos* that Swinburne used to controversial effect in the choruses of his neoclassical drama *Atalanta in Calydon* (1865) and in two other major poems in *Poems and Ballads, First Series*, 'Anactoria' and 'Félise'. Like Sappho in 'Anactoria', the speaker of 'The Leper' derives ecstasy from masochistic sexual love because such love honours 'the mystery of the cruelty of things', Sappho's definition of God (Swinburne 1904, 1.62; and 2000, 51; line 154). Yet, for the speaker of 'The Leper' as for Sappho in 'Anactoria', deriving pleasure from pain is also a means of snatching fire from this sadistic God. Since the scorn of the lady and the scorn of God converge in the speaker's mind, lavishing love upon the lady against her consent (because she is either too ill to resist or dead) is simultaneously to prevail over God:[10]

> Sometimes when service made me glad
> The sharp tears leapt between my lids,
> Falling on her, such joy I had,
> To do the service God forbids.

(lines 77–80)

The syntax makes this passage profoundly troubling: is it a moment of servility (the speaker's tears 'fall' on the woman for joy of tending her) or of rape (the speaker himself 'falls' on to the woman, who is still alive at this point in the poem). 'Service' suggests both sexual servicing and the speaker's ministering role, and seems to imply that the speaker has achieved through his submission to his lady a Christlike exaltation-through-humility. This indeterminacy yields another: is the speaker suggesting that God is so cruel as to forbid compassionate 'service' to a leper (an implication in keeping with his complaints against the God who 'hateth' him (line 89)) – or affirming the 'joy' of having violated a taboo, and raped a dying woman? Though for convenience I have called the speaker 'necrophilic' thus far, it is crucial that the poem is in fact vague on this point. Swinburne strives to hold our moral judgement in suspense; it is impossible to say whether the speaker is beyond the pale, a rapist and a necrophile, or is enacting a paradigm sometimes called 'foolishness for Christ' – that is, flouting social norms in the name of a higher Christian purpose – and bestowing chaste devotion upon a suffering sinner. Swinburne refuses to allow us to keep these alternatives separate; always both open, they contaminate each other as we read. In this way, 'The Leper' strives to locate points of convergence between romantic convention and aberrant sexuality, evil and moral heroism, self-sacrifice and abjection, in order to reveal both the instability of such categories and the tendency of Christian cultures to scapegoat those who confound them.

The clerk's obsessive, Christian love for a disintegrating corpse may be read as a grotesque figure for Browning's efforts to reanimate early Christian history in his religious monologues and thus preserve it from sceptical critique in the present. Similarly, Swinburne's bogus source may be understood as a sly joke on Browning's engagements with the Higher Criticism in poems such as 'Cleon' and 'A Death in the Desert'. Like 'Hymn to Proserpine', 'The Leper' aims to expose, to repeat Swinburne's phrase, 'the viler forms and more hideous outcomes of Christianity, its more brutal aspects and deadlier consequences', which he believed 'lurked' not only in Browning's religious monologues but also in the interstices of the official historical record. In this way, 'Hymn to Proserpine' and 'The Leper' parody the biases of Browning's Christian historicism by flaunting their own polemical investments and 'recovering' decadent or pagan counterhistories, moments of 'holy insurrection' against Christianity's power.

Reflecting upon Swinburne's appropriation of the phrase attributed to Julian the Apostate ('*Vicisti Galilæe*') in 'Hymn to Proserpine', L. M. Findlay suggests that Swinburne identified art with heresy because 'no less than religious hypostasis, aesthetic apostasis bears witness to the need to stand somewhere and for something' (Findlay 1990, 76). The centrality of concepts of heresy and blasphemy to Swinburne's *Poems and Ballads* reveals the extent to which his aestheticism was an audacious attempt to 'stand somewhere and for something' in relation to the Victorian culture of doubt and its sanctification – in Swinburne's own scornful assessment – of a 'failed faith that weeps sceptical tears'.[11] Equally, however, Swinburne's aestheticism reflects the tensions that inhered in his effort to keep alive what he understood as a Romantic tradition of infidelity, and, more broadly, to the complications he faced when he sought to construct atheism – or, to use his preferred term, 'anti-theism' – as an oppositional discourse and as a form of Romantic rebellion.[12] The second half of the Victorian period was an age of blasphemy trials and militant secularism, but also one in which religious doubt was to a large degree cleansed of its ancient stigma and, however controversially and uneasily, integrated into mainstream culture.[13] In his *After Strange Gods: A Primer of Modern Heresy*

(1934), T. S. Eliot complained that blasphemy is 'impossible' in the context of a secularised modernity because the authentic blasphemer 'profoundly believes in that which he profanes'; where there is no deep faith, blasphemy is mere impropriety, or 'bad form' (Eliot 1934, 51–2).[14] Swinburne's poetry suggests he arrived at a similar insight: at a moment when notions of heresy and blasphemy could seem obsolescent, he sought to revive them under the sign of 'aestheticism' in order to preserve religious questioning – and art – from respectability.

NOTES

1 I borrow this phrase from Joss Marsh, who emphasises the prosecutorial character of Victorian literary reviewing. See Marsh 1998, 94.

2 For an account of the case, see Marsh 1998, 90–109.

3 For a discussion of Swinburne's indebtedness to a tradition of Romantic iconoclasm, see Riede 1993, 22–40.

4 For a discussion of the Victorian currency of Gibbon's interpretation of Rome's decline, see Vance 1997, 202–4.

5 The retreat of the 'Sea of Faith' is Arnold's famous metaphor for the Victorian religious crisis in 'Dover Beach' (1867).

6 Swinburne attacks the Victorian conventionalisation of religious doubt both as a literary theme and as a viable stance for Christian believers perhaps most robustly in his essay on Matthew Arnold's poetry, 'Mr. Arnold's New Poems', originally published in the *Fortnightly Review* (1867) and revised for *Essays and Studies* (1875).

7 Rosenberg's chapter on Swinburne (in Rosenberg 2005) is a slightly different revised version of a seminal essay published in *Victorian Poetry* (Rosenberg 1967), which does not contain this reference.

8 The phrase is extrapolated from a passage in Dostoevsky's *The Brothers Karamazov* (1880). See Dostoevsky 1994, 87.

9 'Johannes Agricola' and 'Porphyria's Lover' were first published in the *Monthly Review* in January 1836; they reappeared as a pairing under the title 'Madhouse Cells' in Browning's *Dramatic Lyrics* (1842).

10 I lack space to analyse the disturbing equivalence between rape and heroic anti-theism implicit in 'The Leper'. For a discussion of Swinburne's representations of rape, see Louis 2000, although I am not persuaded by her claim that 'The Leper' highlights the suffering of the victim.

11 I derive this phrase from a passage in the later version of Swinburne's essay on Matthew Arnold published in *Essays and Studies*. Swinburne inserted into this later version a diatribe in French that he ascribed to a spurious 'French critic' and which reads as a thinly veiled attack on Browning and Tennyson's poetics

of religious doubt. Claiming that religious doubt is inartistic, Swinburne deplores 'la pensée qui boite, l'esprit qui louche, l'âme qui a peur et de se soumettre et de se révolter, la foi manquée qui pleure des larmes sceptiques' ('the thought that hobbles, the spirit that squints, the soul which is afraid either to submit or to revolt, the failed faith that weeps sceptical tears'. My translation). See Swinburne 1875a, 131; 1972, 59, 61. Stefano Evangelista discusses the figure of the spurious French critic in Chapter 1 above.

12 For a study of the Romantic tradition of infidelity in relation to literature, see Priestman 2000.

13 For a recent account of how religious doubt lost its associations with sin and heresy and gained wide acceptance in the Victorian period, see Lane 2011.

14 Marsh's *Word Crimes* drew my attention to the appositeness of Eliot's remarks to the status of blasphemy in the Victorian period. See Marsh 1998, 277.

10

WHOSE MUSE? SAPPHO, SWINBURNE, AND AMY LOWELL

Sarah Parker

Swinburne's influence on a number of modernist writers has been remarked upon in several relatively recent critical studies. For example, the poets H. D. and T. S. Eliot provide the focus for comparative studies by Cassandra Laity (1996) and Thaïs E. Morgan (1993b). In this chapter, I propose that the American modernist poet Amy Lowell (1874–1925) should be included in this list, arguing that her work exhibits a number of similarities to Swinburne's poetry.[1] These similarities stem from Swinburne and Lowell's shared understanding of Sappho as an important poetic precursor, muse figure, and homoerotic archetype. I argue that Sappho's influence on Swinburne and Lowell is instrumental in creating an anxiety that subsequent readers and critics 'ward off' by 'forgetting' their work. This results in the devaluation and neglect of both poets despite their considerable contributions to poetry.

From Robert Buchanan to T. S. Eliot, the oft-repeated narrative of Swinburne's devaluation has become a commonplace of Swinburne criticism: as Yisrael Levin has recently noted, 'Critics have discussed, commented on, justified, and deplored Swinburne's unpopularity for almost a century now' and 'the question of his reception has been an integral part of Swinburne studies just as Swinburne himself' (Levin 2010a, 1). Similarly, critical derision of Amy Lowell simmered throughout her career and became more virulent after her death in 1925. Whilst in life Lowell confronted her detractors head-on, once she was dead her critics took the opportunity to 'pounce' (Rollyson 2009, 3). One of the first to do so was Clement Wood, who, just a year after her death, sought to destroy Lowell's then formidable reputation. Wood's biography *Amy Lowell* (1926) focused negatively on Lowell's obesity and commented obliquely that, though she was 'an impassioned singer of her own desires', her love poems 'do not word a common cry of many hearts' (Wood 1926, 173).

Wood's biography unfortunately set a precedent for further critical and biographical studies that read Lowell's poetry via her 'grotesque' corpulent physique and her 'aberrant' desires. Perfunctory treatment in influential studies of modernism, such as Hugh Kenner's *The Pound Era* (1972), set the critical consensus that reduced Lowell 'to a footnote ... in the history of modern poetry' (Munich and Bradshaw 2004, xii). Despite the fact that Lowell features in important recuperative studies of female modernists in the latter decades of the twentieth century, she remains a neglected figure in comparison to her female contemporaries, not even granted a place in Bonnie Kime Scott's anthology *The Gender of Modernism* (1990) where room is found for Pound, Eliot, Lawrence, and Joyce.

Despite a number of attempts to counteract this critical neglect, scholarship on Lowell remains underrepresentative of the crucial role she played in constituting and defending modernist poetics. Lowell was a highly successful practitioner and impresario of the 'New Poetry' in America, using her vast wealth and influential family name to support other poets, such as H. D., Richard Aldington, and D. H. Lawrence.[2] She saw three Imagist volumes through to publication between 1915 and 1917, and published eleven volumes of her own poetry (including three posthumous collections edited by her partner Ada Russell). Although identified with the 'Imagist' label, Lowell's work itself is highly varied, containing long narrative poems, haikus, fixed forms such as ballads, and her own invented form of polyphonic prose. Today she is best known for the love lyrics of *Pictures of the Floating World* (1919), read by many critics as a tribute to her relationship with Russell; Paul Lauter dubs it 'the most fully articulated sequence of lesbian poetry between Sappho and the 1960s' (Lauter 2004, 5).

Interestingly, both Swinburne and Lowell are now the subjects of significant reappraisal. The Swinburne Centenary Conference of 2009, along with Levin's recent essay collection and a special edition of *Victorian Poetry*, bear testament to the fact that interest in Swinburne is probably in a healthier state now than it has ever been since the Victorian period. Similarly, the essay collection *Amy Lowell, American Modern* (2004) instigated a particularly intense moment of Lowell scholarship (Munich and Bradshaw 2004, xxiv). Whatever the vicissitudes of their critical fortunes, existing scholarship on both Swinburne and Lowell has often focused on the important role of Sappho in their work. Swinburne declared Sappho 'the greatest poet who ever was at all' (Swinburne 1959–62, 4.124) and celebrated her in poems such as 'Anactoria' and 'Sapphics' from *Poems and Ballads, First Series* (1866) and 'On the Cliffs' from *Songs of the Springtides* (1880). Sappho's unrivalled status as a powerful muse figure in Swinburne's body of work has been explored in detail by several critical studies.[3] Similarly, scholarship on Lowell has often examined her use of Sappho, particularly in the poem 'The Sisters' from *What's O'Clock* (1925, 459–61). In 'The Sisters', Lowell's speaker depicts Sappho as the first of three inspiring women poets (alongside Elizabeth Barrett Browning and Emily Dickinson), thus figuring her relationship to Sappho in the same sororal terms as Swinburne: 'As brother and sister were we, child and bird. / Since thy first Lesbian word / Flamed on me' (Swinburne 1904, 3.318–19). In her influential essay 'Sapphistries', Susan Gubar places Lowell within a tradition of Sapphic modernism, alongside H. D. and Renée Vivien. However, Gubar argues that, in contrast to these other poets, Lowell's poem exhibits ambivalence towards Sappho. She highlights Lowell's 'problematic limitations' and ultimately rejects her influence: 'for all her attraction to Sappho, Lowell ... implies that the gulf between the ancient tenth muse and the modern woman poet may not be negotiable ... her older "sisters" leave her feeling "sad and self-distrustful"' (Gubar 1984, 58–9).

Critics such as Lillian Faderman and Angela Leighton attribute lesbian writers' ambivalence towards Sappho to the legacy of male writers such as Swinburne and Baudelaire, who portray the Lesbian as an evil vampiric *femme fatale*. Leighton contends that 'Swinburne violently and sadistically appropriates the voice of Sappho for his own fantasies' (Leighton 1992, 301, n.15), whilst Faderman argues that the 'horribly negative terms' in which lesbianism is described by writers such as Vivien and Djuna Barnes are a direct result of their having been exposed to decadent representations of the lesbian as 'a fabricated fantasy image of what would most upset (and arouse) the reader' (Faderman 1981, 265). Faderman even states that Vivien's internalisation of Swinburne's influence literally contributed to her death by inspiring her to drink eau de cologne, like Swinburne's *Lesbia Brandon* (Faderman 1981, 361–2).

However, this view of Swinburne's contribution to lesbian poetics has now been modified. Swinburne, as more recent critics have noted, enabled the lesbian writers that came after him by writing an openly lesbian Sappho for the first time, anticipating Henry Wharton's English translations of Sappho's fragments in *Sappho: Memoir, Text, Selected Renderings, and a Literal Translation* (1885) – the first translation to include the female pronouns in Sappho's love lyrics. Elizabeth Prettejohn writes that 'Swinburne's Sapphic poems of the 1860s were an avowed inspiration for the researches of the amateur scholar' Wharton, and argues that both Swinburne and the artist Simeon Solomon can be credited with moving away from Baudelaire's and Courbet's pornographic interpretations towards a more complex response to Sappho's lesbianism in relation to the notion of art for art's sake (Prettejohn 2008, 120). Swinburne and Solomon's project, she states, marks 'a more important stage in the modern reconfiguration of Sappho's sexuality ... than previous scholarship has acknowledged' (120). Likewise, Catherine Maxwell asserts that 'Swinburne's portrayal of Sappho as a lesbian can be seen as decisive in helping determine the term's modern sexual meaning' (Maxwell 2001, 182).

　　Cassandra Laity has shown that Swinburne enabled modernist women writers who 'discovered in Swinburne's more fluid explorations of sexuality and gender roles a radical alternative to the modernist poetics of male desire' (Laity 1992, 218). For example, for writers such as H. D., Swinburne's *Poems and Ballads* 'articulate[s] a spectrum of desires and gender-disruptions ... which were not available in the high modernist discourse of the 1920s' (Laity 1992, 228). Recalling Gubar's comment on 'the gulf between the ancient tenth muse and the modern woman poet' (Gubar 1984, 58–9), Laity states that modernist lesbian poets 'looked to Swinburne for a more recent and accessible range of poetic conventions which would concretize the "fantasy precursor" they perceived in Sappho' (Laity 1992, 236). In other words, rather than widening the gulf between modernist lesbian poets and Sappho by his supposedly misogynist or pornographic appropriation of her voice, Swinburne in fact brings them *closer* to Sappho owing to *his* greater historical nearness and his own fluid, enabling constructions of gender and sexuality.

　　The relationship I am tracing between Swinburne, Lowell, and Sappho, is informed by Thaïs E. Morgan's conception of intertextuality between Swinburne and T. S. Eliot. Morgan appeals to Michael Riffaterre's notion of intertextuality, noting that '[Riffaterre] expands the dyad characteristic of influence study (the poem and its source) into a triangle involving a minimum of three texts, each of which refers to a "matrix" or shared paradigm of cultural knowledge' (Morgan 1993b, 137). As Morgan explains, 'A typical intertextual triangle consists of the present text; an earlier intertext; and an interpretant text, which is either earlier than or contemporaneous with the text in question, and which mediates between this text and its intertext' (137). This triangular model seems particularly relevant to my exploration of the relationship between Lowell, Swinburne, and Sappho. Taking Lowell's work as the present text, and Sappho's fragments as the intertext, Swinburne's oeuvre occupies the place of the interpretant text.

Diana Collecott argues that Lowell was 'a significant presence between Swinburne's Englishing of Sappho and H. D.'s' (Collecott 1999, 28). In contrast, the lines of influence and intertextuality between Swinburne and Lowell have hitherto received little critical attention. Fortunately, Laity's detailed tracing of Swinburne's influence on H. D. provides a convenient model for my enquiry into the relations between Swinburne, Lowell, and Sappho. As Collecott has shown, Sappho was an important influence on Lowell's friends and Imagist associates, H. D. and Bryher. As Lowell could not read Greek herself, she received Sappho via H. D.'s and Bryher's own experiments in emulating or translating Sapphic lyrics. As a result, a Sapphic aesthetic can be detected in Lowell's own work: her Imagism was influenced by 'the short fragments of Sappho preserved in quotations by later writers' (Snyder 1997, 126). As Laity and Collecott show, these 'quotations by later writers' (such as H. D. and Bryher) were themselves influenced by Swinburne's Sapphic verses. Therefore, Lowell is part of a body of writers who accessed Sappho via Swinburne.

In some respects, the links between Swinburne and Lowell are more obvious than those between Swinburne and H. D. Like Swinburne's, the form and subject matter of Lowell's work often provoked controversy. Reviews of her early work were critical: 'some puzzled, some adverse or angry or openly derisive', ridiculing Lowell's 'bizarre images and weird inventions' (Gould 1975, 140). Lowell also shared Swinburne's much-discussed French influences. She was inspired by French poetic forms, particularly those used by the symbolists Verlaine and Baudelaire, and often 'read Paul Fort and Henri de Régnier aloud' (Gould 1975, 137). Owing to their controversial output and their proudly proclaimed French influences, both Swinburne and Lowell were seen as importing French 'vices'; immorality in Swinburne's case, *vers libre* in Lowell's, although she 'Americanized and adapted the terms at once' to 'unrhymed cadence' (Ribeyrol 2010, 14; Gould 1975, 139).

John Keats was also a major influence on Lowell: she collected his manuscripts and first editions and spent the final years of her life writing his biography. Interestingly, a fragment of an essay on Keats by Swinburne was actually discovered in the Amy Lowell collection at Harvard in 1949.

Cecil Lang notes that the manuscript, auctioned in 1917, 'appears to have been unnoticed by Swinburne's editors and biographers' (Lang 1949, 169). We can speculate that Lowell gained satisfaction from the knowledge that she was taking up the challenge of writing on Keats that Swinburne left unfinished.[4] Lowell mentioned Swinburne, often unfavourably, in a number of her own lectures; for example, criticising his 'confused and redundant imagery' (qtd in Damon 1935, 343). However, something Swinburne and Lowell could agree on was their admiration of Sappho. Not only does Lowell place Sappho at the head of her list of 'sister' poets, she also praised her in lectures: 'the highest poetry is often the most simple. Sappho's "I loved you once, Atthis" gives us the shock of poetry and truth in one' (qtd in Damon 1935, 446). As I shall show, Swinburne's and Lowell's shared Sapphic influences affect their poetry in interconnected ways. This Sapphic influence leads both Swinburne and Lowell to write about courtly love, linking their poetry to Sappho's fragments, which emphasise the speaker's painful distance from or absence of the beloved. This pain is materialised in the form and metre of their work. Reacting to these painful qualities, critics issued remarkably similar complaints against Swinburne's and Lowell's poetry, claiming that they prioritised sound over sense, thus 'attacking' the reader with synaesthetic imagery. In order to ward off the threatening aspects of Swinburne and Lowell's verse – particularly the way in which their work troubled boundaries between the physical body and the text – critics directed their own form of critical 'abuse' at the corpus of the two poets by attacking and insulting their physical bodies.

COURTLY LOVE AND MEDIEVALISM

In his ground-breaking *Swinburne: An Experiment in Criticism* (1972), Jerome McGann draws attention to Swinburne's preoccupation with unrequited love: 'Swinburne's work is dominated from the start by a fascination with ... the theme of lost love ... Swinburne's obsession is essentially a slightly modernized ... version of the topos of the Provençal poet-lover' (McGann 1972, 216). Antony Harrison expands on Swinburne's engagement with medieval literature, discerning 'formal and thematic similarities' between Swinburne's work and troubadour poetry, demonstrating his 'deep engagement with the values and ethos of courtly love literature' (Harrison 1988, 27). From his earliest dramas *Rosamond* (1860) and *Chastelard* (1865) to his later masterpiece *Tristram of Lyonesse*

(1882), Swinburne engaged with the courtly love dynamic characteristic of medieval verse, defining 'passion as a source of suffering' and representing death as 'a release from, as well as a fulfilment of, both physical and spiritual passions' (Harrison 1988, 30, 33). Thematically, Lowell's work is also rooted in the medieval courtly tradition of unrequited love for an unattainable beloved. Lowell is often characterised as a poet who highlights the domestic lesbian 'idyll', her contented relationship with Russell often reflected in her love lyrics. However, Lowell also wrote a series of morbid Gothic narrative poems which led to accusations that she had borrowed from Browning's 'Porphyria's Lover' (Gould 1975, 117). Her early love lyrics, too, contain references to painful unrequited love and vampiric *femmes fatales*. Faderman suggests that these love lyrics originate from the period of Lowell's and Russell's courtship in 1914, during which Lowell begged the reluctant Russell to come and live with her (Faderman 2004, 59–60). Thus, in her love poems to Russell, Lowell presents herself as 'imploring, apologetic, and entirely at the mercy of the beloved' (Faderman 2004, 60).

Several of Lowell's poems are situated in a medieval setting with strongly Keatsian echoes. For example, in a 1914 poem entitled 'In a Castle' (Lowell 1955, 60–1), a courtly knight commits adultery with a lady whose husband is away fighting. The poem, written in Lowell's invented form of 'polyphonic' or cadenced prose, repeatedly calls attention to its medieval setting in a refrain: 'The wide state bed shivers beneath its velvet coverlet. Above, dim, in the smoke, a tarnished coronet gleams dully . . . The arras blows sidewise out from the wall, and then falls back again' (60). Lowell immediately sets up a typical courtly scenario: the crusading knight has attained his 'lady's key, confided with much cunning, whisperingly' (60) and they have arranged an illicit meeting in the absence of her lord: 'Is it guilt to free a lady from her palsied lord, absent and fighting, terribly abhorred?' (60). The knight justifies this adultery using conventional courtly language, emphasising the purity and honour of his love:

> She is so pure and whole. Only because he has her soul will she resign herself to him, for where the soul has gone, the body must be given as a sign. He takes her by the divine right of the only lover. He has sworn to fight her lord, and wed her after. Should he be overborne, she will die adoring him, forlorn, shriven by her great love. (60)

The knight's desire, collapsing metaphysical soul-union with bodily intercourse, echoes the reckless, profane desire expressed by troubadour

Arnaut Daniel: 'Would I were hers in body, not in soul! and that she let me, secretly, into her bedroom! . . . I'll not heed the warning of friend or uncle' (qtd in Press 1971, 188–9). This soul/body union is also suggestive of Keats's 'The Eve of St. Agnes' (1819), from whose manuscript Lowell claimed that 'she learned more about poetic composition' than from any book (Damon 1935, 673).

However, waiting in the chamber, the knight learns that he is not the only man to receive the lady's favour: 'Christ's Death! It is no storm which makes those little chuckling sounds . . . it is his dear lady, kissing and clasping someone!' (60). The second part of the poem cuts to a grim scene, the violent outcome of the knight's discovery of his lady in bed with a page: 'On the velvet coverlet lie two bodies, stripped and fair in the cold grey air . . . At each side of the bed, on the floor, is a head. A man's on this side, a woman's on that, and the red blood oozes along the rush mat' (61). After committing this vengeful double-murder, the knight has killed himself, as we learn from the later reference to 'three corpses . . . growing cold' (61). The knight has left notes on the bodies, addressed to the absent lord on his return. The lady's reads:

> Most noble Lord: Your wife's misdeeds are as a double-stranded necklace of beads. But I have engaged that, on your return, she shall welcome you here. She will not spurn your love as before, you have still the best part of her. Her blood was red, her body white, they will both be here for your delight. The soul inside was a lump of dirt, I have rid you of that with a spurt of my sword point. Good luck to your pleasure. She will be quite complaisant, my friend, I wager. (61)

The unhinged, sadistic tone of this note, inviting the lady's husband to gain 'pleasure' from her dead body, coupled with the knight's phallic reference to 'the spurt of my sword point', implies that he himself may have committed necrophiliac acts on the corpse before ending his own life.

Combining courtly love with perverse, destructive desire, 'In a Castle' shares similarities with Swinburne's 'The Leper' (Swinburne 1904, 1.119–24; 2000, 95–100). Unlike the courtly knight, however, Swinburne's lowly scribe can only watch the beloved from afar:

> I served her in a royal house;
>   I served her wine and curious meat,
> For will to kiss between her brows,
>   I had no heart to sleep or eat.

(lines 5–8)

Though not the object of his lady's affections, the scribe takes part in the courtly scenario by enabling secret meetings with a knight: 'I remember that sundawn / I brought him by a privy way / Out at her lattice' (lines 29–31). Therefore, like 'In a Castle', 'The Leper' depicts an entangled love triangle and the perilous secrecy of an illicit courtly rendezvous.

Despite her meetings with the knight, the Lady proclaims herself 'clean and whole of shame' (line 38), recalling Lowell's knight's view of the lady as 'so pure and whole' (Lowell 1955, 60). According to the logic of courtly love, conventional morality can be overcome by the law of passion. However, as with the lady of 'In a Castle', the beloved's active sexual desire contributes to her downfall:

> Yea, he inside whose grasp all night
> Her fervent body leapt or lay.
> Stained with sharp kisses red and white,
> Found her a plague to spurn away.
>
> (lines 65–8)

The above suggests that the leprous plague that afflicts the lady can be linked to her sexual transgression with the knight: he 'stains' her body with rash-like marks and 'finds' her a plague – the knight's horror implies his own culpability for this (possibly venereal) disease. The connection between disease and sin is assumed by the villagers who 'cast her forth for a base thing / . . . seeing how God had wrought / This curse to plague her' (lines 51–4). Even the scribe connects 'her body of love' with her physical illness (line 48). The lady's position, lying beneath the knight, recalls the knight of 'In a Castle', who remembers 'leap[ing] to cover' his lady 'when she holds out her arms' (Lowell 1955, 60). Lowell's knight also describes the beloved's body as 'white and red', combining her deathly pallor with her spilt blood; in both poems, this image encodes a virginal purity tainted with sexuality. As in Lowell's knight's note, the conclusion to 'The Leper' contains suggestions of necrophilia: 'Her hair, half grey half ruined gold, / Thrills me and burns me in kissing it. / . . . she is dead now, and shame put by' (lines 103–4). In both poems, courtly love is thus connected to unnatural or perverse desire.

Narrative poems aside, in Lowell's love lyrics Lowell's beloveds are at best indifferent, at worst fatal. For example, in the poem 'Absence' (1914), the speaker imagines her heart as a cup, which fills with her own blood when her lover appears: 'When you come, it brims / Red and trembling with blood, / Heart's blood for your drinking; / To fill your mouth with love / And the bittersweet taste of a soul' (Lowell 1955, 41). These lines echo Sappho's famous description of eros as 'bittersweet' in Fragment 130 (Campbell 1994, 147), an implacable force combining pleasure and pain. This fragment also provides the opening line of Swinburne's 'Anactoria': 'My life is bitter with thy love' (Swinburne 1904, 1.57; 2000, 47). The vampiric Sappho uses images of blood to describe erotic commingling and the pulsing rhythm of poetry: 'I feel thy blood against my blood: my pain / Pains thee' (line 12). However, this passion becomes a painful surfeit of pleasure, as Sappho longs to consume and destroy Anactoria entirely:

> That I could drink thy veins as wine, and eat
> Thy breasts like honey! that from face to feet
> Thy body were abolished and consumed,
> And in my flesh thy very flesh entombed!
>
> (lines 111–14)

A comparable desire for total consumption or merging with the beloved is seen in the eucharistic imagery of Lowell's 'In Excelsis' (1925):

> I drink your lips,
> I eat the whiteness of your hands and feet.
> My mouth is open,
> As a new jar I am empty and open.
> Like white water are you who fill the cup of my mouth.
>
> (Lowell 1955, 444)

This wish for erotic consummation in death is characteristic of chivalric discourses. For example, in Swinburne's 'Satia te Sanguine' (1904, 1.86–8; 2000, 70–2), the speaker is drained by the beloved: 'You suck with a sleepy red lip / The wet red wounds in his heart. / You thrill as his pulses dwindle, / You brighten and warm as he bleeds' (lines 59–62). Similarly, in Lowell's poem 'A Gift' (1914), the speaker gives herself to the beloved in the form of words in 'little jars', knowing that this unrequited love will ultimately be fatal: 'When I shall have given you the last one, / You will have the whole of me, / But I shall be dead' (Lowell 1955, 41).

SAPPHO AND COURTLY LOVE

The two poets' interest in courtly love has its origins in Sappho, who repeatedly takes unrequited desire as her theme. For example, her famous 'Ode to Aphrodite' (Fragment 1) entreats the goddess to help her win the love of an indifferent woman. The poem concludes with Aphrodite promising Sappho: 'If she runs away, soon she shall pursue; if she does not accept gifts, why, she will give them instead; and if she does not love, soon she shall love even against her will' (Campbell 1994, 55). Fragment 31 voices a similarly unrequited desire, as, from across the room, the speaker watches her beloved talking with a man: 'He seems as fortunate as the gods to me, the man who sits opposite you and listens to your sweet voice and lovely laughter' (Campbell 1994, 79). Owing to the frequency of this theme in Sappho's verse, Page duBois has defined the Sapphic aesthetic as an 'aesthetic of distance' and unattainability, which values 'the absent object of desire' (duBois 1995, 53).

This absence and unattainability have painful physical effects on the speaker, as seen in Fragment 31: 'my tongue is snapped, at once a subtle fire has stolen beneath my flesh, I see nothing with my eyes, my ears hum, sweat pours from me, a trembling seizes me all over, I am greener than grass, and it seems to me that I am little short of dying' (Campbell 1994, 81). This physical reaction to desire is also frequently seen in troubadour verse. For example, Jaufré Rudel's depiction of the effects of desire clearly echoes Sappho's Fragment 31: 'I am stricken by joy which slays me, and by a pang of love which ravishes my flesh, whence will my body waste away; and never ... from any blow did I so languish' (qtd in Press 1971, 34–5).[5] Jaime Hovey argues that the unrequited desire depicted in both Sappho's lyrics and European courtly love poetry offered twentieth-century lesbian poets an enabling literary tradition by transforming the thwarted aspects of homoerotic longing into a heroic lesbian chivalry. By rewriting 'sterility' as exalted, spiritualised desire and encoding the dangers inherent in homoerotic love in its tragic, violent plots, courtly love models permitted a simultaneous confirmation and denial of desire for lesbian writers such as Lowell, making 'a degraded love honourable' (Hovey 2004, 81). In arguing that the courtly love tradition was 'flexible enough to sustain carnal superstructures built on its ethereal Platonic foundation', Harrison also suggests how the courtly love model could appeal to homo-erotically inclined writers (Harrison 1988, 34).

As Karla Jay (1988) has shown, Natalie Barney and Renée Vivien drew their dynamic of courtly love from Sappho, with one performing the role of unattainable lady, the other the suppliant page. These roles feature in Vivien's *A Woman Appeared to Me* (1904), when one of the characters imagines herself reincarnated in ancient Lesbos:

> I was only a sullen and awkward child when an older playmate took me to the temple where Psappha was invoking the Goddess. I heard the Ode to Aphrodite ... Psappha cared nothing for me. But I loved her, and when later I developed the body of a woman, my sobs of desire were directed toward her. (Vivien 1982, 8)

For Vivien, the pain of unrequited love is linked to Sappho, who is incomparable and unapproachable artistically and sexually. In *Notes on Poems and Reviews* (1866) Swinburne figured his relationship to Sappho in similar terms of unbridgeable distance, writing of his Sapphic imitations: "'It is as near as I can come; and no man can come close to her'" (Swinburne 2000, 407). Harrison shows that Swinburne advocated 'an attitude of aloof submission and reverence before a female idol' (Harrison 1988, 27). However, Yopie Prins argues this was a 'self-reviling pose' from which Swinburne derived pleasure; in this 'scenario of domination and submission' Swinburne is 'only too eager to give [Sappho] the upper hand' (Prins 1999, 122–3).

Lowell experiences a similar distance in 'The Sisters' as the speaker longs to observe Sappho: 'Just to watch the crisp sea sunshine playing on her hair / And listen, thinking all the while 'twas she / Who spoke' (Lowell 1955, 459). As Gubar observes, Lowell does not actually *speak* to Sappho directly (Gubar 1984, 58). In her love lyrics, the beloved's presence is also consistently invoked through her distance or absence; for example, in 'The Taxi', 'The lamps of the city prick my eyes / So that I can no longer see your face. / Why should I leave you to wound myself upon the sharp edges of the night?' (Lowell 1955, 43). This poem recalls Sappho's Fragment 16 in which she is reminded of 'Anactoria who is not here' (Campbell 1994, 67). Just as Anactoria's presence is marked through her absence, Lowell's love lyrics also transform 'the pain of separation into an eloquent tribute to the beauty of desire' (Hovey 2004, 81). This painful desire not only serves as a sign of courtly love and Sapphic influence but is also reproduced in the formal properties of both Swinburne's and Lowell's work.

SADOMASOCHISTIC SAPPHO AND THE PLEASURES AND PAINS OF FORM

Formally, Lowell's poems (with the exception of the haikus) are seldom 'clean', sparse, and classical, despite the strict dictates of Imagism. Her poems were considered by some 'excessive': in a letter to Lowell (14 November 1916), D. H. Lawrence criticised Lowell's poetry as 'pure sensation without concepts', while Louis Untermeyer claimed that her work is 'best in its portrayal of colors and sounds, of physical perceptions rather than the reactions of emotional experience' (Lawrence 1985, 50; Untermeyer 1930, 231). Alice Corbin Henderson criticised Lowell's 'spiritual poverty, the manufactured stage-passion, the continuous external glitter with no depth beneath, the monotony of style ... [and] the endless emphasis on form' (Henderson 1919, 166). As Melissa Bradshaw notes, '[t]his charge of paying attention only to surfaces, of an excess of detail belying a paucity of content' resembles Robert Buchanan's criticisms of Swinburne and 'the Fleshly School of Poetry' (Bradshaw 2000, para. 2). In his 1866 review of *Poems and Ballads*, Buchanan claimed, 'Absolute passion is there none; elaborate attempts at thick colouring supply the place of passion' (Buchanan in Hyder 1970, 32). Maxwell argues that this attitude towards Swinburne persists into the early twentieth century, in a different form: 'If early critics were bothered by the content of these poems, later critics ... defended themselves against the verse by claiming there was nothing there; Swinburne's sonorous lyricism and metrical fluency were deemed by his detractors to be all sound and precious little sense' (Maxwell 2006, 8). This attitude is epitomised in T. S. Eliot's criticisms of Swinburne in his 1920 essay 'Swinburne as Poet': Eliot rejects Victorian moral objections to Swinburne's verse, only to assert a different kind of 'morbidity', one 'not of human feeling but of language' and claims that 'his meaning is merely the hallucination of meaning' (Eliot 1920a, 149).

Therefore, in the case of both Lowell *and* Swinburne, their innovative use of form and rhythm is seen to disguise an underlying shallowness. Indeed one reviewer noted that while Lowell's 'virtues are her own ... her faults are the faults of Swinburne; namely a prodigality of poetic energy which is not richness but confusion' (qtd in Bradshaw 2000, para. 1). Harriet Monroe associates this poetic energy with physical pain, writing that '[Lowell] delights in the rush and clatter of sounds, in the kaleidoscopic glitter of colors', and noting that 'In a few poems in the imagist anthologies ... one's ears and eyes feel fairly battered' (Monroe 1926, 81).

This reaction recalls Prins's analysis of Swinburne's 'Sapphic Sublime', in which she argues that he conceived of Sappho's rhythms as beatings inflicted on his body. Prins links this to Swinburne's painful public school education in classical metre, his flagellant writings, and the images of Sappho as schoolmistress. Swinburne thus casts Sappho in the role of 'singing mistress ... who teaches Swinburne the striking power of her poetry by forcing him to submit to its rhythm' (Prins 1999, 122). Poems such as 'Anactoria' dramatise this 'Sapphic scene of instruction', as Anactoria's limbs become a lyre on which Sappho cruelly plays: 'Would I not hurt thee perfectly? ... / Strike pang from pang as note is struck from note, ... / Take thy limbs living and new- mould with these / A lyre of many faultless agonies?' (Swinburne 1904, 1.61; 2000, 51). Swinburne also associates the sublime power of the sea with this disciplining rhythm, drawing yet another connection with Sappho, whose body ends up in the sea after she leaps from the Leucadian cliff.

Swinburne experimented with recreating Sapphic form, transforming Greek lyric rhythms into English metre, most notably in the poem 'Sapphics' (1904, 1.204–7; 2000, 163–5). Prins notes that these Sapphic metres can only be seen, not heard 'for Sappho's song can only be made "visible" by the conversion of rhythm into a metrical pattern ... a written form that appeals to the eye instead of the ear' (Prins 1999, 145). For Swinburne, therefore, Sappho becomes 'the embodiment of a rhythm that ... increasingly turns into an abstract metrical principle' (Prins 1999, 120). Lowell, too, experimented with Sapphic form. As Adrienne Munich observes, poems such as 'The Letter', 'Opal', and 'A Spring of Rosemary' (all 1919) alternate long and short lines, creating a visual resemblance to Sapphic stanzas (Munich 2004, 16). Several critics have noted how Sappho's lyrics were a key inspiration for the Imagist group – not only for Lowell but also for H. D., Richard Aldington, and Ezra Pound (Collecott 1999, 103–34). In addition, Lowell's experimentation with spare Japanese forms drew on the brevity and concentration of image associated with Sappho's fragments. But whilst Swinburne sees Sappho in terms of strict rhythm, Lowell emphasises 'the apparent freedom with which Sappho was able to let her poetic imagination soar' appreciating 'the robust eroticism, expressed without restraints ... that permeates the songs of Sappho' (Snyder 1997, 128). This is illustrated by her description of Sappho in 'The Sisters', in which she is contrasted with Elizabeth Barrett Browning:

> Sapho could fly her impulses like bright
> Balloons tip-tilting to a morning air
> And write about it. Mrs. Browning's heart
> was squeezed in stiff conventions. So she lay
> Stretched upon a sofa, reading Greek
> And speculating, as I must suppose,
> In just this way on Sapho.

(Lowell 1955, 459)

Ultimately both Swinburne and Lowell make use of Sappho as the poet who represents the poetry *they* want to write. Prins suggests that we consider Swinburne's use of Sappho in terms of a 'highly self-conscious nineteenth-century discourse on metre' (Prins 1999, 155). In contrast, Lowell utilised Sappho to promote free verse, insisting that rhythm and cadence were the heart of Sappho's *and* modernist practice: as she explains, '[i]f the modern movement in poetry could be defined in a sentence, the truest thing which could be said of it ... would be that it is a movement to restore the audible quality to poetry' (Lowell 1930, 23). In this way, Lowell could be said to be attempting to reverse Swinburne's Sapphic alchemy, turning poetry from strict English metre to be appreciated on the page, back into cadenced song to be performed aloud.

Lowell's 'polyphonic prose' was based on 'the rhythm of the speaking voice' (qtd in Thacker 2004, 107). Lowell conceived of this form in terms of 'tides' and 'waves' of differing sound effects. But, whilst for Lowell such fluidity suggested freedom and sensuality, for Swinburne it represented the strictly rhythmical patterns of nature: '[Swinburne's] sea is a fluid and formless mass given structure by the rhythms of the waves and the tides and the coast's outlines' (Walsh 2010, 51). Thus, Lowell rejects Swinburne's version of strict Sapphic metre, projecting this on to Barrett Browning, whose 'heart' (and poetry) is 'squeezed in stiff conventions'.

This rejection of Victorian prosody is characteristic of modernist poets more generally, who viewed such 'regulation of rhythm ... [as] an unnatural and mechanical imposition of meter' (Prins 1999, 172). Swinburne's imagery was also criticised by modernists, with Lowell referring to 'the Swinburne of confused and redundant imagery' (qtd in Damon 1935, 343). Charlotte Ribeyrol points out that Swinburne's synaesthetic imagery contributed to accusations of his 'fleshliness', indicating 'a loss of control over the senses, once again paradoxically contained within a rigid form' (Ribeyrol 2010, 113). These synaesthetic 'attacks' threateningly blurred the boundaries between self and other, thus 'pass[ing] on the burden of sensitivity in that they assault their readers with multiple stimuli' (Maxwell 2001, 196).

Despite her own criticisms, Lowell became accused of the same 'sins' as Swinburne. Polyphonic prose was itself 'very much a synaesthetic experience' arranging 'the visual elements of language in a painterly composition' (Thacker 2004, 116). As a result, Lowell's detractors complained that she assaulted the senses with overwrought imagery, mixed metaphors, and attacks of sound, at the expense of distinct images and clearly defined subject matter. Harriet Monroe's complaint that when reading the pyrotechnic Lowell 'one's ears and eyes feel fairly battered' (Monroe 1926, 81) recalls a character in Swinburne's novel Lesbia Brandon who complains that 'things in verse hurt one' (Swinburne 1952, 148). Therefore the fusion of pleasure and pain connected to Sappho was played out in the form and imagery of both Swinburne and Lowell's work. Their poetry, assaulting the senses through rhythmical form and synaesthetic images, disrupts the boundary between the body and the text, and is thus linked to the pain of unrequited Sapphic desire. Ultimately, criticism of the pain inflicted by their verses was projected onto their physical appearance, thus marking their bodies as sites of abuse.

CRITICAL ABUSE AND THE POET'S BODY

In my opening, I noted that Lowell and Swinburne have both been critically marginalised. This can be attributed, in part, to the way both poets have been unfairly caricatured in biographical and critical studies of their work that often exhibit a fixation with their physical abnormalities. For example, Lowell's obesity led her to be called the 'hippopoetess' by her modernist peers, whilst Swinburne's slight build and red hair attracted the ridicule of Max Beerbohm and Edmund Gosse in diminishing caricatures and written portraits which describe his body in terms of effeminacy (Bradshaw 2004, 171; Prins 1999, 156–62; Maxwell 2006, 4–7). In both cases, criticism of the body becomes virtually indistinguishable from criticism of the work, creating stereotypes that unfortunately endure to this day. Referring to T. S. Eliot's influential criticisms of Swinburne, Thaïs E. Morgan remarks that Eliot particularly feared Swinburne as he exemplifies the 'perfect' poet, scholar, and critic, representing 'a rival to Eliot in all three of these roles' (Morgan 1993b, 142). Eliot's fear of Swinburne recalls Harold Bloom's Oedipal theories of father/son poetic rivalry. However, Cassandra Laity, in her work on H. D. and Swinburne, suggests that Eliot's attitude is based on the male modernists' fear of 'feminisation' at the hands of the previous literary movement. She argues that, 'Contrary to Harold Bloom's Oedipal model of father-son combat, male modernists appear to have perceived their Romantic precursors as insidiously possessive "foremothers", whose influence threatened to feminise both their psyches and their art' (Laity 1992, 219).

Depictions of Swinburne as weak and feminine – 'long-ringleted, flippant-lipped, down-cheeked, amorous-lidded' in the words of Buchanan – imply that he is a castrated figure, an impotent and sexless servant to a dominant female power: 'utterly and miserably lost to the Muses' (Buchanan in Hyder 1970, 32). Maxwell suggests that poetic law itself can be understood as 'the law of the mother', represented by Sappho and the muses, a law that Swinburne submitted himself to; as she asserts, 'Swinburne's honouring of female power is undisguised ... the female principle is dominant in his work' (Maxwell 2001, 191, 181). The fact that Swinburne openly admitted his ultimate poetic inspiration was female – a female of ambiguous sexuality, at that – and celebrated her repeatedly, only intensifies the anxiety that his influence might feminise, corrupt, and possess the virile modernist.

Swinburne's slight form appears to have allowed his critics to take his work equally lightly. I suggest we can understand Amy Lowell as a kind of inverted Swinburne, a female whose immense bulk contributed to her critical neglect. As Munich and Bradshaw observe, Lowell's poetic achievements have been eclipsed by an emphasis on her physical appearance and eccentric behaviour: 'It is her corpulence and her love of cigars (not her considerable literary contributions) that have kept Amy Lowell in literary memory' (Munich and Bradshaw 2004, xxiii). Lowell was famously attacked by Pound for 'taking over' the Imagist movement; Pound then dismissed the movement as 'Amygisme'. Repeatedly, Pound criticised the 'mushy technique' and 'general floppiness' of Lowell's poetry in terms that suggest the fluidity and softness associated with the female body (qtd in Bradshaw 2004, 172). Testifying to Pound's repugnance toward Lowell's body, Collecott writes that Pound saw himself as 'the first line of defence against "Amy" and "*slop*"' (Collecott 1999, 163). The threatening liquidity Pound perceived in Lowell links her to Swinburne's vision of the sea, associated with the feminine power he connected to Sappho.

Pound's criticisms of Lowell's work recall what Leslie Heywood has

defined as the 'anorexic aesthetic' of modernism. She writes that 'In both
the high modernist artist and the anorexic there is a rejection and a will to
eliminate the feminine ... to shape the "base material" into a "higher,"
masculine form' (Heywood 1996, 61). Therefore, the modernist emphasis
on 'hardness, paring down, and reducing the poetic body can be read as a
corollary for the ... reduction or elimination of the female body' (101).
Following Heywood's theory, one could suggest that Lowell threatened to
overwhelm, squash, and spill all over Pound's neatly chiselled Imagism
with her boundary-dissolving excess, performed in her poetic experimen-
tation and embodied in her obesity. Like the Swinburnian female that
Buchanan denounces as a 'large-limbed, sterile creature' (qtd in Prins
1999, 159), Lowell's size also disrupts boundaries of gender and sexuality.
Surveying depictions of Lowell's body, Bradshaw writes that 'fat female
bodies evade easy classification, destabilize categories, invite paradox.
They are at once pathetic and threatening, weak and overpowering.
Overwhelmingly feminine, with their exaggerated secondary sexual char-
acteristics, they are, at the same time, perceived as disconcertingly
masculine in their bulk' (Bradshaw 2004, 179). Alison Pease has shown
that Swinburne's poetry embodied the same boundary-defying qualities:
threatening to 'destabilize the socially constructed norms of male and
female behaviour', the 'unrestrained and repetitive sexuality of the poems
exacts a transgression by which all passions and all people become the
same, and that sameness is reflected ... in a bestial, sensual chaos that
tends to collapse constructed taxonomies' (Pease 1997, 43, 45). A similar
fear of boundary-defying chaos is certainly suggested by a letter that
Pound wrote to Margaret Anderson (22 April 1921), betraying his fear that
Lowell would overwhelm, smother, and possess him. He asks: 'Ought one
to be distracted, ought one to be asked to address that perpetual mother's
meeting, ... that cradle of on-coming Amys???' (qtd in Munich and
Bradshaw 2004, xiv). Pound's image of monstrous maternity and the
threat of engulfment by multiple Amys, suggest that the violent, anxious
reactions Lowell elicited in the male modernists link her to those other
overwhelming poetic 'foremothers': Swinburne and Sappho.

    To conclude, this chapter has suggested a number of ways in which
Sappho, Swinburne, and Lowell are connected. Drawing on Michael
Riffaterre's and Thaïs E. Morgan's concept of intertextuality, I have shown
how these three poets form a triangular 'matrix' of complex cultural
cross-influences (Morgan 1993b, 137). In particular, this chapter has
demonstrated how Amy Lowell's response to Sappho is mediated by

Swinburne's earlier versions of the 'Tenth Muse'. As a result of this inter-textual influence, both Swinburne and Lowell connect Sapphic desire to medieval courtly love, figuring such desire in terms of distance and unat-tainability. They embody this painful separation through the Sapphic form of 'suffering meter' (Prins 1999, 140). This formal experimentation and use of synaesthesia threaten boundaries between physical bodies and bodies of poetry, leading to similar criticism of both poets that attacks their physical bodies and their bodies of poetry as threateningly feminine and queer. Understanding the importance of Sappho to Swinburne and Lowell – not just as a lesbian icon but as an early 'courtly lover' and formal experimenter – leads to greater understanding of their own strange, complex poetic bodies, and why they have elicited such derision and fear.

NOTES

1   Amy Lowell's early collections are *A Dome of Many-Coloured Glass* (1912) and *Sword Blades and Poppy Seeds* (1914). In 1915 she became the editor of the anthology series *Some Imagist Poets*. Despite periods of long illness, which began in 1916, Lowell published six more volumes of poems (including Chinese and Japanese translations), two more Imagist anthologies, critical studies, and a two-volume biography of Keats (1925). She died of a stroke in May 1925. Three more volumes of her poetry were published posthumously, edited by Ada Dwyer Russell. The first of these, *What's O'Clock* (1925), won the Pulitzer Prize in 1926.

2   'The New Poetry' encompasses various kinds of modernist experimentation practised by American poets in the early twentieth century, including direct treatment of the image (as opposed to rhetorical flourishes), *vers libre* or 'free verse', and unconventional punctuation. This kind of poetic experimentation was resisted as bogus, obscure, or even immoral by many American readers. For Amy Lowell's role in promoting the 'New Poetry', see Marek 2004.

3   Zonana (1990) emphasises Sappho's role as Swinburne's muse and his under-standing of her as a spiritual 'sister'; Morgan (1984, 1992) explores Swinburne's utilisation of the lesbian body to voice alternative masculinities; similarly Dellamora (1990) argues that Swinburne's Sapphic poems embody a complex male homoerotic/queer desire; Prins (1999) focuses on Swinburne's use of strict Sapphic metre in relation to his flagellant fantasies; Maxwell (2001) examines Sappho as a powerful feminine force in Swinburne's work and the source of his blurring of boundaries of gender and sexuality.

4   Swinburne was commissioned to write the essay on Keats for *The English Poets* Series, as Lowell would have known from her copy of Gosse's edition of Swinburne's letters (1919). For the letter to Gosse (6 October 1879) in which

Swinburne agrees to undertake the Keats essay, see Swinburne 1919a, 2.37 and Swinburne 1959–62, 4.100–1. Swinburne briefly met Lowell's ancestor, the poet James Russell Lowell (letter to E. C. Stedman, 4 April 1882), a meeting recounted in Swinburne 1919a, 2.102–3, and Swinburne 1959–62, 4.264–5.

5 Though it is difficult to posit a direct influence of Sappho on Rudel, Fragment 31 was one of the few Sappho poems to survive in near-complete form from antiquity through the medieval period via citation by other writers. It was included in Longinus' treatise *On the Sublime* (copied into manuscript form during the tenth century) and was adapted by the Roman poet Catullus in his Poem 51 (see Higgins 1996). Ovid's *Heroides* also famously recounts Sappho's love for Phaon, so we can expect medieval writers such as Petrarch, Boccacio, and Chaucer, who read and admired Ovid (see Ziolkowski 2005, 25–6), to associate Sappho with courtly or unrequited love.

11

ATMOSPHERE AND ABSORPTION: SWINBURNE, ELIOT, DRINKWATER

Catherine Maxwell

T. S. Eliot's 1920 essay on Swinburne had a lasting impact on the critical fortunes of the poet. Some have tried to claim that Eliot's comments were complimentary or at least a dispassionate analytic assessment, although it seems to me that Eliot's tactic is accurately summed up by Rikky Rooksby in an essay on Swinburne's reception when he writes that 'Eliot marginalized Swinburne by damning with faint praise' (Rooksby 1993, 4). It is true that Eliot uses the word 'genius' of the poet when he asserts that 'Only a man ȯf genius could dwell so exclusively and consistently among words as Swinburne' (Eliot 1920a, 150), but the term clearly did not hold over-whelmingly positive connotations for Eliot, as can be seen in his essay on Blake which follows 'Swinburne as Poet' in *The Sacred Wood* (1920). There, Blake, rebuked for lacking 'a framework of accepted and traditional ideas which would have prevented him from indulging in a philosophy of his own', is compared unfavourably with Dante. For Eliot, the medieval poet's possession of such a framework 'is one of the reasons why Dante is a classic, and Blake only a poet of genius' (158). In Eliot's view the 'genius' tends to the waywardly idiosyncratic, a quality that removes him from influential 'classic' status and keeps him locked in a world of his own that has no relevance to the present moment. Thus Eliot at the end of his essay on Swinburne, having conceded the 'singular life' of the poet's language, nonetheless refuses to allow it any part in contemporary literary experimentation, contrasting it with 'the language which is more important to us' such as 'the prose of Mr. James Joyce or the earlier Conrad' (150).

Eliot's 'faint praise' may have been mistaken as complimentary by some, but when set alongside his other critical remarks on Swinburne – the bulk of which are negative or hostile – it becomes evident that he was not interested in doing his Victorian predecessor any favours. As Rooksby has shown, the 1920 essay did long-term damage to Swinburne's reputation, with many happy to take the modernist poet's view as the critical last word. Eliot's readers would also have in mind his many other less restrained attacks on Swinburne that help reinforce the negative implications of his essay.

A brief and by no means comprehensive survey of his published comments on the poet begins with his 1917 essay, 'Reflections on *Vers Libre*' in which he deprecates the 'trick' of Swinburne's metrical technique (Eliot 1965, 185). Eliot continues this deprecation in his pamphlet *Ezra Pound: His Metric and Poetry* of the same year, on which I'll say more later.[1] In April 1918 he declares in an otherwise critical review of an essay collection by Alice Meynell, 'she wins our hearts ... when she denounces Swinburne' (Eliot 1918, 61). More adverse remarks follow in a disparaging essay on Rudyard Kipling, 'Kipling Redivivus' of 1919, and come to a head in the two famous essays that make Swinburne their particular focus – 'Swinburne as Critic' and 'Swinburne as Poet' – first published in the *Athenæum* in September 1919 and January 1920 respectively and then reprinted in *The Sacred Wood* later in 1920.[2] This collection also includes 'Euripides and Professor Murray', which originally came out just after 'Swinburne as Poet'. This is another piece that takes a passing swipe at Swinburne who, to Eliot's disapproval, was an obvious influence on the poetic translations of the eminent classicist Gilbert Murray (Eliot 1920a, 74, 75).[3] Also included in *The Sacred Wood* is 'The Perfect Critic', originally published as two articles in July 1920, which compares the decadent writer Arthur Symons unfavourably with Swinburne as critic, but nonetheless makes it clear that Swinburne's superiority is only relative, suggesting that in any case Symons's criticism is negatively influenced by Swinburne's poetry (Eliot 1920a, 5–7).[4] During 1921 Eliot had a brief skirmish with George Saintsbury in the pages of the *Times Literary Supplement*, after the older critic tried to claim the chorus 'Before the beginning of Time' (from *Atalanta in Calydon*) as 'metaphysical' (Eliot 1921b; Saintsbury 1921). In 1926 Eliot was on the attack again in his Clark lecture on metaphysical poetry, given at Trinity College, Cambridge, declaring that 'the imagery of Shelley and Swinburne is merely careless' and that 'Shelley and Swinburne had a vague statement of intellectual order'. Refining on this, he adds, 'When I assert that neither Shelley's nor Swinburne's verse will bear close examination, I do not imply that they were fools ... But their minds were like clocks hurriedly put together by the hand of a child; there is no real intimacy between the thought and the feeling in their work' (Eliot 1993, 175). He also took this opportunity to repudiate once more Saintsbury's characterisation of Swinburne as metaphysical (Eliot 1993, 204).

Thereafter Swinburne comes in for rebuke in Eliot's review of Pound's *Personae* published in *The Dial* in 1928, where he writes: 'Swinburne's form is uninteresting, because he is literally saying next to nothing, and unless you mean something with your words they will do nothing for you' (Eliot 1928, 6). Five years later Eliot was evidently still of the same opinion, as we can see when he mentions Swinburne in an unpublished lecture on Edward Lear given at Scripps College, Claremont, in January 1933. According to the college newspaper, Eliot, discussing poetry and meaning, signalled that 'Swinburne achieves his effects by rhythm and emotional use of words, the intellectual content being negligible' and that 'Swinburne gives the illusion of profound meaning where there is no meaning whereas Lear does not mean to mean anything' (Baker 1983, 566). There is perhaps a hint of concession in Eliot's Turnbull lectures of 1933 at Johns Hopkins when he cites some lines from Swinburne's 'Before the Mirror' which he had disparaged at least twice before and admits that they have some validity: 'I can see that what Swinburne was after was a particular association of our feeling towards violets and feelings towards small pathetic fragile human beings' (Eliot 1993, 272). However, lest this should sound like relenting, his essay on Tennyson's 'In Memoriam' of 1936 informs us that 'Tennyson is the master of Swinburne and the versification of Swinburne, himself a classical scholar, is often crude and sometimes cheap in comparison with Tennyson's' (Eliot 1936, 175–6). In later years Eliot substantially revised his initial poor opinion of Kipling, but Swinburne was never similarly rehabilitated, although the issue of his status hangs in the air in the revisionary Kipling essay of 1941 when Eliot remarks that 'Kipling's debt to Swinburne is considerable' but fails to specify how (Eliot 1957, 230).[5] Yet in 1946, reflecting on the state of poetry as it faced Pound in the first decade of the twentieth century, Eliot remarked, 'The question was still: where do we go from Swinburne? and the answer appeared to be, nowhere' (Eliot in Russell 1950, 25).

In reviewing this collection of remarks, most of them gibes, questions come to mind about the extent of Eliot's knowledge of the poet. How well did he know Swinburne's work and how exactly did he read him? The purpose of this chapter is not so much to deplore Eliot's view of Swinburne (although, of course, I do) but rather to explore the context for it and, in so doing, to shed some light on Eliot's resistance to Swinburne. While the first part of this chapter considers the milieu in which Eliot was writing and responding to poetry, the second part provides what would seem to be a significant and somewhat surprising new source for many of the views and ideas expressed in Eliot's influential essay of 1920.

In 'Swinburne as Poet' Eliot had been keen to represent an enthusiasm for Swinburne as an affair of adolescence, something to be put aside with the onset of adulthood. He coolly solicits his readers' agreement that 'we do not (and I think the present generation does not) greatly enjoy Swinburne, and that ... (a more serious condemnation) at one period of our lives we did enjoy him and now no longer enjoy him' (Eliot 1920a, 145). We might reasonably assume from this that Eliot had himself enjoyed reading Swinburne at an earlier stage in his life. Yet four years later Eliot would claim that he had encountered Swinburne too late to get 'anything out of [him]'. Writing to Pound on 22 December 1924, he declared:

> Probably the fact that Swinburne and the poets of the nineties were entirely missed out of my personal history counts for a great deal. I never read any of these people until it was too late for me to get anything out of them, and until after I had assimilated other influences which made it impossible for me to accept the Swinburnians at all. The only exception to the above is Rossetti. I am as blind to the merits of those people as I am to Thomas Hardy. (Eliot 1996, 394–5; 2009, 2.557)

This sounds suspiciously defensive, as if Eliot is trying to edit his personal history. Indeed this account is contradicted by his note to 'On the Development of Taste' that forms part of the introductory lecture (1932) to his Harvard lecture series collected in *The Use of Poetry and the Use of Criticism* (1933). In this note he describes an encounter with Edward FitzGerald's *Rubáiyát* that made the world seem 'painted with bright delicious and painful colours. Thereupon I took the usual adolescent course with Byron, Shelley, Keats, Rossetti, Swinburne' (Eliot 1933, 33). Eliot nonetheless emphasises the immaturity of this phase, which lasted 'until my nineteenth or twentieth year', adding that 'we must not confuse the intensity of the poetic experience in adolescence with the intense experience of poetry' (Eliot 1933, 34). Various of Eliot's early poems written between 1907 and 1909 before he discovered his Laforguian style have a generic late Victorian wistfulness, faintly reminiscent of

Swinburne's elegiac strain, while a more lurid note sounds in 'Circe's Palace' of November 1908:

> Around her fountain which flows
> With the voice of men in pain
> Are flowers that no man knows.
> Their petals are fanged and red
> With hideous streak and stain;
> They sprang from the limbs of the dead. —
> We shall not come here again.

(Eliot 1967, 26; 1969, 598)

It is perhaps from the embarrassments of such obvious indebtedness, an indebtedness that reads like an unintentionally bad parody of Swinburne, that Eliot was anxious to free himself, though his editor Christopher Ricks notes various echoes from Swinburne that crop up throughout the more formative poetry of 1909–17 collected in *Inventions of the March Hare* (Eliot 1996).

Yet Eliot's more mature poetry is not immune from Swinburne's influence. Cassandra Laity has convincingly identified 'A Leave-Taking' as a source for 'Prufrock' as well as suggesting that Eliot's recurrent images of drowning are indebted to the Victorian poet (Laity 2004, 436). David Ned Tobin hears Swinburne's presence in 'sounding chants' like 'Blown hair is sweet, brown hair over the mouth blown, / Lilac and brown hair' from 'Ash-Wednesday' (Tobin 1983, 94; Eliot 1969, 93). I have proposed Swinburne's late poem 'A Rosary' from *A Channel Passage and Other Poems* (1904) as a possible source for the imagery in the rose-garden episode in 'Burnt Norton' (Maxwell 1994, 101–4). Both David Riede and I have respectively noted that Eliot's use of the mythic method in *The Waste Land* (1921) is preceded by the example of Swinburne's own powerful myth-making in poems such as 'Itylus' from *Poems and Ballads* (1866) and the later 'On the Cliffs' from *Songs of the Springtides* (1880) which conspicuously incorporates translated fragments from Sappho and Aeschylus as well as encrypted allusive echoes to Homer, Milton, Keats, Matthew Arnold, and Whitman (Riede 1978; Maxwell 2001). Eliot's fascination with Philomela and Tiresias is anticipated by Swinburne's own preoccupation with these figures. Swinburne's *The Sisters: A Tragedy* (1892), a contemporary verse drama inspired by Elizabethan models, might just possibly have had an influence on Eliot's *The Family Reunion* (1939), his attempt at writing a modern verse drama inspired by Greek tragedy. Both plays are set in country houses in the north of England and feature dysfunctional aristocratic families haunted by the past. Jean Overton Fuller has also pointed out how Swinburne's experimental rendering of everyday speech as blank verse in his play 'is precisely what T. S. Eliot did in *The Cocktail Party* and other works' (Fuller 1968, 282). Eliot might well have encountered *The Sisters* as one of the plays in the collected five-volume *Tragedies of Algernon Charles Swinburne* of 1905, an edition that includes the 'Stuart plays' he mentions elsewhere (Eliot 1920a, 144).

All of this raises the question, how much of Swinburne did Eliot read or know? His 1920 essay was initially written as a review of Edmund Gosse and Thomas Wise's *Selections from Swinburne* (1919), the first selection published since the 1887 collection authorised by the poet himself that omits many of his best-known poems. Broaching the question 'how much must be read of a particular poet', Eliot remarks that

> Of Swinburne, we should like to have the *Atalanta* entire, and a volume of selections which should certainly contain *The Leper, Laus Veneris* and *The Triumph of Time*. It ought to contain many more, but there is perhaps no other single poem which it would be an error to omit. A student of Swinburne will want to read one of the Stuart plays and dip into *Tristram of Lyonesse*. But almost no one, to-day, will wish to read the whole of Swinburne. (Eliot 1920a, 144)

'Itylus' and 'Before the Mirror' are two other poems specifically mentioned by Eliot in this essay. Both along with 'The Triumph of Time' appear in *Selections from Swinburne*, but the other texts do not. Eliot's review specifically discusses the tenor of 'the first *Poems and Ballads*' (149), which includes 'The Leper' and 'Laus Veneris', so he was clearly familiar with that volume.

Both 'Swinburne as Poet' and 'Swinburne as Critic', although written as reviews, were undoubtedly stimulated by Eliot's work as an extension lecturer during the period 1916–19. As Ronald Schuchard has shown, Eliot began giving extension lectures on modern French literature for Oxford in 1916, moving on to teach a class on modern English literature for London University in October that same year. Although this course ranged from Tennyson to Meredith, Swinburne did not appear on the syllabus. He did, however, appear on the syllabus of two later courses on Victorian litera-ture that commenced in the autumn of 1917, although the first, 'A Course of Twenty-Five Lectures on Victorian Literature', lists only the titles of the lectures, Lecture 13 being 'A Poet of Liberty – A. C. Swinburne'

(Schuchard 1974, 293). The other course, a continuation of the previous year's class in modern English literature, featured Swinburne as the fourth topic to be treated (after D. G. Rossetti and before Pater). The brief notes on the lecture schedule are as follows:

> The pure romantic. Relation to Pre-Raphaelitism. 'Paganism'. His early attitude. His championship of liberty. Merits and faults of his poetry. Read: Selections from *Poems and Ballads*; *Atalanta in Calydon*, selections from *Songs Before Sunrise*.
> Swinburne as prose writer. Comparison with Shelley, as a poet. (Schuchard 1974, 294).

We can assume that in addition to the listed works Eliot himself had probably 'read one of the Stuart plays and dip[ped] into *Tristram of Lyonesse*'. In 'Swinburne as Critic' he also mentions Swinburne's play *The Duke of Gandia* (1908) as an Elizabethan-inspired drama that he finds wanting (1920a, 23).

'Swinburne as Critic' – in *The Sacred Wood* part of a larger survey titled significantly 'Imperfect Critics' – reveals that Eliot had consulted much of Swinburne's dramatic criticism. He mentions 'the *Contemporaries of Shakespeare*, the *Age of Shakespeare* and the books on Shakespeare and Jonson' (20).[6] In this essay Eliot is somewhat grudgingly warmer about Swinburne, admitting that 'With all his superlatives, his judgment, if carefully scrutinized, appears temperate and just', that 'his taste [is] sensitive and discriminating', and that 'we cannot say that his thinking is faulty or perverse – up to the point at which it is thinking' (19, 20). He also avers 'His great merit as a critic ... is that he was sufficiently interested in his subject-matter and knew quite enough about it; ... a rare combination in English criticism'. Even so, Swinburne is deemed to be 'an appreciator and not a critic' and his failure to ask the kinds of questions Eliot believes are significant makes his work 'an introduction rather than a statement' (24, 19, 20).

Eliot seems to have read Swinburne's criticism in a fairly measured and attentive fashion but the same cannot be said for his reading of Swinburne's poetry. In his Clark lectures of 1926, he says of Crashaw's poetry: 'you cannot race through it as you not only can, but must, race through Swinburne even at his best' (Eliot 1993, 179). In fact the very opposite of this is true; while an initial pacey reading of Swinburne may give a sense of his vital energy, it is necessary to partner this with a reading that resists the rush in order to attend to the complexity of meaning and allusion. Eliot accused Swinburne of carelessness on more than one occasion but, if his own reading had been slower and more considered, he would have realised that the poet was perfectly justified in his choices. For example, in 'Swinburne as Poet' Eliot selects the opening lines from the Second Chorus in *Atalanta*:

> Before the beginning of years
> > There came to the making of man
> Time with a gift of tears;
> > Grief with a glass that ran.
> (Eliot 1920a, 148; Swinburne 1904, 4.258; Swinburne 2000, 258)

He then comments:

> This is not merely 'music': it is effective because it appears to be a tremendous statement, like statements made in our dreams; when we wake up we find that the 'glass that ran' would do better for time than for grief, and that the gift of tears would be as appropriately bestowed by grief as by time. (148–9)

In his elegant essay on *Atalanta*, Maurice Bowra remarks of Eliot's preferred revision:

> It is too obvious. [Swinburne] wishes to surprise, to say something unexpected, and he is justified for it is perfectly true that time brings tears and that grief devours our days. He rises above the commonplace to something else, and his way of doing it is to use words and ideas in unexpected combinations, so we keep awake and move from shock to delighted shock. (Bowra 1950, 238)

John Rosenberg similarly dismisses Eliot's reversal as 'trite' and, noting how the whole chorus is about 'the terrible ambiguity of the gods' gifts to men', remarks:

> As we read the lines, we are half aware of the conventional imagery underlying them, our mind reacting as does our ear to a departure from regular rhythm, half hearing the normal beat and half hearing the eccentric. (Rosenberg 1967, 133)

To take another example: discussing Swinburne's choice of words, Eliot asserts 'he uses the most general word, because his emotion is never particular, never in direct line of vision, never focused', and, in support of this, he quotes from 'The Triumph of Time':

> There lived a singer in France of old
> By the tideless, dolorous, midland sea.
> In a land of sand and ruin and gold
> There shone one woman, and none but she.
> (Eliot 1920a, 147; Swinburne 1904, 1.44; Swinburne 2000, 39)

Eliot adds:

You see that Provence is the merest point of diffusion here. Swinburne defines the place by the most general word, which has for him its own value. 'Gold,' 'ruin,' 'dolorous': it is not merely the sound that he wants, but the vague associations of idea that the words give him. He has not his eye on a particular place. (147)

In point of fact Swinburne's lines describe two places. The first is France (the home of Jaufré Rudel, the twelfth-century Provençal singer) and the second the home of Rudel's apocryphal amour, the Lady of Tripoli. Swinburne is more precise than Eliot gives him credit for. Southern France borders on the Mediterranean, an almost landlocked 'midland' sea that Swinburne despised and thought pitiable or 'dolorous' for its tameness, its lack of vital tides (20 January 1882; Swinburne 1959–62, 4.254). The Lady, on the other hand, lives in Tripoli in Lebanon, an arid but wealthy country that by the twelfth century had already amassed the ruins of previous occupying nations.

Eliot's own negligence is evident. His Clark lecture rebukes Swinburne for the carelessness of his imagery but in the example he gives (Eliot 1993, 174) – perhaps imperfectly recalled from 'Swinburne as Poet' (Eliot 1920a, 148) – he misquotes Swinburne's lines from 'Before the Mirror' – 'Snowdrops that plead for pardon / And pine for fright' – as 'Violets that plead for pardon / And pine for fright', a misprision that ruins not only the sound values of Swinburne's line but also its sense by removing the impression of intense whiteness which is the main point of the comparison. He repeats the same mistake in his Turnbull lecture seven years later but there at least reluctantly acknowledges that Swinburne's lines do have some applicability (Eliot 1993, 272).

Eliot's aggression towards Swinburne and other leading Victorians has long been attributed to his sense of belatedness.[7] David Ned Tobin declares in his thoughtful study of Eliot's Victorian inheritance:

What emerges on Eliot's part is an ambivalent, wavering point of view, and a subtle strategy of defense: unmistakable signs of 'the anxiety of influence.' His references to poets like Tennyson and Kipling indicate a profound familiarity with their work, coupled with a need to distance it, evaluate it, sometimes misrepresent or belittle it – and finally, to come to terms with it. (Tobin 1983, 91)

Arguably, though, Eliot did not finally 'come to terms' with Swinburne as he may have done with other Victorian precursors, possibly because Swinburne exercised a priority that must have been especially galling. When he encountered Swinburne's lead in so many key areas – Elizabethan drama, Blake, Baudelaire, Mallarmé, Greek-inspired myth-making, avant-gardism, dramatic experimentation – Eliot cannot have been pleased to find himself a latecomer. Yet there is another important element in Eliot's negative treatment of Swinburne that specifically helped him to sideline his precursor as outdated.

The new tenets of poetry-making as expressed in the doctrines of Imagism allowed Eliot, in company with other poets keen to define themselves as authentically modern, to pit themselves against a Victorian heritage that Ezra Pound and others saw as characterised by vagueness, by the 'crepuscular spirit'.[8] 'Vague' is a favourite word of various late Victorians despised by Eliot such as Swinburne's prose successor Walter Pater and Pater's friend, the female aesthetic writer Vernon Lee (see Eliot 1971, 26, 27, 40, 41). For these writers 'vague' is a word that is often used to denote an imaginative suggestiveness that works through subconscious or indirect association. Writing in 'The School of Giorgione' (1877) of lyrical poetry as 'the highest and most complete form of poetry', Pater comments that its 'very perfection . . . often seems to depend, in part, in a certain suppression or vagueness of mere subject, so that the meaning reaches us by ways not distinctly traceable by the understanding' (Pater 1980, 108). Lee's essay 'Faustus and Helena: Notes on the Supernatural in Art' (1880) makes the vague an attribute of and a precondition for the supernatural. Writing of our 'transient delight in the impossible and the vague', she explains how 'We moderns seek in the world of the supernatural a renewal of the delightful semi-obscurity of vision and keenness of fancy of our childhood' (Lee 2006, 312).[9] This kind of vagueness then is antithetical to Pound's *Imagisme*, which was in his words, 'Objective – no slither; direct . . . straight talk'.[10] The famous preface to *Some Imagist Poets: An Anthology* of 1915, a collection planned and assembled mainly by Richard Aldington and H. D., declared among other things that it was essential that poetry 'present an image' and 'should render particulars exactly and not deal in vague generalities'. Thus poets must 'produce poetry that is hard and clear, never blurred nor indefinite' (Aldington and H. D. et al., 1915, vii).

In 1970 Wallace Martin suggested Théodule Ribot's *Essai sur l'imagina-
tion créatrice* (1900; English edition 1906) as a book that may have
influenced the Imagist aesthetic, citing in particular its last section that
distinguishes between the 'plastic' and the 'diffluent imagination' (Martin
1970, 200–1). For Ribot, the plastic imagination 'has for its special charac-
ters clearness and precision of form; more explicitly those forms whose
materials are clear images ... giving the impression of reality'; while the
diffluent imagination, allied to 'the romantic state of mind', 'consists of
vaguely-outlined, indistinct images that are evoked and joined according
to the least rigorous modes of association'. Diffluent images 'have an
impressionist mark ... They act less through a direct influence than by
evoking, suggesting, whispering; they permit a glance, a passing glimpse:
we may justly call them crepuscular or twilight ideas' (Ribot 1906, 184,
195–7). As Martin points out, that word 'crepuscular' recurs strikingly in
Pound's poem, 'Revolt: Against the Crepuscular Spirit in Modern Poetry',
collected in *Personae* (1909) (Martin 1970, 201).[11] In his discussion of the
diffluent imagination Ribot also mentions the 'pre-Raphaelites' whom he
perceives as 'effacing forms, outlines, semblances, colors ... to *paint*
emotion' (Ribot 1906, 204). Whether or not Pound or Eliot knew Ribot's
work, his association of the vague and the indistinct with the 'romantic
state of mind', Pre-Raphaelitism, and impressionism is usefully pertinent
when considering Eliot's treatment of Swinburne's visual aesthetic as
tainted by a Romanticism deemed old-fashioned and 'adolescent'.

Two years after *Some Imagist Poets*, Eliot echoes its creators' sentiments
when reviewing Pound's poetry in *Ezra Pound: His Metric and Poetry*. Citing
two lines from the second chorus of Swinburne's *Atalanta*, a poem he
disliked enough to censure on more than one occasion, he comments:
'Instead of slightly veiled and resonant abstractions such as / *Time with a
gift of tears, / Grief with a glass that ran* / – of Swinburne, or the mossiness
of Mallarmé, Pound's verse is always definite and concrete, because he
has a definite emotion behind it' (Eliot 1965, 170). Swinburne could do
particularity perfectly well if he chose – one only has to look at a poem
such as 'The Sundew' (Swinburne 1904, 1.186–7) – and indeed he is often
more particular than his detractors realise, but, as his preferred technique
is to multiply perception and suggestion, it is easy to see how for Eliot his
poetry would become the epitome of despised Victorian vagueness, anti-
thetical to the now privileged 'definite and concrete'. In 'Swinburne as
Poet', Eliot, questioning the conventional linkage of Swinburne's verse
with music rather than visual imagery, asserts testily 'There is no reason

why verse intended to be sung should not present a sharp visual image', and he later complains that Swinburne's 'emotion is never particular, never in direct line of vision, never focused' (Eliot 1920a, 146, 147). Commenting on his word choice in the quoted lines from 'The Triumph of Time', Eliot adds: 'it is not merely the sound that he wants, but the *vague* associations of idea that the words give him' (147; my emphasis). And earlier in the essay, he proclaims 'For what he gives is not images and ideas and music, it is one thing with a curious mixture of suggestions of all three' (146). The blurring that Eliot finds in Swinburne's verse he also finds in his criticism where 'there is the same curious mixture of qualities to produce Swinburne's own effect, resulting in the same blur, which only the vigour of the colours fixes' (Eliot 1920a, 24).

That suggestive blurring is an example of what Pound might have identified as 'crepuscular' or, in his essay 'Lionel Johnson', as late Victorian 'muzziness': 'The "nineties" have chiefly gone out because of their muzziness, because of a softness derived, I think, not from books but from impressionist painting' (Pound 1954, 363). Pound's image, like Eliot's 'blur', evokes visual impressionism but terms like 'vague', 'crespuscular', and 'muzziness' perhaps also hark back to aesthetic writers' fondness for the word or notion of 'atmosphere', meaning the temperament, spirit, or ambience of a writer or artist's style or world. Swinburne, for example, describes the painter Simeon Solomon's prose poem *A Vision of Love Revealed in Sleep* (1871) as 'Dim and vague as the atmosphere of such work should be' (Swinburne 1871a, 570). While Pater uses the actual term 'atmosphere' far more frequently, Swinburne's critical writing abounds in metaphors of atmospheric light, temperature, and weather that describe his response to different writers and artists. Such effects find a counterpart in two nineteenth-century artists dear to him whose works might be thought to offer a visual analogue to his poetic style. As Rosenberg points out (Rosenberg 1967, 149), Swinburne had a life-long love of Turner, the painter who declared to Ruskin 'Atmosphere is my style', and who supposedly claimed that 'indistinctness is my forte' (Ruskin 1956–58, 1.273; Bailey 1997, 277). 'I was brought up on him ... and simply revel in everything of his', Swinburne enthused in 1901 (Swinburne 1959–62, 6.152, note). Turner is the natural precursor of later atmospheric painters such as Whistler and the French impressionists, and Whistler was for many years a close friend of the poet's; Swinburne admired and celebrated his paintings in 'Before the Mirror' and the essay 'Notes on Some Pictures of 1868' (Swinburne 1904, 1.129–31; 1875a, 372–3).

In his own protest against the crepuscular, Eliot rebukes Gilbert
Murray for his translations of Euripides that 'blur the Greek lyric to the
fluid haze of Swinburne' (Eliot 1920a, 74), while elsewhere he accuses
Arthur Symons of producing translations that envelop Baudelaire 'in the
Swinburnian violet-coloured London fog of the "nineties"' (Eliot 1936,
70).[12] Moreover, if the pervasive general 'atmosphere' of a particular
writer's work allows it to stand alone as an independent creative realm or
world, as Pater remarked when in 1868 he said of the poetry of William
Morris 'The atmosphere on which its effect depends belongs to no actual
form of life' (Pater 1868, 300), then this self-sufficiency potentially violates
the modernist desire for a clear match between language and the exact
particulars of an actual world. Hence Eliot's later discomfort with
Swinburne's 'language, [which] uprooted, has adapted itself to an inde-
pendent life of *atmospheric* nourishment' (Eliot 1920a, 149; my emphasis).
The earth-bound plant turned air-plant lives independently because
supported by the atmosphere that surrounds it.

In the 'Supplementary Reading' that he prescribed for his extension
lectures, Eliot lists as the sole work of secondary criticism Edward
Thomas's *Algernon Charles Swinburne: A Critical Study*, one of the first
critical monographs on the poet, which had appeared in 1912. Thomas,
who was commissioned to write studies of both Swinburne and Pater,
was clearly ambivalent about both these aesthetic writers and often
deeply critical. Although he is not the most powerful influence on Eliot's
'Swinburne as Poet', there are a number of telling points of comparison
such as the charge of vagueness, as for example when he says of
Swinburne's 'Hesperia': 'In the whole opening passage of this poem there
is the same accumulation, aided by the *vague*, as in "region of stories" and
"capes of the past oversea"' (Thomas 1912, 97; my emphasis). And here is
Thomas on the atmosphere of Swinburne's poetry:

> Swinburne has almost no magic felicity of words. He can astonish and melt
> but seldom thrill, and when he does it is not by any felicity of as it were
> God-given inevitable words. He has to depend on sound and an *atmosphere*
> of words which is now and then concentrated and crystallized into an
> intensity of effect which is almost magical, perhaps never quite magical.
> This *atmosphere* comes from a vocabulary very rich in words connected with
> objects and sensations and emotions of pleasure and beauty, but used, as I
> have said, somewhat lightly and even in appearance indiscriminately. No
> poet could be poorer in brief electric phrases, pictorial, or emotional. (96–7;
> my emphasis)

This analysis picks up on other several ideas that resurface in Eliot's essay where Swinburne's self-sufficient poetry is denied music, visual impact, and emotion.

However, if Eliot's views seem indebted to Thomas, then this debt is even more strongly marked and startling with regard to another Swinburne critic, the Georgian poet John Drinkwater. This debt is particularly surprising in that in 1921, in his 'London Letter' published in *The Dial*, Eliot would aggressively savage Drinkwater's poetry: 'I cannot point to any existing society which produces finer average specimens than Mr Drinkwater ... The most obvious thing to say, the thing which makes it difficult for the critic to say more, is that the work of Mr Drinkwater is dull, supremely dull' (Eliot 1921a, 450). Dull as a poet though he may have seemed to Eliot, that did not stop him leaning heavily on Drinkwater's monograph *Swinburne: An Estimate*, published in 1913, a year after Thomas's study. If he hadn't come across it earlier, Eliot might possibly have read Drinkwater's book in the British Library when he was studying there to prepare for his extension lectures (Ackroyd 1984, 74). My evidence for influence is purely textual, my claim being that Eliot drew heavily on Drinkwater's first chapter titled 'Lyric Technique'; although, apart from the strong coincidence of views and vocabulary, one might also note that the supporting quotation from Shakespeare's *The Winter's Tale* – 'daffodils that come before the swallow dares' (4.4.118–19) – which Eliot misattributes to *Macbeth* in 'Swinburne as Poet' (148) is cited by Drinkwater on p. 3 of this chapter.[13]

Like Thomas, Drinkwater is also critical of Swinburne, although he has a better sense of his achievement and his criticism is tempered by his sense of Swinburne's significance for English literature. What is striking about his opening chapter on 'Lyric Technique', whether one agrees with it or not, is a relatively sophisticated analysis of the relationship between language and referentiality that strikingly anticipates many of the points that Eliot will raise in 'Swinburne as Poet'. So strong is the coincidence that it is hard to believe that Eliot had not read Drinkwater's monograph.

Let me then briefly summarise the chief points of comparison, starting with the fact that both Drinkwater and Eliot stress the need for selection with Swinburne. Drinkwater declares 'he needs selection more than any of his fellows' (13), while Eliot writes that 'there are [poets] who need be read only in selections' and comments that 'almost no one, to-day, will wish to read the whole of Swinburne' (144). In the original *Athenæum* review, he remarks of the Gosse–Wise anthology that 'the present selection is a good one', adding that 'almost no-one will wish to read the whole of Swinburne. A selection is therefore necessary and is also sufficient' (Eliot 1920b, 72). At the same time both critics acknowledge what they see as the inherent difficulty of selecting Swinburne. Drinkwater writes 'The misfortune is that whilst with other poets a glance is sufficient to tell us which pages to pass over and which to absorb, each page of Swinburne has to be examined carefully before any determination can be made' (13), while Eliot states 'The necessity and difficulty of a selection are due to the peculiar nature of Swinburne's contribution' (144). Both critics thus emphasise Swinburne's difference from other poets, with Drinkwater noting that 'The most immediate impression gathered from a close acquaintance with Swinburne's lyric poetry is its curious distinctiveness from all other poetry … We see first the curious distinctiveness of this body of poetry from all others, the strange resemblance within itself of its corporate parts' (1, 6); Eliot, similarly, observes 'the peculiar nature of Swinburne's contribution, which, it is hardly too much to say, is of a very different kind from that of any other poet of equal reputation' (144), and he comments subsequently that 'he did something that had not been done before' (145).

It is, however, in specifying how Swinburne's difference resides in his unique use of poetic language that Eliot's echo of Drinkwater is most pronounced. Yet, while both critics see Swinburne's poetry as somehow flawed or lacking, they do not have identical views. Drinkwater, interestingly, sees all poetic language, not just Swinburne's, as having what he calls 'an independent life of its own'; he claims 'Language in its working has *an independent life of its own*, and it is by the strict adjustment of this life to the poet's thought and vision that he achieves the perfect proportion of his art' (my emphasis). For him, then, Swinburne's flaw lies in an insufficient pliability of this language to 'changing moods and adventurous thoughts' (9). Commenting on a typical example, he notices how 'The mood, grave, reflective, restrained, has been twisted in its growth; its life has been sacrificed to the *life of the poet's language*' (10; my emphasis), and criticises Swinburne's 'fostering in language this absolute instead of relative life' (11). Drinkwater suggests that Swinburne does not provide enough 'spirit of vision' (14), making his poetry too purely an affair of linguistic control, although this can occasionally result in something admirable:

> Language, accepting the freedom and separateness that this poet bestowed upon it, was at times merciless in the abuse of privilege, but there were also times when it gave something in return. The *very words themselves* became at moments a *world* for Swinburne, a mood. The phenomenon was one …

without a parallel in poetry, but it was in poetry nevertheless ... Contrary
to all experience, Swinburne did from time to time write poetry of unmis-
takable beauty and integrity, that sprang from no discoverable spiritual
impulse, but was created out of *the life of language itself*, words growing, as
it were, into a dual being of vision and form. (14; my emphasis)

Reflecting on some lines from Swinburne's 'Hesperia', he also proposes
that 'Although there is in [those lines] no emotion drawn from the poet's
brooding and exultation over life, there is yet an emotion. *The life of
language* has borne witness that it has *a temperament, a passion, of its own*.
Again there is discoverable *no* distinction of thought or intensity of
personal feeling behind the expression' (19; my emphasis).

Eliot's investment in a poetic language that, properly, 'in a healthy
state, presents the object, is so close to the object that the two are identi-
fied' (149), prevents him from acknowledging the independence of all
poetic language; for him, it is the independence of Swinburne's poetic
language *per se* that marks him off from others: '[Language and the
object] are identified in the verse of Swinburne solely because the object
has ceased to exist, because the meaning is merely the hallucination of
meaning, because language, uprooted, has adapted itself to an independ-
ent life of atmospheric nourishment' (149). Eliot also concedes that 'His
language is not, like the language of bad poetry, dead. It is very much
alive, with *this singular life of its own*' (150; my emphasis). As with
Drinkwater, although for somewhat different reasons, Swinburne's poetry
represents for Eliot a self-sufficient, independent 'world', and, as in
Drinkwater, the emotion of this poetic world is 'impersonal'. Eliot asserts
that 'The *world* of Swinburne does not depend upon some other world
which it simulates; it has the necessary completeness and self-sufficiency
for justification and permanence. It is impersonal, and no one else could
have made it' (149; my emphasis). For both Drinkwater and Eliot, the
feeling or emotion of Swinburne's poetry is a matter of poetic language.
Eliot's remarks that 'his emotion is never particular' (147) and 'the human
feelings ... in Swinburne's case do not exist. The morbidity is not of
human feeling but of language' (149) follow on from Drinkwater's decla-
ration that '*The life of language* has borne witness that it has *a temperament,
a passion, of its own*'.

When they come to examine Swinburne's word usage, both
Drinkwater and Eliot agree on his privileging of the general meaning over
the particular. Drinkwater declares that 'we are conscious always in his
best poetry of a *general* significance presiding over the *particular* occasion

of the word's use' (Drinkwater 25; my emphasis), while Eliot affirms that
'He is concerned with the meaning of the word in a peculiar way: he
employs, or rather "works," the word's meaning. ... he uses the most
general word, because his emotion is never *particular*, never in direct line
of vision, never focused; it is emotion reinforced, not by intensification,
but by expansion' (147; my emphasis).

Nonetheless Drinkwater sees this
general significance working to good effect in the opening to the chorus
from *Atalanta* already mentioned, 'Time, with a gift of tears, / Grief, with
a glass that ran', and asserts 'There is a meaning in these lines of wider
range than that of the actual statement. The horizons are thrown back
across a larger world by some secret property of the words' (24), while
Eliot deems the same lines a seeming 'tremendous statement' that turns
out to be empty (148–9).

Drinkwater and Eliot even evince apparent similarities in their conclu-
sions as they ponder the state of literary writing after Swinburne,
although on close inspection they have very different ideas about
Swinburne's legacy. Drawing his chapter to its close, Drinkwater congrat-
ulates Swinburne for the 'superb achievement' of the energy found in his
'lyrical language and measures', and he writes: 'After Swinburne, poetry is
finding for itself new channels of expression, new distribution and appli-
cation of eternal principles. It will sing of the recurring and elemental
manifestations which are life, but it will sing with a difference' (36).
Drinkwater thus implicitly sees Swinburne's poetry as instrumental in
helping forge those 'new channels of expression' while Eliot, apparently
conceding that Swinburne was 'a man of genius', nonetheless diminishes
his influence when he states finally that 'But the language which is more
important to us is that which is struggling to digest and express new
objects, new groups of objects, new feelings, new aspects, as, for instance,
the prose of Mr. James Joyce or the earlier Conrad' (150). Crucially, when
Drinkwater adds 'In the remote future a day will call for another
Swinburne to sing the glorious summary of the poetic succession now at
its birth' (36), he constructs a continuity, a succession. His vision suggests
that the new developments build on the old and that Swinburne will have
poetic heirs. Eliot, on the other hand, poses a dramatic discontinuity that
assigns Swinburne to oblivion, but significantly in doing so he suddenly
switches his focus from poetry to prose, to Joyce and Conrad, an artful
move that raises the question of whether a later poet can, as his example
would suggest, cut himself off from the poetic tradition and his predeces-
sors so easily.

As we are now well aware, thanks to the work of Frank Kermode, Perry Meisel, and others, Eliot, who placed such a heavy value on the literary tradition, was not above making his own highly selective adjustments to that tradition to suit his purposes, such as eliding Romantic and Victorian precursors whose influence pressed uncomfortably and embarrassingly close. Various of Eliot's early essays thus symbolically attack and sideline Swinburne in order to promote his own modernist credentials, with 'Swinburne as Poet' the chief case in point. Although it is clear from 'Swinburne as Poet' that Eliot does not precisely replicate Drinkwater's views but adapts them to his own modernist point of view, it is deeply ironic that this essay, so carefully positioned as a self-conscious statement of innovative modernist values, is nonetheless so deeply indebted to the work of a Georgian poet and critic whom he publicly despised. In an essay on Philip Massinger (1920) included in *The Sacred Wood*, Eliot noted that 'Immature poets imitate; mature poets steal', adding 'bad poets deface what they take, and good poets make it into something better' (Eliot 1920a, 125). This quip may itself be 'stolen' from Drinkwater who in his book on Swinburne observes that 'Genius can be no common thief, but it absorbs everything' (34). Whether or not Eliot's thefts can be considered as improvements, his own wayward 'genius' absorbed and recycled not only key elements of his inconvenient Victorian precursor but also, more specifically, what was useful to him in a source much nearer to hand.

NOTES

1 T. S. Eliot, 'Reflections on *Vers Libre*', *New Statesman* 8.204 (3 March 1917), 518–19, reprinted in Eliot 1965, 183–89; *Ezra Pound: His Metric and Poetry* (New York: Alfred K Knopf, 12 November 1917), reprinted in Eliot 1965, 162–82.

2 T. S. Eliot, 'Swinburne and the Elizabethans', *Athenæum* 4664 (19 September 1919), 909–10. Review by Eliot of Swinburne's *Contemporaries of Shakespeare*, ed. Edmund Gosse and Thomas J. Wise. Reprinted, with an additional paragraph as 'Swinburne as Critic', in Eliot 1920a, 17–24; 'Swinburne', *Athenæum* 4681 (16 January 1920), 72–3, reprinted with revisions as 'Swinburne as Poet', in Eliot 1920a, 144–50.

3 T. S. Eliot, 'Euripides and Gilbert Murray: A Performance at the Holborn Empire', *Art and Letters* 3.2 (Spring 1920), 36–43. Reprinted as 'Euripides and Professor Murray', in Eliot 1920a, 71–7.

4 T. S. Eliot, 'The Perfect Critic' [I] *Athenæum* 4706 (9 July 1920), 40–1; 'The Perfect Critic' [II], *Athenæum* 4708 (23 July 1920), 102–4, reprinted in Eliot 1920a, 1–16.

5 T. S. Eliot, 'Rudyard Kipling', originally published as the introduction to *A Choice of Kipling's Verse* (Faber & Faber, 1941), and reprinted in Eliot 1957, 228–51.

6 Eliot also recommended *The Age of Shakespeare* and *A Study of Ben Jonson* as 'interesting, though misleading' to his students for his lecture course on Elizabethan literature in 1918 (Schuchard 1974, 301).

7 See also Meisel 1987, Morgan 1993b, and Laity 2004.

8 Ezra Pound, 'Revolt: Against the Crepuscular Spirit in Modern Poetry', in Pound 1977, 96.

9 See also my chapter on Lee and vagueness in Maxwell 2008, 114–65.

10 Ezra Pound, Letter to Harriet Monroe (October 1912) in Pound 1951, 45.

11 Martin notes that Ribot sees the 'plastic imagination' exemplified in the work of the Parnassians, in particular Théophile Gautier (Martin 1970, 201), who was much admired by Pound and Eliot.

12 Eliot takes the phrase 'fluid haze' from another vague Victorian. See Tennyson's *The Princess*, 2.101.

13 My thanks to Jeremy Noel-Tod for alerting me to the misattribution. Eliot possibly may have been recalling the lines about 'the temple haunting martlet' from *Macbeth* (1.6.4) although a 'martlet' is a house martin.

REFERENCES

Ackroyd, Peter. 1984. *T. S. Eliot*. London: Hamish Hamilton.

Adorno, Theodor W. 1991. 'On Lyric Poetry and Society' (1957). In *Notes to Literature*. Ed. Rolf Tiedemann. Tr. Shierry Weber Nicholsen. New York: Columbia University Press. 1.37–54.

[Aldington, Richard, H. D., et al.]. 1915. Preface. *Some Imagist Poets: An Anthology*. Boston and New York: The Riverside Press, Houghton Mifflin Co. v–viii.

Alexander, Jonathan. 1996. 'Sex, Violence, and Identity: A. C. Swinburne and the Uses of Sadomasochism'. *Victorian Newsletter* 90, 33–6.

'Amateur'. 1862. 'Music'. *Spectator* (12 April), 410.

Anderson, Amanda. 1998. 'Cosmopolitanism, Universalism, and the Divided Legacies of Modernity'. In *Cosmopolitics: Thinking and Feeling Beyond the Nation*. Eds Pheng Cheah and Bruce Robbins. Minneapolis: University of Minnesota Press. 265–89.

Anderson, Amanda. 2001. *The Powers of Distance: Cosmopolitanism and the Cultivation of Detachment*. Princeton: Princeton University Press.

Anderson, Amanda. 2005. 'Victorian Studies and the Two Modernities'. *Victorian Studies* 47:2, 195–203.

Anonymous. [John Nichol]. 1858. 'The *Saturday Review* on Love and Marriage'. *Undergraduate Papers* 2, 90–6.

Anonymous. 1862a. Review of *Modern Love*. *Athenæum* (31 May), 719–20.

Anonymous. 1862b. Review of *Modern Love*. *London Review* (13 September), 237–8.

Anonymous. 1866. 'Mr Swinburne and His Critics'. *Fraser's Magazine for Town and Country* 74:443 (November), 635–48.

Anonymous. 1868. 'Rossetti's Art-Criticisms', *Saturday Review* 25:665 (16 May), 663–4.

Anonymous. 1869. Review of *Translations from Charles Baudelaire. With a Few Original Poems by R. H. Shepherd*. *Athenæum* (21 August), 237–8.

Anonymous. 1883. 'Swinburne's New Volume'. *New York Times* (18 July), 3.

Anonymous. 1890. 'Mr Swinburne's Lyrics'. *Edinburgh Review* 171:350 (April), 429–52.

Anonymous. 1899a. 'The Reverse at Ladysmith'. *The Times* (1 November), 7.

Anonymous. 1899b. 'The Disaster at Ladysmith: Further Despatch from Sir G. White'. *The Times* (2 November), 5.

Anonymous. 1909. 'Algernon Charles Swinburne'. *Eton College Chronicle* 1270 (13 May), 471–2.

Appiah, Kwame Anthony. 1998. 'Cosmopolitan Patriots'. In *Cosmopolitics: Thinking and Feeling Beyond the Nation*. Eds Pheng Cheah and Bruce Robbins. Minneapolis: University of Minnesota Press. 91–114.

Appiah, Kwame Anthony. 2005. *The Ethics of Identity*. Princeton: Princeton University Press.

Appiah, Kwame Anthony. 2006. *Cosmopolitanism: Ethics in a World of Strangers*. New York: W. W. Norton.

Arnold, Edwin et al. 1895. 'Who Should be Poet Laureate?' *The Idler Magazine: An Illustrated Monthly* 7, 400–19.

Arnold, Matthew. 1869. *Culture and Anarchy, An Essay in Political and Social Criticism*. London: Thomas Nelson & Sons.

Arnold, Matthew. 1962. *Lectures and Essays in Criticism*. Ed. R. H. Super. Ann Arbor: University of Michigan Press.

Arnold, Matthew. 1965. *Culture and Anarchy*. Ed. R. H. Super. Ann Arbor: University of Michigan Press.

Arnold, Matthew. 1968. *Literature and Dogma: An Essay towards a Better Apprehension of the Bible*. In *Dissent and Dogma*. Ed. R. H. Super. Ann Arbor: University of Michigan Press. 139–411.

Bailey, Anthony. 1997. *Standing in the Sun: A Life of J. M. W. Turner*. London: Sinclair-Stevenson.

Baird, Julian. 1971. 'Swinburne, Sade, and Blake: The Pleasure-Pain Paradox'. *Victorian Poetry* 9 (Spring–Summer), 49–76.

Baker, William. 1983. 'T. S. Eliot on Edward Lear: An Unnoted Attribution'. *English Studies* 64:6, 564–6.

Barrett, Dorothea. 1993. 'The Politics of Sado-Masochism: Swinburne and George Eliot'. In *The Whole Music of Passion*. Eds Rikky Rooksby and Nicholas Shrimpton. Aldershot and Burlington, VT: Scolar Press. 107–19.

Battiscombe, Georgina. 1981. *Christina Rossetti: A Divided Life*. London: Constable.

Baudelaire, Charles. 1993. *The Flowers of Evil* (1857). Tr. James McGowan. Oxford: Oxford University Press.

Baum, Paull F. (ed.). 1937. *Dante Gabriel Rossetti: Poems, Ballads and Sonnets*. New York: Doubleday, Doran, & Co.

Bernal, Martin. 1987. *Black Athena, The Afroasiatic Roots of Classical Civilization, The Fabrication of Greece 1785–1985*. New Brunswick, NJ: Rutgers University Press.

Birchfield, James D. 1980. 'New light on the Swinburne-Leith Correspondence'. *Kentucky Review* 1, 52–63.

Blair, Kirstie. 2006a. 'Swinburne's Spasms: *Poems and Ballads* and the "Spasmodic School"'. *Yearbook of English Studies* 36:2, 180–96.

Blair, Kirstie. 2006b. *Victorian Poetry and the Culture of the Heart*. Oxford: Oxford University Press.

Bond, Ronald. 1992. 'Leprosy'. In *A Dictionary of Biblical Tradition in English Literature*. Ed. David Jeffrey. Grand Rapids, MI: William B. Eerdmans.

Bonnecase, Denis and Sébastien Scarpa (eds). 2010. *Tombeau pour Swinburne*. Paris: Éditions ADEN.

Bowra, Maurice. 1950. *The Romantic Imagination*. Oxford: Oxford University Press.

Bradshaw, Melissa. 2000. 'Modernizing Excess: Amy Lowell and the Aesthetics of Camp'. www.english.illinois.edu/maps/poets/g_l/amylowell/about.htm.

Bradshaw, Melissa. 2004. 'Remembering Amy Lowell: Embodiment, Obesity, and the Construction of a Persona'. In *Amy Lowell, American Modern*. Eds Adrienne Munich and Melissa Bradshaw. New Brunswick, NJ and London: Rutgers University Press. 167–85.

Bragman, Louis J. 1934. 'The Case of Algernon Swinburne: A Study in Sadism'. *Psychoanalytic Review* 21, 59–74.

Brake, Laurel. 2010. 'Culture Wars?: Arnold's *Essays in Criticism* and the Rise of Journalism, 1865–1895'. In *Conflict and Difference in Nineteenth-Century Literature*. Eds Dinah Birch and Mark Llewellyn. Basingstoke and New York: Palgrave Macmillan. 201–12.

Bright, Michael. 1996. *Robert Browning's Rondures Brave*. Athens: Ohio University Press.

Brisson, Luc. 1997. *Le Sexe incertain, Androgynie et hermaphrodisme dans l'Antiquité gréco-romaine*. Paris: Les Belles Lettres.

Browning, Robert. 2005. *The Major Works*. Ed. Adam Roberts. Intr. Daniel Karlin. Oxford: Oxford University Press.

[Buchanan, Robert.] 1866. Review of A. C. Swinburne's *Poems and Ballads*. *Athenæum*, 4 August. Reprinted in *Swinburne: The Critical Heritage*. Ed. Clyde K. Hyder. London: Routledge & Kegan Paul. 1970. 30–4.

Buchanan, Robert ['Thomas Maitland']. 1871. 'The Fleshly School of Poetry'. *Contemporary Review* 18 (October), 334–50.

Calhoun, Craig. 2002. 'The Class Consciousness of Frequent Travellers: Towards a Critique of Actually Existing Cosmopolitanism'. In *Conceiving Cosmopolitanism: Theory, Context, and Practice*. Eds Steven Vertovec and Robin Cohen. Oxford: Oxford University Press. 86–109.

Campbell, David A. (ed.). 1994. *Greek Lyric I: Sappho & Alcaeus*. Loeb Classical Library. Cambridge, MA and London: Harvard University Press.

Carter, John. 1959. *William Johnson Cory 1823–1892: A Great Eton Master*. Cambridge: Rampant Lions Press.

Chaucer, Geoffrey. 1974. *The Works of Geoffrey Chaucer*. Ed. F. N. Robinson. 2nd ed. Oxford: Oxford University Press.

Christ, Carol T. 1984. *Victorian and Modern Poetics*. Chicago and London: University of Chicago Press.

Clements, Patricia. 1985. *Baudelaire and the English Tradition*. Princeton: Princeton University Press.

Cohen, Mitchell. 1992. 'Rooted Cosmopolitanism'. *Dissent* 39:4, 478–83.

Coleridge, Samuel Taylor. 1959. *Collected Letters of Samuel Taylor Coleridge*. Volume 4. Ed. Earl Leslie Griggs. Oxford: Clarendon Press.

Collecott, Diana. 1999. *H. D. and Sapphic Modernism, 1910–1950*. Cambridge: Cambridge University Press.

Connolly, T. E. 1964. *Swinburne's Theory of Poetry*. New York: New York State University Press.

Conway, Moncure D. 1868. Review of *William Blake: A Critical Essay*. *Fortnightly Review* 3 n.s. (February), 216–20.

Cornish, Francis Warre. 1897. *Extracts from the Letters and Journals of William Cory*. Ed. Francis Warre Cornish. Oxford: Private publication.

Costigan, Giovanni. 1972. 'William Johnson Cory: A Great Victorian Teacher'. *The Cornhill* 1072, 234–56.

Cronin, Richard. 2002. 'The Spasmodics'. In *A Companion to Victorian Poetry*. Eds Richard Cronin, Alison Chapman, and Antony H. Harrison. Oxford: Blackwell. 291–305.

Damon, S. Foster. 1935. *Amy Lowell: A Chronicle, with Extracts from Her Correspondence*. Boston: Houghton Mifflin.

'Dark Blue'. 1871. In *Publishers' Circular* (1 March), 140.

'Dark Blue'. 1966–89. In *Wellesley Index to Victorian Periodicals, 1824–1900*. Eds Walter Houghton, Esther Rhoads Houghton, and Jean Slingerland. 5 vols. London: Routledge & Kegan Paul. Toronto: University of Toronto Press. 4.178–83.

Dellamora, Richard. 1990. *Masculine Desire: The Sexual Politics of Victorian Aestheticism*. Chapel Hill and London: University of North Carolina Press.

Disch, Thomas M. 2002. 'Roundeaux and Roundels'. In *An Exaltation of Forms: Contemporary Poets Celebrate the Diversity of Their Art*. Eds Annie Finch and Kathrine Varnes. Ann Arbor: University of Michigan Press. 279–89.

Dobell, Sydney. 1875. *The Poetical Works of Sydney Dobell*. Ed. John Nichol. 2 vols. London: Smith, Elder.

Doolittle, H. [H. D.]. 1992. *Asphodel* (1922). Ed. Robert Spoon. Durham, NC and London: Duke University Press.

Dostoevsky, Fyodor. *The Brothers Karamazov*. Tr. Ignat Avsey. Oxford: Oxford University Press, 1994.

Douglas, Mary. 2007. *Thinking in Circles: An Essay on Ring Composition*. New Haven and London: Yale University Press.

Dowling, Linda. 1989. 'Ruskin's Pied Beauty and the Construction of a "Homosexual" Code'. *Victorian Newsletter* 75, 1–8.

Dowling, Linda. 1994. *Hellenism and Homosexuality in Victorian Oxford*. Ithaca and London: Cornell University Press.

Drinkwater, John. 1913. *Swinburne: An Estimate*. London and Toronto: J. M. Dent & Sons, Ltd.

'Dry Point'. 1862. 'Fine Arts. The Preparation for the Royal Academy'. *Spectator* (12 April), 409–10.

duBois, Page. 1995. *Sappho Is Burning*. Chicago: University of Chicago Press.

Eagleton, Terry. 2007. *How to Read a Poem*. Oxford: Blackwell Publishing.

Eliot, Simon. 2000. '"Hotten: Rotten: Forgotten"?: An Apologia for a General Publisher'. *Book History* 3, 61–93.

Eliot, Simon. 2004. 'John Camden Hotten'. In *Oxford Dictionary of National Biography*. Oxford: Oxford University Press.

Eliot, T. S. 1918. 'Professional or . . .' (Review featuring Alice Meynell's *Hearts of Controversy*). *Egoist* 5:4 (April), 61.

Eliot, T. S. 1919. 'Kipling Redivivus'. *Athenæum* 4665 (9 May 1919), 297–8.

Eliot, T. S. 1920a. *The Sacred Wood: Essays on Poetry and Criticism*. London and New York: Methuen.

Eliot, T. S. 1920b. 'Swinburne'. *Athenæum* 4681 (16 January 1920), 72–3.

Eliot, T. S. 1921a. 'Prolegomena to Poetry', in 'London Letter'. *The Dial* 70:4 (March), 448–53.

Eliot, T. S. 1921b. Letter (3 November) to the *Times Literary Supplement* 1033, 716.

Eliot, T. S. 1928. 'Isolated Superiority' (Review of *Personae: The Collected Poems of Ezra Pound*). *The Dial* 84:1 (January), [4]-7.

Eliot, T. S. 1933. *The Use of Poetry and the Use of Criticism*. London: Faber & Faber.

Eliot, T. S. 1934. *After Strange Gods: A Primer of Modern Heresy*. London: Faber & Faber.

Eliot, T. S. 1936. *Essays Ancient and Modern*. London: Faber & Faber.

Eliot, T. S. 1943. *Four Quartets*. New York: Harcourt Brace Jovanovich.

Eliot, T. S. 1957. *On Poetry and Poets*. London: Faber & Faber.

Eliot, T. S. 1965. *To Criticize the Critic*. London: Faber & Faber.

Eliot, T. S. 1967. *Poems Written in Early Youth*. London: Faber & Faber.

Eliot, T. S. 1969. *Complete Poems and Plays*. London: Faber & Faber.

Eliot, T. S. 1971. *The Waste Land: A Facsimile and Transcript of the Original Drafts including the Annotations of Ezra Pound*. Ed. Valerie Eliot. London: Faber & Faber.

Eliot, T. S. 1993. *The Varieties of Metaphysical Poetry: The Clark Lectures at Trinity, Cambridge, 1926, and the Turnbull Lectures at The Johns Hopkins University, 1933*. Ed. Ronald Schuchard. London: Faber & Faber.

Eliot, T. S. 1996. *Inventions of the March Hare: Poems 1909–1917 by T. S. Eliot*. Ed. Christopher Ricks. London: Faber & Faber.

Eliot, T. S. 2009. *The Letters of T. S. Eliot*. Eds Valerie Eliot and Hugh Haughton. Volume 2: *1923–1925*. London: Faber & Faber.

Evangelista, Stefano. 2009. *British Aestheticism and Ancient Greece: Hellenism, Reception, Gods in Exile*. Basingstoke and New York: Palgrave Macmillan.

Evangelista, Stefano. 2010. 'Swinburne's Galleries'. *Yearbook of English Studies* 40:1 and 40:2, 160–79.

Evangelista, Stefano. 2011. 'Lessons in Greek Art: Jane Harrison and Aestheticism'. *Women's Studies* 40:4, 513–36.

Evans, Lawrence. 1970. *The Letters of Walter Pater*. Oxford: Clarendon.

Faderman, Lillian. 1981. *Surpassing the Love of Men: Romantic Friendship and Love between Women from the Renaissance to the Present*. London: The Women's Press.

Faderman, Lillian. 2004. '"Which, Being Interpreted, Is as May Be, or Otherwise": Ada Dwyer Russell in Amy Lowell's Life and Work'. In *Amy Lowell, American Modern*. Eds Adrienne Munich and Melissa Bradshaw. New Brunswick, NJ and London: Rutgers University Press. 59–76.

Farrar, F. W. 1868. 'On Greek and Latin Verse Composition as a General Branch of Education'. In *Essays on a Liberal Education*. Ed. F. W. Farrar. Macmillan: London. 205–39.

Findlay, L. M. 1990. 'The Art of Apostasy: Swinburne and the Emperor Julian'. *Victorian Poetry* 28:1, 69–78.

Fiske, Shanyn. 2008. *Heretical Hellenism: Women Writers, Ancient Greece, and the Victorian Popular Imagination*. Athens: Ohio University Press.

Freud, Sigmund. 1961. *Beyond the Pleasure Principle* (1920). Tr. James Strachey. New York: Norton.

Fuller, Jean Overton. 1968. *Swinburne: A Critical Biography*. London: Chatto & Windus.

Garland, Tony W. 2009. 'Brothers in Paradox: Swinburne, Baudelaire, and the Paradox of Sin'. *Victorian Poetry* 47:4, 633–45.

Gautier, Théophile. n.d. *The Complete Works of Théophile Gautier*. Tr. and ed. S. C. De Sumichrast. 12 vols. London: Athenæum Press.

Gibson, Ian. 1978. *The English Vice: Beating, Sex and Shame in Victorian England and After*. London: Duckworth.

Gissing, George. 1974. 'Tyrtaeus' (1889). *Gissing Newsletter* 10:3, 2–4.

Gladstone, William Ewart. 1858. *Studies on Homer and the Homeric Age*. 3 vols. Oxford: Oxford University Press.

Gladstone, William Ewart. 1877. 'The Colour-Sense'. *The Nineteenth Century* 8, 366–88.

Goldhill, Simon. 2002. *Who Needs Greek? Contests in the Cultural History of Hellenism*. Cambridge & New York: Cambridge University Press.

Gosse, Edmund. 1893. 'Christina Rossetti'. *The Century* 46, 211–17.

Gosse, Edmund. 1896. *Critical Kit-Kats*. London: Heineman.

Gosse, Edmund. 1917. *The Life of Algernon Charles Swinburne*. London: Macmillan.

Gould, Jean. 1975. *Amy: The World of Amy Lowell and the Imagist Movement*. New York: Dodd, Mead, & Company.

Gubar, Susan. 1984. 'Sapphistries'. *Signs* 10:1, 43–62.

Hall, Jason David. 2011a. 'Materializing Meter: Physiology, Psychology, Prosody'. *Victorian Poetry* 49:2, 179–97.

Hall, Jason David (ed.). 2011b. *Meter Matters: Verse Cultures of the Long Nineteenth Century*. Athens: Ohio University Press.

Harrison, Antony H. 1988. *Swinburne's Medievalism: A Study in Victorian Love Poetry*. Baton Rouge and London: Louisiana State University Press.

Harrison, Antony H. 1990. *Victorian Poets and Romantic Poems: Intertextuality and Ideology*. Charlottesville: University Press of Virginia.

Harrison, Jane Ellen. 1913. *Ancient Art and Ritual*. London: Williams and Norgate.

Harrison, Jane Ellen. 1915. *Alpha and Omega*. London: Sidgwick & Jackson.

Henderson, Alice Corbin. 1919. 'On "The Movement"'. *Poetry: A Magazine of Verse* (June), 159–67.

Henderson, Philip. 1974. *Swinburne: The Portrait of a Poet*. Routledge: London.

Heywood, Leslie. 1996. *Dedication to Hunger: The Anorexic Aesthetic in Modern Culture*. Berkeley and London: University of California Press.

Higgins, Dolores. 1996. 'Sappho's Splintered Tongue: Silence in Sappho 31 and Catullus 51'. In *Re-Reading Sappho: Reception and Transmission*. Ed. Ellen Greene. Berkeley: University of California Press. 68–78.

Hirst, F. W. 1927. *Early Life and Letters of John Morley*. 2 vols. London: Macmillan & Co.

Hollinger, David A. 1995. *Postethnic America: Beyond Multiculturalism*. New York: Basic Books.

Hovey, Jaime. 2004. 'Lesbian Chivalry in Amy Lowell's *Sword Blades and Poppy Seed*'. In *Amy Lowell, American Modern*. Eds Adrienne Munich and Melissa Bradshaw. New Brunswick, NJ and London: Rutgers University Press. 77–89.

Hughes, Linda K. 2007. 'What the Wellesley Index Left Out: Why Poetry Matters to Periodical Studies'. *Victorian Periodicals Review*, 40:2 (Summer), 91–125.

Hughes, Randolph (ed.). 1952. *Lesbia Brandon, by Algernon Charles Swinburne: An Historical and Critical Commentary Being Largely a Study (and Elevation) of Swinburne as a Novelist*. London: The Falcon Press.

Hulme, T. E. 1998. 'Romanticism and Classicism' (1912). In *Selected Writings*. Ed. Patrick McGuinness. Manchester: Carcanet. 68–83.

Hutton, R. H. 1896. 'Tennyson'. In *Literary Essays*. London: Macmillan. 361–436.

Hyder, Clyde K. 1931. 'The Medieval Background of Swinburne's "The Leper"'. *PMLA* 46:4, 1280–8.

Hyder, Clyde K. 1966. *Swinburne Replies*. Syracuse: Syracuse University Press.

Hyder, Clyde K. (ed.). 1970. *Swinburne, The Critical Heritage*. London and Boston: Routledge & Kegan Paul.

Hyder, Clyde K. (ed.). 1972. *Swinburne as Critic*. London and Boston: Routledge & Kegan Paul.

Japp, Alexander Hay [H. A. Page]. 1878. 'Parody and Parodists'. *The British Quarterly Review* 67, 173–93.

Jay, Karla. 1988. *The Amazon and the Page: Natalie Clifford Barney and Renée Vivien*. Indiana: Indiana University Press.

Jenkins, Ian. 2001. *Cleaning and Controversy: The Parthenon Sculptures (1811–1939)*. London: British Museum Press.

Johnson [Cory], William. 1861. *Eton Reform*. London: Longman.

Johnson [Cory], William. 1868. 'On the Education of the Reasoning Faculties'. In *Essays on a Liberal Education*. Ed. F. W. Farrar. Macmillan: London. 313–63.

Johnson [Cory], William. 1898. *Hints for Eton Masters*. London: Henry Frowde.

Keats, John. 1982. *John Keats: Complete Poems*. Ed. Jack Stillinger. Cambridge, MA: Belknap Press.

Keirstead, Christopher M. 2011. *Victorian Poetry, Europe, and the Challenge of Cosmopolitanism*. Columbus: Ohio State University.

Kernahan, Coulson. 1917. *In Good Company*. London: John Lane.

Kuduk, Stephanie. 2001. '"A Sword of a Song": Swinburne's Republican Aesthetics in *Songs before Sunrise*'. *Victorian Studies* 43:2, 253–78.

Lafourcade, Georges. 1928. *La Jeunesse de Swinburne*. 2 vols. Publications de la Faculté des Lettres de Strasbourg. Paris and Oxford: Société D'Édition, Les Belles Lettres and Humphrey Milford, Oxford University Press.

Lafourcade, Georges. 1932. *Swinburne: A Literary Biography*. London: G. Bell.

Laity, Cassandra. 1992. 'H. D. and A.C. Swinburne: Decadence and Sapphic Modernism'. In *Lesbian Texts and Contexts: Radical Revisions*. Eds Karla Jay and Joanne Glasgow. London: Onlywomen Press. 217–40.

Laity, Cassandra. 1996. *H. D. and the Victorian Fin de Siècle*. Cambridge: Cambridge University Press.

Laity, Cassandra. 2004. 'T. S. Eliot and A. C. Swinburne: Decadent Bodies, Modern Visualities, and Changing Modes of Perception'. *Modernism/Modernity* 11, 425–48.

Landy, Joshua. 2009. 'Modern Magic: Jean-Eugène Robert-Houdin and Stéphane Mallarmé'. In *The Re-Enchantment of the World: Secular Magic in a Rational Age*. Eds Joshua Landy and Michael Saler. Stanford: Stanford University Press. 109–25.

Lane, Christopher. 1999. *The Burdens of Intimacy: Psychoanalysis and Victorian Masculinity*. Chicago: University of Chicago Press.

Lane, Christopher. 2011. *The Age of Doubt: Tracing the Roots of Our Religious Uncertainty*. New Haven: Yale University Press.

Lang, Cecil Y. 1949. 'Swinburne on Keats: A Fragment of an Essay'. *Modern Language Notes* 64:3 (March), 168–9.

LaPorte, Charles and Jason R. Rudy. 2004. 'Introduction: Spasmodic Poetry and Poetics'. *Victorian Poetry* 42:4, 422–8.

Largier, Niklaus. 2007. *In Praise of the Whip: A Cultural History of Arousal*. New York: Zone Books.

Lauter, Paul. 2004. 'Amy Lowell and Cultural Borders'. In *Amy Lowell, American Modern*. Eds Adrienne Munich and Melissa Bradshaw. New Brunswick, NJ and

London: Rutgers University Press. 1–8.

Lawrence, D. H. 1985. *The Letters of D. H. Lawrence and Amy Lowell: 1914–1925*. Eds E. Claire Healey and Keith Cushman. Santa Barbara: Black Sparrow Press.

Lee, Vernon. 2006. 'Faustus and Helena: Notes on the Supernatural in Art' (1880). In *Hauntings and Other Fantastic Tales*. Eds Catherine Maxwell and Patricia Pulham. Peterborough, ON: Broadview. 291–319.

Leighton, Angela. 1992. *Victorian Women Poets: Writing Against the Heart*. New York and London: Harvester Wheatsheaf.

Levin, Yisrael. 2010a. 'Introduction'. *A. C. Swinburne and the Singing Word: New Perspectives on the Mature Work*. Ed. Yisrael Levin. Farnham and Burlington, VT: Ashgate. 1–9.

Levin, Yisrael. 2010b. 'Solar Erotica: Swinburne's Myth of Creation'. In *A. C. Swinburne and the Singing Word*. Ed. Yisrael Levin. Farnham and Burlington, VT: Ashgate. 55–72.

Levin, Yisrael. 2011. '"But the Law Must Be Poetic": Swinburne, Omond, and the New Prosody'. In *Meter Matters: Verse Cultures of the Long Nineteenth Century*. Ed. Jason David Hall. Athens: Ohio University Press. 178–95.

Louis, Margot K. 1990. *Swinburne and His Gods: The Roots and Growth of an Agnostic Poetry*. Montreal and Kingston: McGill-Queen's University Press.

Louis, Margot K. 1999. 'Proserpine and Pessimism: Goddesses of Death, Life, and Language from Swinburne to Wharton'. *Modern Philology* 96, 312–46.

Louis, Margot K. 2000. 'Swinburne on Rape'. *The Journal of Pre-Raphaelite Studies* 9:2, 55–68.

Louis, Margot K. 2009a. 'Erotic Figuration in Swinburne's *Tristram of Lyonesse*, Canto 2: The Vanishing Knight and the Drift of Butterflies'. *Victorian Poetry* 47:4, 647–59.

Louis, Margot K. 2009b. *Persephone Rises 1860–1927, Mythography, Gender and the Creation of a New Spirituality*. Farnham and Burlington, VT: Ashgate.

Lowell, Amy. 1925. *What's O'Clock*. Boston: Houghton Mifflin Co.

Lowell, Amy. 1930. 'Poetry as a Spoken Art' (1916). *On Poetry and Poets*. Boston: Houghton Mifflin. 10–23.

Lowell, Amy. 1955. *The Complete Poetical Works of Amy Lowell*. Boston: Houghton Mifflin.

Lutz, Deborah. 2011. *Pleasure Bound: Victorian Sex Rebels and the New Eroticism*. New York: W. W. Norton.

McGann, Jerome. 1972. *Swinburne: An Experiment in Criticism*. Chicago: University of Chicago Press.

McGann, Jerome. 2008. 'Swinburne, "Hertha", and the Voice of Language'. *Victorian Literature and Culture* 36, 283–97.

McGann, Jerome. 2009. 'Wagner, Baudelaire, Swinburne: Poetry in the Condition of Music'. *Victorian Poetry* 47:4, 619–32.

Mackenzie, Faith Compton. 1950. *William Cory: A Biography*. London: Constable.

McSweeney, Kerry. 1981. *Tennyson and Swinburne as Romantic Naturalists*. Toronto: University of Toronto Press.

'Maitland, Thomas' [Robert Buchanan]. 1871. 'The Fleshly School of Poetry. Mr. D. G. Rossetti'. *Contemporary Review* 18 (October), 334–50.

Marcus, Steven. 1966. *The Other Victorians: A Study in Sexuality and Pornography in Mid-Nineteenth Century England*. London: Weidenfeld & Nicolson.

Marek, Jayne E. 2004. 'Amy Lowell, *Some Imagist Poets*, and the Context of the New Poetry'. In *Amy Lowell, American Modern*. Eds Adrienne Munich and Melissa Bradshaw. New Brunswick, NJ and London: Rutgers University Press. 154–66.

Marsh, Jan. 1994. *Christina Rossetti: A Literary Biography*. London: Cape.

Marsh, Jan. 1996. 'The Spider's Shadow: Christina Rossetti and the Dark Double Within'. In *Beauty and the Beast: Christina Rossetti, Walter Pater, R. L. Stevenson and Their Contemporaries*. Eds Pieter Liebiegts and Wim Tigges. Amsterdam: Rodopi. 21–30.

Marsh, Joss. 1998. *Word Crimes: Blasphemy, Culture, and Literature*. Chicago: University of Chicago Press.

Martin, Meredith. 2012. *The Rise and Fall of Meter: Poetry and English National Culture, 1860–1930*. Princeton: Princeton University Press.

Martin, Meredith and Yisrael Levin. 2011. 'Victorian Prosody: Measuring the Field'. *Victorian Poetry* 49:2, 149–60.

Martin, Wallace. 1970. 'The Sources of the Imagist Aesthetic'. *PMLA* 85, 196–204.

Matthews, A. V. 1999. 'Aestheticism's True Colors: The Politics of Pigment in Victorian Art, Criticism, and Fashion'. In *Women and British Aestheticism*. Eds Talia Schaffer and Kathy Alexis Psomiades. Charlottesville and London: University Press of Virginia. 172–91.

Maxwell, Catherine. 1994. 'Eliot's *Four Quartets* and Swinburne's "A Rosary"'. *Explicator* 52:101–4.

Maxwell, Catherine. 2001. *The Female Sublime from Milton to Swinburne: Bearing Blindness*. Manchester: Manchester University Press.

Maxwell, Catherine. 2003. 'Swinburne: Style, Sympathy, and Sadomasochism'. *Journal of Pre-Raphaelite Studies* 12, 86–96.

Maxwell, Catherine. 2006. *Swinburne*. Writers and Their Work. Tavistock: Northcote House.

Maxwell, Catherine. 2008. *Second Sight: The Visionary Imagination in Late Victorian Literature*. Manchester: Manchester University Press.

Maxwell, Catherine. 2009. 'Swinburne and Thackeray's *The Newcomes*.' *Victorian Poetry* 47:4, 733–46.

Maxwell, Catherine. 2010a. 'Swinburne's Friendships with Women Writers'. In *A. C. Swinburne and the Singing Word: New Perspectives on the Mature Work*. Ed. Yisrael Levin. Farnham and Burlington, VT: Ashgate. 127–47.

Maxwell, Catherine. 2010b. 'Whistlerian Impressionism and the Venetian Variations of Vernon Lee, John Addington Symonds, and Arthur Symons'.

Yearbook of English Studies 40:1 and 40:2, 217–45.

Meisel, Perry. 1987. *The Myth of the Modern*. New Haven: Yale University Press.

Meyers, L. Terry and Rikky Rooksby (eds). 2009. '"A hundred sleeping years ago": in commemoration of Algernon Charles Swinburne'. (Special centenary issue). *Victorian Poetry* 47: 4.

Millgate, Michael. 2004. *Thomas Hardy: A Biography Revisited*. Oxford: Oxford University Press.

Monroe, Harriet. 1926. *Poets and Their Art*. New York: Macmillan.

Monsman, Gerald. 1998. *Oxford University's Old Mortality Society: A Study in Victorian Romanticism*. Lewiston, NY and Lampeter: Edward Mellen Press.

Montiglio, Silvia. 2005. *Wandering in Ancient Greek Culture*. Chicago and London: University of Chicago Press.

Morgan, Monique R. 2007. 'Lyric Narrative Hybrids in Victorian Poetry'. *Literature Compass* 4, 917–34.

Morgan, Thaïs. 1984. 'Swinburne's Dramatic Monologues: Sex and Ideology'. *Victorian Poetry* 22:2, 175–95.

Morgan, Thaïs E. 1992. 'Male Lesbian Bodies: The Construction of Alternative Masculinities in Courbet, Baudelaire and Swinburne'. *Genders* 15, 37–57.

Morgan, Thaïs. 1993a. 'Reimagining Masculinity in Victorian Criticism: Swinburne and Pater'. *Victorian Studies* 36:3, 315–32.

Morgan, Thaïs. 1993b. 'Influence, Intertextuality and Tradition in Swinburne and Eliot'. In *The Whole Music of Passion: New Essays on Swinburne*. Eds Rikky Rooksby and Nicholas Shrimpton. Aldershot: Scolar Press. 136–47.

Morgan, Thaïs. 1996. 'Perverse Male Bodies: Simeon Solomon and Algernon Charles Swinburne'. In *Outlooks: Lesbian and Gay Visual Cultures*. Eds Peter Horne and Reina Lewis. London: Routledge. 61–85.

[Morley, John]. 1866. 'Mr Swinburne's New Poems'. *Saturday Review* 22 (4 August), 145–7. Also reprinted in *Swinburne: The Critical Heritage*. Ed. Clyde K. Hyder. London: Routledge. 1970. 33–40.

[Morley, John, Editor]. 1868. 'Critical Notices'. *Fortnightly Review* 3 (June), 713–15.

Munich, Adrienne. 2004. 'Family Matters: Genealogies and Intertexts in Amy Lowell's "The Sisters"'. In *Amy Lowell, American Modern*. Eds Adrienne Munich and Melissa Bradshaw. New Brunswick, NJ and London: Rutgers University Press. 9–26.

Munich, Adrienne and Melissa Bradshaw. 2004. 'Introduction'. In *Amy Lowell, American Modern*. New Brunswick, NJ and London: Rutgers University Press. xi–xxvi.

Nasson, Bill. 2010. *The War for South Africa: The Anglo-Boer War 1899–1902*. Cape Town: Tafelberg.

Nicolson, Harold. 1926. *Swinburne*. London: Macmillan.

Nietzsche, Friedrich. 2000. *The Birth of Tragedy* (1872). Tr. Douglas Smith. Oxford: Oxford University Press.

Ober, William R. 1979. *Boswell's Clap and Other Essays: Medical Analyses of Literary Men's Afflictions*. Carbondale: Southern Illinois University Press.

Østermark-Johansen, Lene. 2002a. 'Swinburne's Serpentine Delights: The Aesthetic Critic and the Old Master Drawings in Florence'. *Nineteenth-Century Contexts* 24:1, 49–72.

Østermark-Johansen, Lene. 2002b. 'Serpentine Rivers and Serpentine Thought: Flux and Movement in Walter Pater's Leonardo Essay'. *Victorian Literature and Culture* 30, 455–82.

Østermark-Johansen, Lene. 2002c. 'The Death of Euphues: Euphuism and Decadence in Late-Victorian Literature'. *English Literature in Transition* 45, 4–25.

Packer, Lona Mosk. 1963. 'Swinburne and Christina Rossetti: Atheist and Anglican'. *University of Toronto Quarterly* 33, 30–42.

Paden, W. D. 1962. 'Swinburne and the *Spectator* in 1862, and Walter Bagehot'. In *Six Studies in Nineteenth-Century English Literature and Thought*. Eds Harold Orel and George J. Worth. *Humanistic Studies* 35. Lawrence, Kansas: University of Kansas Publications. 91–115.

Paglia, Camille. 2001. *Sexual Personae: Art and Decadence from Nefertiti to Emily Dickinson*. London and New Haven: Yale University Press.

Parry, Jonathan. 2006. *The Politics of Patriotism: English Liberalism, National Identity and Europe, 1830–1886*. Cambridge: Cambridge University Press.

Pastoureau, Michel. 2002. *Bleu, Histoire d'une couleur*. Paris: Éditions du Seuil.

Pater, Walter. 1868. 'Poems by William Morris'. *The Westminster Review* 90, n.s. 34, 300–12.

Pater, Walter. 1910. *The Library Edition of the Works of Walter Pater*. 10 vols. London: Macmillan.

Pater, Walter. 1980. *The Renaissance: Studies in Art and Poetry, The 1893 Text*. Ed. Donald L. Hill. Berkeley and Los Angeles: University of California Press.

Pease, Alison. 1997. 'Questionable Figures: Swinburne's *Poems and Ballads*'. *Victorian Poetry* 35:1, 43–56.

Peters, Robert L. 1965. *The Crowns of Apollo: Swinburne's Principles of Literature and Art*. Detroit: Wayne State University Press.

Plato. 1980. *The Symposium*. Ed. Kenneth Dover. Cambridge: Cambridge University Press.

Poulet, Georges. 1979. *Les Metamorphoses du cercle* (1961). 2nd ed. Paris: Flammarion, 1979.

Pound, Ezra. 1951. *The Letters of Ezra Pound 1907–1941*. Ed. D. D. Paige. London: Faber & Faber.

Pound, Ezra. 1954. *The Literary Essays of Ezra Pound*. Ed. with an Introduction by T. S. Eliot. London: Faber & Faber.

Pound, Ezra. 1977. *Collected Early Poems of Ezra Pound*. Ed. Michael John King. London: Faber & Faber.

Pound, Ezra. 1991. *Ezra Pound's Poetry and Prose, Contributions to Periodicals*. 11 vols. Eds Lea Baechler, A. Walton Litz, and James Longenbach. New York, London: Garland.

Pound, Ezra. 1997. *Selected Poems 1908–1959*. London: Faber & Faber.

Praz, Mario. 1970. *The Romantic Agony* (1933). Tr. Angus Davidson. 2nd ed. Oxford: Oxford University Press.

Press, Alan R. (ed.). 1971. *Anthology of Troubadour Lyric Poetry*. Austin: University of Texas Press.

Prettejohn, Elizabeth. 2008. 'Solomon, Swinburne, Sappho'. *Victorian Review* 34:2, 103–28.

Priestman, Martin. 2000. *Romantic Atheism: Poetry and Freethought 1780–1830*. Cambridge: Cambridge University Press.

Prins, Yopie. 1999. *Victorian Sappho*. Princeton: Princeton University Press.

Prins, Yopie. 2000. 'Victorian Meters'. In *The Cambridge Companion to Victorian Poetry*. Ed. Joseph Bristow. Cambridge: Cambridge University Press. 89–113.

Prins, Yopie. 2004. 'Voice Inverse'. *Victorian Poetry* 42:1, 43–59.

Prins, Yopie. 2005. 'Nineteenth-Century Homers and the Hexameter Mania'. In *Nation, Language, and the Ethics of Translation*. Eds Sandra Berman and Michael Wood. Princeton: Princeton University Press. 203–28.

Prochaska, Frank. 2000. *The Republic of Britain 1760–2000*. New York: Penguin Putnam.

Psomiades, Kathy. 1997. *Beauty's Body: Femininity and Representation in British Aestheticism*. Stanford: Stanford University Press.

Pulham, Patricia. 2007. 'Tinted and Tainted Love: The Sculptural Body in Olive Custance's Poetry'. *Yearbook of English Studies* 37:1, 161–76.

Pulham, Patricia. 2008. *Art and the Transitional Object in Vernon Lee's Supernatural Tales*. Aldershot: Ashgate.

Rader, R. W. 1976–77. 'The Dramatic Monologue and Related Lyric Forms'. *Critical Inquiry* 3, 131–51.

Ribeyrol, Charlotte. 2010. 'A Channel Passage: Swinburne and France'. In *A. C. Swinburne and the Singing Word: New Perspectives on the Mature Work*. Ed. Yisrael Levin. Farnham and Burlington, VT: Ashgate. 107–25.

Ribot, Théodule. 1906. *Essay on the Creative Imagination*. Tr. Albert H. N. Baron. Chicago and London: Open Court and Kegan Paul, Trench, Trübner & Co., Ltd.

Riede, David. 1978. *Swinburne: A Study of Romantic Mythmaking*. Charlottesville: University Press of Virginia.

Riede, David 1993. 'Swinburne and Romantic Authority'. In *The Whole Music of Passion: New Essays on Swinburne*. Eds Rikky Rooksby and Nicholas Shrimpton. Aldershot and Brookfield, VT: Scolar Press. 22–39.

Riede, David. 2002. 'The Pre-Raphaelite School'. In *A Companion to Victorian Poetry*. Eds Richard Cronin, Alison Chapman, and Antony Harrison. Oxford: Blackwell. 305–20.

Riede, David. 2010. 'Afterword'. In A. C. Swinburne and the Singing Word: New Perspectives on the Mature Work. Ed. Yisrael Levin. Farnham: Ashgate. 167–79.

Robson, Catherine. 2005. 'Standing on the Burning Deck: Poetry, Performance, History'. PMLA 120:1, 148–62.

Rollyson, Carl. 2009. Amy Lowell Among Her Contemporaries. Bloomington: ASJA Press.

Rooksby, Rikky. 1985. 'Swinburne in Miniature: A Century of Roundels'. Victorian Poetry 23, 249–65.

Rooksby, Rikky. 1988. 'Swinburne Without Tears: A Guide to the Later Poetry'. Victorian Poetry 26, 413–30.

Rooksby, Rikky. 1990. 'A Short Note on the Swinburne Manuscripts at Worcester College, Oxford'. The Victorians Institute Journal 18, 175–83.

Rooksby, Rikky. 1993. 'A Century of Swinburne'. In The Whole Music of Passion: New Essays on Swinburne. Eds Rikky Rooksby and Nicholas Shrimpton. Aldershot and Brookfield, VT: Scolar Press. 1–21.

Rooksby, Rikky. 1997. A. C. Swinburne: A Poet's Life. Aldershot and Brookfield, VT: Scolar Press.

Rooksby, Rikky and Nicholas Shrimpton (eds). 1993. The Whole Music of Passion: New Essays on Swinburne. Aldershot and Brookfield, VT: Ashgate.

Rosenberg, John D. 1967. 'Swinburne'. Victorian Studies 11:2, 131–52.

Rosenberg, John D. 2005. Elegy for an Age: The Presence of the Past in Victorian Literature. London and New York: Anthem Press.

The Rossetti Archive. www.rossettiarchive.org.

Rossetti, Christina. 1850. 'Dream Land'. The Germ: Thoughts Towards Nature in Poetry, Literature, and Art 1, 20.

Rossetti, Christina. 1875. Goblin Market, The Prince's Progress and Other Poems. A New Edition. London: Macmillan.

Rossetti, Christina. 1885. Time Flies. London: SPCK.

Rossetti, Christina. 1896. New Poems, Hitherto Unpublished or Uncollected. Ed. W. M. Rossetti. London: Macmillan.

Rossetti, Christina. 1904. The Poetical Works of Christina Rossetti. Ed. W. M. Rossetti. London: Macmillan.

Rossetti, Christina. 1997–2004. The Letters of Christina Rossetti. 4 vols. Ed. Antony H. Harrison. Charlottesville: The University Press of Virginia.

Rossetti, Christina. 2001. Christina Rossetti: The Complete Poems. Ed. Betty S. Flowers. London: Penguin.

Rossetti, D. G. 1881. Poems. London: Ellis & White.

Rossetti, D. G. 1937. Poems, Ballads, and Sonnets. Ed. Paull Franklin Baum. New York: Doubleday Doran.

Rossetti, William Michael. 1866. Swinburne's Poems and Ballads. A Criticism. London: John Camden Hotten.

Rossetti, William Michael. 1904. Preface to The Poetical Works of Christina Rossetti.

London: Macmillan. vii–xiv.

Rossetti, William Michael. 1906. *Some Reminiscences*. 2 vols. London: Brown, Langham, & Co.

Rossetti, William Michael. 1990. *Selected Letters of William Michael Rossetti*. Ed. Roger Peattie. University Park: Pennsylvania State University Press.

Rudy, Jason R. 2009. *Electric Meters: Victorian Physiological Poetics*. Athens: Ohio University Press.

Ruskin, John. 1903–12. *The Complete Works of John Ruskin*. Eds E. T. Cook and Alexander Wedderburn. London: George Allen.

Ruskin, John. 1956–59. *The Diaries of John Ruskin*. Eds Joan Evans and John Howard Whitehouse. 3 vols. Oxford: Clarendon Press.

Russell, Peter. 1950. *Ezra Pound: A Collection of Essays*. London and New York: Peter Nevill Ltd.

Rutland, W. R. 1931. *Swinburne, A Nineteenth Century Hellene, With Some Reflections on the Hellenism of Modern Poets*. Oxford: Blackwell.

Saintsbury, George. 1921. Letters (27 October and 10 November) to the *Times Literary Supplement* Nos 1032 and 1034, 698, 734.

Saville, Julia F. 2009a. 'Cosmopolitan Republican Swinburne: The Immersive Poet as Public Moralist'. *Victorian Poetry* 47:4, 691–713.

Saville, Julia F. 2009b. 'Nude Male Alfresco Swimmers: The Prehistory of a Nineteenth-Century Republican Trope'. *Word and Image* 25:1, 56–74.

Saville, Julia F. 2011. 'Swinburne Contra Whitman: From Cosmopolitan Republican to Parochial English Jingo?' *ELH* 78:2, 479–505.

Savory, Jerold J. 1984. 'Once a Week'. In *British Literary Magazines*. Volume 3: *The Victorian and Edwardian Age, 1837–1913*. Ed. Alvin Sullivan. Westport, CT and London: Greenwood Press. 287–91.

Schuchard, Ronald. 1974. 'T. S. Eliot as an Extension Lecturer, 1916–1919'. *Review of English Studies* n.s. 25, no. 98, 163–73; no. 99, 292–304.

Sedgwick, Eve. 1993. 'A Poem Is Being Written'. In *Tendencies*. Durham, NC: Duke University Press. 177–214.

Shakespeare, William. 2003. *Hamlet, Prince of Denmark*. Ed. Philip Edwards. Cambridge: Cambridge University Press.

Shannon, Richard. 1974. *The Crisis of Imperialism: 1865–1915*. London: Hart-Davis, MacGibbon.

Shelley, Percy Bysshe. 2009. *The Major Works*. Eds Zachary Leader and Michael O'Neill. Oxford: Oxford University Press.

Shrimpton, Nicholas. 1993. 'Swinburne and the Dramatic Monologue'. In *The Whole Music of Passion: New Essays on Swinburne*. Eds Rikky Rooksby and Nicholas Shrimpton. Aldershot and Brookfield, VT: Scolar Press. 52–72.

Sieburth, Richard. 1984. 'Poetry and Obscenity: Baudelaire and Swinburne'. *Comparative Literature* 36:4, 343–53.

Snyder, Jane McIntosh. 1997. *Lesbian Desire in the Lyrics of Sappho*. New York:

Columbia University Press.

Spectator Advertisements for Cornhill and Fraser's. 1862. Spectator (31 May), 614.

Spectator Table of Contents. 1862. Spectator (28 June), 701.

Stewart, Susan. 1984. On Longing: Narratives of the Miniature, the Gigantic, the Souvenir, the Collection. Baltimore and London: Johns Hopkins University Press.

[Swinburne, Algernon Charles.] 1857. 'Modern Hellenism'. Undergraduate Papers 1, 38–40.

Swinburne, Algernon Charles. 1858. Review of The Monomaniac's Tragedy, and Other Poems, by Ernest Wheldrake. Undergraduate Papers 2:3, 97–102.

Swinburne, Algernon Charles. 1862a. 'Charles Baudelaire: Les Fleurs du Mal'. Spectator (6 September), 998–1000.

Swinburne, Algernon Charles. 1862b. '"Les Misérables" Parts II and III'. Spectator (21 June), 694–5.

Swinburne, Algernon Charles. 1862c. 'Dead Love'. Once a Week 7:172 (11 October), 432–4.

Swinburne, Algernon Charles. 1862d. 'The Fratricide'. Once a Week 6:138 (15 February), 215.

Swinburne, Algernon Charles. 1862e. 'Mr George Meredith's "Modern Love"'. Spectator (7 June), 632–33.

Swinburne, Algernon Charles. 1864. Dead Love. London: John W. Parker & Son.

Swinburne, Algernon Charles. 1866. Notes on Poems and Reviews. London: John Camden Hotten.

Swinburne, Algernon Charles. 1867a. 'Mr Arnold's New Poems'. Fortnightly Review 2 (October), 414–45.

Swinburne, Algernon Charles. 1867b. 'Morris's "Life and Death of Jason"'. Fortnightly Review 2 (July), 19–28.

Swinburne, Algernon Charles. 1868a. William Blake: A Critical Essay. London: John Camden Hotten.

Swinburne, Algernon Charles. 1868b. 'Ave atque Vale. In Memory of Charles Baudelaire'. Fortnightly Review 3 (January), 71–6.

Swinburne, Algernon Charles. 1869. 'Intercession'. Fortnightly Review 6 (November), 509–10.

Swinburne, Algernon Charles. 1870a. 'The Poems of Dante Gabriel Rossetti'. Fortnightly Review 7:41, 551–79. Subsequently published in Algernon Charles Swinburne. Essays and Studies. London: Chatto & Windus. 1875. 60–109.

Swinburne, Algernon Charles. 1870b. 'The Complaint of Monna Lisa'. Fortnightly Review 7 (February), 176–9.

Swinburne, Algernon Charles. 1871a. 'Simeon Solomon: Notes on his "Vision of Love" and Other Studies'. Dark Blue 1:5 (July), 568–77.

Swinburne, Algernon Charles. 1871b. 'The End of a Month'. Dark Blue 1 (April), 217–20.

Swinburne, Algernon Charles. 1872a. Under the Microscope. London: D. White.

Swinburne, Algernon Charles. 1872b. Review of John Nichol's *Hannibal: A Historical Drama* in 'Critical Notices'. *Fortnightly Review* 12 (December), 751–53.

Swinburne, Algernon Charles. 1875a. *Essays and Studies*. London: Chatto & Windus.

Swinburne, Algernon Charles. 1875b. *George Chapman*. London: Chatto & Windus.

Swinburne, Algernon Charles. 1881. 'Tennyson and Musset'. *Fortnightly Review* 29:170 (February), 129–53.

Swinburne, Algernon Charles. 1883. *A Century of Roundels*. London: Chatto & Windus.

Swinburne, Algernon Charles. 1904. *The Poems of Algernon Charles Swinburne*. 6 vols. London: Chatto & Windus.

Swinburne, Algernon Charles. 1905. *The Tragedies of Algernon Charles Swinburne*. 5 vols. London: Chatto & Windus.

Swinburne, Algernon Charles. 1916. *Ernest Clouët, A Burlesque*. Ed. Edmund Gosse. London: Printed for Private Circulation.

Swinburne, Algernon Charles. 1919a. *The Letters of A. C. Swinburne*. 2 vols. Eds Edmund Gosse and T. J. Wise. New York: John Lane.

Swinburne, Algernon Charles. 1919b. *Selections from A. C. Swinburne*. Eds Edmund Gosse and Thomas James Wise. London: William Heinemann.

Swinburne, Algernon Charles. 1925–27. *The Complete Works of Algernon Charles Swinburne*. 20 vols. The Bonchurch Edition. London and New York: William Heinemann Ltd and Gabriel Wells.

Swinburne, Algernon Charles. 1952. *Lesbia Brandon*. Ed. Randolph Hughes. London: The Falcon Press.

Swinburne, Algernon Charles. 1959–62. *The Swinburne Letters*. 6 vols. Ed. Cecil Y. Lang. New Haven: Yale University Press.

Swinburne, Algernon Charles. 1964. 'Les Amours Étiques, Félicien Cossu', and 'Les Abîmes par Ernest Clouët'. In *New Writings by Swinburne or Miscellanea Nova et Curiosa: Being a Medley of Poems, Critical Essays, Hoaxes and Burlesques*. Ed. Cecil Y. Lang. Syracuse: Syracuse University Press. 88–96; 97–102.

Swinburne, Algernon Charles. 1966. *Swinburne Replies*. Ed. Clyde K. Hyder. Syracuse: Syracuse University Press.

Swinburne, Algernon Charles. 1972. *Swinburne as Critic*. Ed. Clyde K. Hyder. London and Boston: Routledge & Kegan Paul.

Swinburne, Algernon Charles. 1974. *A Year's Letters*. Ed. Francis Jacques Sypher. New York: New York University Press.

Swinburne, Algernon Charles. 1997. *Algernon Charles Swinburne*. Ed. Catherine Maxwell. Everyman's Poetry. London: J. M. Dent.

Swinburne, Algernon Charles. 2000. *Poems and Ballads & Atalanta in Calydon*. Ed. Kenneth Haynes. London: Penguin.

Swinburne, Algernon Charles. 2004a. *Swinburne's Major Poems and Selected Prose*.

Eds Jerome McGann and Charles Sligh. New Haven: Yale University Press.

Swinburne, Algernon Charles. 2004b. *Uncollected Letters of Algernon Charles Swinburne*. Ed. Terry L. Meyers. 3 vols. London: Pickering & Chatto.

Symonds, John Addington. 1890. *Essays, Speculative and Suggestive*. 2 vols. London: Chapman & Hall.

Symonds, John Addington. 1893. *In the Key of Blue and Other Prose Essays*. London: Elkin Matthews & John Lane.

Symonds, John Addington. 1902. *Studies of the Greek Poets* (1873, 1876). 2 vols. London: Adam & Charles Black.

Symonds, John Addington. 1967–69. *Letters of John Addington Symonds*. 3 vols. Eds Herbert M. Schueller and Robert L. Peters. Detroit: Wayne State University Press.

Symonds, John Addington. 1975. 'A Problem in Greek Ethics' (1883). In *Sexual Inversion* (1897). Havelock Ellis and John Addington Symonds. New York: Arno Press. 163–251.

Symonds, John Addington. 1984. *The Memoirs of John Addington Symonds*. Ed. Phyllis Grosskurth. New York: Random House.

Symonds, John Addington. 2005. 'Eudiades'. In *Tales of Ancient Greece* (1878). New York: AstroLogos Books. 1–33.

Sypher, F. J. 1974. 'Introduction'. *Undergraduate Papers. An Oxford Journal (1857–58)*. Delmar, NY: Scholars' Facsimiles & Reprints. xi–xxxviii.

Thacker, Andrew. 2004. 'Unrelated Beauty: Amy Lowell, Polyphonic Prose, and the Imagist City'. In *Amy Lowell, American Modern*. Eds Adrienne Munich and Melissa Bradshaw. New Brunswick, NJ and London: Rutgers University Press. 104–19.

Thomas, Donald. 1979. *Swinburne: The Poet in His World*. London: Weidenfeld & Nicolson.

Thomas, Edward. 1912. *Algernon Charles Swinburne: A Critical Study*. London: Martin Secker.

Tinkler-Villani, Valeria. 1999. 'Atheism and Belief in Shelley, Swinburne and Christina Rossetti'. In *Victorian Keats and Romantic Carlyle: The Fusions and Confusions of Literary Periods*. Ed. C. C. Barfoot. Amsterdam: Rodopi. 323–37.

Tobin, David Ned. 1983. *The Presence of the Past: T. S. Eliot's Victorian Inheritance*. Ann Arbor, MI: UMI Research Press.

Tucker, Herbert F. 1985. 'Dramatic Monologue and the Overhearing of Lyric'. In *Lyric Poetry: Beyond New Criticism*. Eds Chaviva Hošek and Patricia Parker. Ithaca and London: Cornell University Press.

Tucker, Herbert F. 1993. '*Aurora Leigh*: Epic Solutions to Novel Ends'. In *Famous Last Words: Changes in Gender and Narrative Closure*. Ed. Alison Booth. Charlottesville and London: University Press of Virginia. 62–85.

Tucker, Herbert F. 1996. 'When the Soul Had Hips: Six Animadversions on Psyche and Gender in Nineteenth-Century Poetry'. In *Sexualities in Victorian Britain*.

Eds Andrew H. Miller and James Eli Adams. Bloomington: Indiana University Press. 157–86.

Tucker, Herbert F. 2008. *Epic: Britain's Heroic Muse: 1790–1910*. Oxford: Oxford University Press.

Turner, Frank M. 1981. *The Greek Heritage in Victorian Britain*. New Haven and London: Yale University Press.

Undergraduate Papers 1–3. 1857–58.

Untermeyer, Louis. 1930. *Modern American Poetry: A Critical Anthology*. New York: Harcourt Brace & Company.

Vance, Norman. 1997. *The Victorians and Ancient Rome*. Oxford: Blackwell Publishing.

Vernant, J.-P. 1996. *La Mort dans les yeux: figures de l'autre en Grèce ancienne*. Paris: Éditions du Seuil.

Vincent, John. 1997. 'Flogging Is Fundamental: Applications of the Birch in Swinburne's *Lesbia Brandon*'. In *Novel Gazing: Queer Readings in Fiction*. Ed. Eve Kosofksy Sedgwick. Durham, NC: Duke University Press. 269–95.

Vivien, Renée. 1982. *A Woman Appeared to Me* (1904). Tr. Jeanette H. Foster. Tallahassee, FL: The Naiad Press.

Wagner-Lawlor, Jennifer. 1996. 'Metaphorical "Indiscretion" and Literary Survival in Swinburne's "Anactoria"'. *Studies in English Literature, 1500–1900* 36:4, 917–34.

Walkowitz, Rebecca. 2006. *Cosmopolitan Style: Modernism beyond the Nation*. New York: Columbia University Press.

Wallace, Jennifer. 1997. *Shelley and Greece: Rethinking Romantic Hellenism*. London: Macmillan; New York: St Martin's Press.

Walsh, John A. 2010. '"A Quivering Web of Living Thought": Conceptual Networks in Swinburne's *Songs of the Springtides*'. In *A. C. Swinburne and the Singing Word*. Ed. Yisrael Levin. Farnham and Burlington, VT: Ashgate. 29–53.

Weiner, Stephanie Kuduk. 2005. *Republican Politics and English Poetry, 1789–1874*. New York: Palgrave Macmillan.

Weiner, Stephanie Kuduk. 2010. 'Knowledge and Sense Experience in Swinburne's Late Poetry'. In *A. C. Swinburne and the Singing Word*. Ed. Yisrael Levin. Farnham and Burlington, VT: Ashgate. 11–28.

Welby, T. Earle. 1926. *A Study of Swinburne*. London: Faber & Gwyer.

Wellesley Index to Victorian Periodicals, 1824–1900. 1966–89. Eds Walter Houghton, Esther Rhoads Houghton, and Jean Slingerland. 5 vols. London: Routledge & Kegan Paul.

Wilde, Oscar. 1968. 'Mr Swinburne's Last Volume' (1889). In *The Artist as Critic: Critical Writings of Oscar Wilde*. Ed. Richard Ellman. New York: Random House. 146–9.

Wilson, F. A. C. 1969. 'Swinburne's "Dearest Cousin": The Character of Mary Gordon'. *Literature and Psychology* 19, 89–99.

Wise, Thomas J. 1919. *A Bibliography of the Writings in Prose and Verse of Algernon*

Charles Swinburne. 2 vols. London: Richard Clay & Sons, Ltd.

Wise, Thomas J. 1927. Volume 20: *Bibliography.* In *The Complete Works of Algernon Charles Swinburne.* 20 vols. The Bonchurch Edition. London and New York: William Heinemann Ltd and Gabriel Wells.

Wood, Clement. 1926. *Amy Lowell.* New York: Harold Vinal.

Ziolkowski, Theodore. 2005. *Ovid and the Moderns.* Ithaca: Cornell University Press.

Zonana, Joyce. 1990. 'Swinburne's Sappho: The Muse as Sister-Goddess'. *Victorian Poetry* 28, 39–51.

INDEX

Note: numbers in *italic* refer to illustrations